History of Child Saving in the United States, 1893

AT THE

Twentieth National Conference of Charities and Correction in Chicago, June, 1893

REPORT OF THE COMMITTEE ON THE HISTORY OF CHILD-SAVING WORK

C. D. Randall, Coldwater, Mich.; C. L. Brace, New York; Chas. W. Birtwell, Boston; Mrs. M. R. W. Wallace, Chicago; Homer Folks, Philadelphia; Francis Wayland, New Haven; Mrs. C. E. Dickinson, Denver; Mrs. Sarah B. Cooper, San Francisco; S. J. Hathaway, Marietta, Ohio; Mrs. Samuel Cushman, Deadwood, So. Dakota; D. Solis Cohen, Portland, Ore.; Charles Martindale, Indianapolis; Mrs. Virginia T. Smith, Hartford, Conn.; H. W. Lewis, Owatonna, Minn.

PRESENTED TO THE CONFERENCE
AS THE CONTRIBUTION OF THE COMMITTEE

PRINTED FOR THE COMMITTEE BY GEO. H. ELLIS,
141 FRANKLIN STREET, BOSTON
1893

CONTENTS.

PAGE

INTRODUCTION. By C. D. Randall, *Chairman*, ... v

THE CHILDREN'S AID SOCIETY OF NEW YORK. ITS HISTORY, PLANS, AND RESULTS. By Charles Loring Brace, ... 1

FAMILY LIFE VERSUS INSTITUTION LIFE. By Miss Sophie E. Minton, . . 37

THE MASSACHUSETTS SYSTEM OF CARING FOR STATE MINOR WARDS. By Mrs. Anne B. Richardson, ... 54

NON-SECTARIAN ENDOWED CHILD-SAVING INSTITUTIONS. By Lyman P. Alden, ... 68

THE KINDERGARTEN IN ITS BEARINGS UPON CRIME, PAUPERISM, AND INSANITY. By Mrs. Sarah B. Cooper, ... 86

SAVING THE CHILDREN: SIXTEEN YEARS' WORK AMONG THE DEPENDENT YOUTH OF CHICAGO. By Oscar L. Dudley, ... 99

THE HISTORY OF CHILD-SAVING WORK IN CONNECTICUT. By Mrs. Virginia T. Smith, ... 116

CHILDREN'S HOMES IN OHIO. By S. J. Hathaway, ... 131

CHILD-SAVING WORK IN PENNSYLVANIA. By Homer Folks, ... 138

THE HISTORY OF CHILD-SAVING WORK IN THE STATE OF NEW YORK. By William Pryor Letchworth, ... 154

STATE PUBLIC SCHOOLS FOR DEPENDENT AND NEGLECTED CHILDREN. By G. A. Merrill, ... 204

STATEMENT FROM THE TRUSTEES OF THE STATE PRIMARY AND REFORM SCHOOLS OF MASSACHUSETTS. By Mrs. Glendower Evans, ... 227

THE CATHOLIC PROTECTORY OF NEW YORK · ITS SPIRIT AND ITS WORKINGS FROM ITS ORIGIN TO THE PRESENT, ... Appendix

INTRODUCTION.

The Committee on the History of Child-saving Work of the Twentieth National Conference of Charities and Correction has prepared this volume of monographs as the contribution of the committee to the labors of the Conference and for distribution among its members. There is no effort in the work to produce a continuous history of child-saving in the United States. That would involve a research and compilation that will be practicably impossible until the official reports of the States shall furnish data and statistics which are now almost entirely wanting. And it is doubtful whether at this time and for the purposes of this convention such a history, if it could be produced, would be of the most value. In general history we are most attracted by the decisive battles, by the aggressive movements of rulers against their subjects, and by the uprising and assertion of an oppressed and determined people. We judge mainly by the greater movements in social history. In the history of child-saving in this country, especially since the organization of this National Conference, there have been certain prominent movements which have had much to do in determining methods in child-saving. The object of this volume is to present some of these principal movements, and in a form where they can be, in outline, examined and contrasted.

The committee desired to obtain a larger collection of monographs, but was not able to secure co-operation in all places where it was solicited. The fact that each writer bears the expenses of publishing his paper has had its influence in limiting the collection. But through the kindness of the writers the volume will contain an interesting and valuable history of the movements which will throw the most light on child-saving in this country.

The brief time allotted each committee at the Conference held at the time of the Columbian Exposition would not permit the presentation of any extended history of child-saving. This committee appreciated deeply and keenly that there was no question in social economy of so much vital interest and importance as that relating to the reformation and reinstatement of delinquent children and the care and education of dependent children. The highest interests of the State and the future welfare of the children are deeply involved in the proper treatment of delinquent and dependent children. Being so convinced, this committee has undertaken in this volume to call a more extended attention to the subject of child-saving than could be given in a brief report in the convention, with the hope that this effort may lead to a more extended examination of different methods, to the end that the best system will become more an exact science than now. Allowing for the unlike conditions in the different States, there must be an ideal system, which, with modifications to suit conditions, will come to be accepted and adopted generally. It is believed that some of the features of the ideal system will be found to be foreshadowed in some of the papers in this. volume.

That there is need of a uniform and correct system cannot be doubted. There are now about as many systems as there are States. In most of the States dependent children are yet provided for in the county poorhouses, which are admitted nurseries of crime and pauperism. In them the child often spends years associated with the insane, the idiotic, and with adult paupers, the mental, moral and physical wrecks of their own debased lives. In the larger number of the States there are no proper reformatories or industrial schools for minor delinquents; nor is there any classification of prisoners, the young child being placed in contaminating association with adult criminals in the same jail, workhouse, or prison.

The same want of uniformity between States exists in penalties for crime, in efforts for reformation, in prison discipline, and in aid for discharged prisoners. Both adult and minor crime and pauperism could be more effectually and more rapidly reduced under an ideal system, uniform among the States. For that ideal system, in charitable, reformatory, and prison work the National Conference of Charities and Correction has now labored for twenty years, and has had more to do than any other factor in solving some of the most difficult problems in social science.

The light emanating from this Conference has been turned so strongly on the evils of old systems, especially on the old county system for dependent children, the association of children with adults in prisons and jails, that abuses have disappeared in many places. This Conference will yet have much to do in securing uniformity and advancement.

The monographs in this volume have been prepared at the request of this committee. The writers are well known, and their ability to write on the several subjects treated by them will be conceded. The Hon. WILLIAM PRYOR LETCHWORTH, LL.D., is an ex-President, of the Eleventh National Conference of Charities and Correction, ex-Chairman of the Sixth, Eighth, Tenth, and Twelfth National Conferences of Charities and Correction, and chairman of the Committee on Dependent and Delinquent Children of the New York State Board of Charities.

Mr. GALEN A. MERRILL is an ex-State agent and assistant superintendent of the Michigan State Public School, and the superintendent of the Minnesota State Public School.

Mr. CHARLES LORING BRACE is the secretary of the Children's Aid Society of New York, and the successor of his father of the same name.

Mrs. SARAH B. COOPER, of California, has long been prominently connected with the promotion of kindergartens.

Mr. HOMER FOLKS, for some time connected with the Pennsylvania system for providing homes for children, is now an official in the Charity Organization Society of New York.

Mr. Lyman P. Alden is ex-superintendent of the Michigan State Public School, and superintendent of the Rose Orphan Home of Terre Haute, Ind.

Mr. S. J. Hathaway, a lawyer, is a trustee of one of the Ohio Orphan Homes for dependent children.

Mr. Oscar L. Dudley is secretary and general manager of the Illinois School of Agriculture and Manual Training for Boys, and has had sixteen years' experience in child-saving in Chicago.

Mrs. Virginia T. Smith is a member of the State Board of Charities of Connecticut.

Mrs. Anne B. Richardson is a member of the State Board of Lunacy and Charity of Massachusetts.

Miss Sophie E. Minton is chairman of Committee on Children of the State Charities Association of New York.

The New York Catholic Protectory monograph is prepared by some one connected with the institution, the author's name being omitted. As the paper originates with the institution, its statements are authentic.

Mrs. Glendower Evans furnishes a statement from the trustees of the Massachusetts State Primary and Reform Schools.

To these writers the thanks of the committee are cordially and gratefully extended.

The reader of these monographs will inquire, Which presents the better method? Each may be approximately right under its special conditions. Each has its merits and defects. In the densely crowded city all children may not find a home or occupation. The agricultural West and manufacturing towns open a field. On the farm the child finds opportunities sufficient; and at the forge and the bench he may become not only self-supporting, but a skilled expert. Private charity is always commendable. It is of ancient origin, and has blessed the world and sweetened dependent child life alone for ages. Public charity, more modern, is stronger in its power, when fully and properly exerted. Both are to be encouraged and continued. And yet out of them all cannot there be matured a system which should include both private and public, and which should be brought to a higher perfection, under which all children should be protected from ill treatment, should be reformed if delinquent, and should be cared for if dependent, all being restored to the kind and elevating influences of good home life?

The crucial test of the best method to be found in the light of this age is, Which one will soonest fit the child for a good family home, and restore the child to it? It is no matter to the child whether it is cared for and restored by public or private agencies. There are some who will throw doubts upon this position, but the general view is that the family home is better for the child than an institution. This paper is not to argue that question, if there be any question. Without referring to all the institutions and methods herein described, reference is made to three systems the most dissimilar, and first to the State Public School systems of Michigan, Wisconsin, Minnesota, and Rhode Island on one hand, and the New York and California system on the other. Under the first the laws of the State compel the management to use diligence to restore children to family life; and under the second the State pays for the support of the children in private and generally sectarian institutions while the children are inmates, with no requisition, supervision, or control to secure the placing in homes. The State system secures the early finding of homes, while the other holds out the temptation for retaining the children for the compensation afforded to mainly support the institution in which the children are placed. Probably the most noted example of State aid to sectarian schools will be found in the Catholic Protectory herein described. This institution has done a great deal of good in the past, and does it now. Those connected with its management have proved their unselfish devotion. In the main, its work is to be highly commended.

The Protectory was invited by this committee to give a history of its work, so that its side of the story might be heard, as there has been much criticism regarding the large number of inmates, over two thousand on the average, kept there. It is to be regretted that the Protectory has not furnished the facts most desirable to know. It does not tell us how many children have been received since its organization, how many have been returned to their families, how many have been indentured or adopted, how many have been taught trades in or out of the institution, and, generally, what has become of the children. The report does not tell us the average detention in the Protectory, the supervision given indentured children, how far indentured children are protected, and what has been the results relative to the children placed out. It does not tell us how much it now annually receives from the public and how much from private sources, and whether the State pays for enough or more than to support it. We are left in the dark in regard to all these facts. Mr. Letchworth and Miss Minton in their able papers call attention to the questions which have arisen relative to public control to secure administration of sectarian institutions, for the better protection of children and the State regarding prompt placing of children in family homes from them.

This whole matter is very ably presented by Mrs. Josephine Shaw Lowell, for a long time member of the New York State Board of Charities, in her report for 1890, and to which reference is made. Many of the facts suggested as wanting in the history of the Protectory herein will be found in the published annual reports. From Mrs. Lowell's report it will be seen that there was received by the Protectory in 1889 : —

From the city	$263,341.48
" private sources	2,458.36
" all other sources	44,087.93
Total receipts for 1889	$309,887.77

The number of children cared for that year was 2,255. The per capita expense was about $137. This showing is not unusual as to expense. The main question here will be, Is it necessary that so great a number should be supported in one institution, and is the massing of so great a number for the good of the children? These are very serious questions, and they are receiving consideration in New York and California. New Hampshire has just authorized the support of dependent children in private institutions at public expense with no more restrictions than in New York and California. Mrs. Lowell says: "New York City supports an average population of about 14,000 boys and girls, at an expense of $1,500,000 annually, in institutions controlled by private individuals. . . . . There is no official of New York City who knows or has a right to know whether these thousands of children are trained in idleness or industry, in virtue or vice." She has much to say, and forcibly, against the system.

The third instance as a contrast will be found in the Ohio system, which appears to meet with much favor in that State. In 1891 there were in that State forty-five public homes for dependent children; and there was invested in their plants $1,432,750, and the number of children in them was 2,359,—about $600 per capita, for plant. In 1887 Ohio paid to support the children in these homes $312,254, and cared for during the year 3,573. New York that year paid for supporting 20,205 children in private or sectarian asylums about $2,000,000, and California under the New York system paid $231,215 to support 3,600.

As an instance of the State system, Michigan, with about double the population of California, in 1887 had only about 200 dependent children to support; and this was done at a cost of about $35,000. Child dependency in that State had been gradually reduced since the system was put in operation in 1874 from 600 dependent children then to only about 200 in 1887, though the population had increased about fifty per cent. No State supporting children in private asylums can make such a showing. The children cost less because they are out in homes and the State is relieved of their support. The main features of the system will be found explained in the biennial reports of the Michigan State Public School, where much more will be found to commend the system to all. Mr. Merrill's paper in this volume describes this system so fully that little need be said here.

This preface is not intended to compare the different systems of child-saving. It is to call attention to some of the leading features of the various systems, in order to invite investigation and discussion. As a resident of Michigan, the writer naturally considers the Michigan system the most perfect, as it is most radical and efficient in restoring children to family life from institutions for delinquent as well as dependent children. But in that system there are yet serious defects. Its Reform School for Boys at Lansing has for many years been one of the best conducted in the country. But there are too many boys confined there. The law is at fault. Boys are sent there as truants from school, made criminals because they did not attend school. Many are sent there for first and slight offence, when suspension of sentence or some light punishment would have been sufficient, and saved them from prison taint. Many boys are sent there who were never criminals at heart. The average number might be reduced to two hundred and fifty to three hundred at least. Our Girls' Industrial School at Adrian has fine buildings, and, on the whole, is a model institution. But the girls are kept too long. These are faults which occur in all States. But the one thing especially lacking in Michigan is the want of public supervision and control of all private or sectarian institutions for children. There is no supervision or control over such institutions in Michigan. They receive and can hold during minority the children that come into their custody, and public authority does not interfere. This condition exists in most of the States.

There are some features which are suggested in the future ideal system for dependent and delinquent children : —

1. State supervision and control of all public and private institutions for children, to secure full protection to children in their custody.

2. No child to be placed in an institution except on judicial approval and finding that it is a delinquent or dependent.

3. All institutions required to place dependent children in an approved family home within a reasonable time.

4. The supervision and protection of all indentured children during minority.

5. The State to furnish aid to public institutions only, but to give full encouragement otherwise to private charities, reserving supervision and control.

6. The protection of ill-treated children by the execution of stringent provisions of law, to the extent of the deprivation of parental custody where necessary.

7. The radical separation of dependent and delinquent children.

These are considered to be some of the essentials to a more perfect system, as shown by experience and the best thought of the present.

C. D. RANDALL,

Chairman.

COLDWATER, MICH.

CHILD SAVING.

THE CHILDREN'S AID SOCIETY OF NEW YORK.

ITS HISTORY, PLAN, AND RESULTS.

COMPILED FROM THE WRITINGS AND REPORTS OF THE LATE

CHARLES LORING BRACE,

THE FOUNDER OF THE SOCIETY, AND FROM THE RECORDS OF THE SECRETARY'S OFFICE.

The first circular of the Children's Aid Society ushered in a new movement in the charitable world. It is dated March, 1853, and was prepared by the late Charles Loring Brace, the secretary of the society. In this circular the plan of all the subsequent work of the society is clearly stated; and the principles which underlie these plans, then so novel, are now admitted on every side as the proper form of charitable effort among destitute or neglected children. Individual influence and home life as better than institutional life; the lessons of industry and self-help as better than alms; the implanting of moral and religious truths in union with the supply of bodily wants; and the entire change of circumstances as the best cure for the defects of the children of the lowest poor,— these principles, first brought to the attention of the public in the society's first appeal, and for years so much contested, are now recognized as settled methods in the science of charity.

As stated in the circular: "This society has taken its origin in the deeply settled feeling of our citizens that something must be done to meet the increasing crime and poverty among the destitute children of New York. Its objects are to help this class by opening Sunday meetings and industrial schools, and gradually, as means shall be furnished, by forming lodging-houses and reading-rooms for

CHARLES LORING BRACE,
Founder of the Children's Aid Society.

children and by employing paid agents, whose sole business shall be to care for them.

" As Christian men, we cannot look upon this great multitude of unhappy, deserted, and degraded boys and girls without feeling our responsibility to God for them. The class increases: immigration is pouring in its multitudes of poor foreigners who leave these young outcasts everywhere in our midst. These boys and girls, it should be remembered, will soon form the great lower class of our city. They will influence elections; they may shape the policy of the city; they will assuredly, if unreclaimed, poison society all around them. They will help to form the great multitude of robbers, thieves, and vagrants, who are now such a burden upon the law-respecting community. . . .

" In one ward alone of the city, the eleventh, there were in 1852, out of 12,000 children between the ages of five and sixteen years, only 7,000 who attended school and only 2,500 who went to Sabbath-school, leaving 5,000 without the common privileges of an education, and about 9,000 destitute of public religious influence. In 1852 the warden of the City Prison reported that one-fourth of the commitments to this prison and nearly one-half of those charged with petty offences had not attained the age of twenty-one years. The number of arrests averaged one inhabitant out of every fourteen persons, or seventy in each 1,000. . . .

" In view of these evils we have formed an association which shall devote itself entirely to this class of vagrant children. We do not propose in any way to conflict with existing asylums and institutions, but to render them a hearty co-operation, and at the same time to fill a gap, which of necessity they have all lacked. A large multitude of children live in the city who cannot be placed in asylums, and yet who are uncared for and ignorant and vagrant. We propose to give to these work, and to bring them under religious influence. A central office has been taken, and Mr. Charles L. Brace has been engaged to give his whole time to efforts for relieving the wants of this class. As means shall come in, it is designed to district the city, so that hereafter every ward may have its agent, who shall be a friend to the vagrant child. Boys' Sunday meetings have already been formed. With these we intend to connect industrial schools. We hope, too, especially, to be the means of draining the city of these children, by communicating with farmers, manufacturers, or families in the country, who may need such employment. When homeless boys are found by our agents, we mean to get them homes in the families of respectable persons, and to put them in the way of an honest living. We design, in a word, to bring humane and kindly influences to bear on this forsaken class. . . .

"We call upon all who recognize that these are the little ones of Christ, all who believe that crime is best averted by sowing good influences in childhood, all who are friends of the helpless, to aid us in our enterprise."

This circular was issued from the office, No. 683 Broadway, corner of Amity Street, by the secretary of the society, Charles L. Brace.

With him were associated as trustees the following gentlemen: Benjamin J. Howland, John L. Mason, William C. Gilman, William L. King, Charles W. Elliott, Augustine Eaton, J. L. Phelps, M.D., James A. Burtus, Moses G. Leonard, William C. Russell, J. Earl Williams, A. D. F. Randolph.

Of these the first president was Judge John L. Mason, and the first treasurer, J. Earl Williams, Esq.

Before the formation of the society, in February of 1853, Mr. Brace and several of his friends had been at work among the vagrant boys of the city in organizing "Boys' Meetings." It was seen that these boys would not enter the Sabbath-schools or churches, and accordingly informal meetings were opened on Sundays for them alone. The first of these meetings was started by members of the Carmine Street Presbyterian Church in 1848. Encouraged by the success of this, similar ones were established by Mr. Brace, Mr. Russell, Mr. Howland, Mr. King, and others, in the Five Points, Eighth Avenue, and elsewhere, and also with Judge Mason in Avenue D, from which arose the "Wilson School." All these gentlemen felt the need of some general organization to aid children, which should devote itself through its agents entirely to the interests of this neglected class, with the special object of providing work and new homes for the poor and degraded children of New York. Mr. Brace urged the formation of such an association in the daily press, and at length the gentlemen engaged in this work met to discuss this idea. Finally, in February, 1853, the association was formed under the name of the "Children's Aid Society"; and Mr. Brace was requested to assume the management of it as secretary. He was at that time busied in literary and editorial pursuits, but had expected soon to carry out the purpose of his special training, and to become a preacher; but "the call" of the neglected and outcast was too strong for him to listen to any other, and the humble charity under his extraordinary powers of organization became a moral and educational movement so profound and earnest as to repay the life-endeavors of any man.

One of the most energetic members of this new body, in the beginning, was Mr. William C. Russell, a man of great earnestness of character. With him was associated Mr. Benjamin J. Howland, of peculiar compassion of nature, a Unitarian. Then on the other side, theologically, was Judge John L. Mason, one of the pillars of the Presbyterian Church. His accurate legality of mind and solidity of character were of immense advantage to the youthful association. With him, representing the Congregationalists, was a very careful and judicious man, engaged for many years in Sunday-school and similar missions, Mr. William C. Gilman. The Dutch Reformed were represented by an experienced friend of education, Mr. Mahlon T. Hewitt; and the Presbyterians, again, by one of such gentleness and humanity that all sects might have called him brother, Mr. William L. King. To these was added one who was a great impelling force in this humane movement, a man of large generous nature, with a high and refined culture, who did more to gain support for this charity with the business community where he was so influential than any other man, Mr. John Earl Williams.

In a subsequent year was elected a gentleman who especially represented a religious body that has always profoundly sympathized with this enterprise, Mr. Howard Potter, the son of the eminent Episcopal Bishop of Pennsylvania. Mr. Potter is still trustee. Through him and Mr. Robert J. Livingston, who was chosen a few years after, the whole accounts of the society were subsequently put in a clear shape, and the duties of the trustees in supervision made distinct and regular.

This association, which from such small beginnings has grown to so important dimensions, was thus formed in 1853, and was subsequently incorporated in 1855, under the general act of the State of New York in relation to Charitable Associations.

The public — so profound was the sense of these threatening evils — immediately came forward with its subscriptions, the first large gift (fifty dollars) being from the wife of the principal property-holder in the city, Mrs. William B. Astor.

SULLIVAN STREET INDUSTRIAL SCHOOL.

Erected in 1892 by Mrs. Joseph M. White and Miss Mathilda W. Bruce.

Most touching was the crowd of wandering little ones who immediately found their way to the office. Ragged young girls who had nowhere to lay their heads; children driven from drunkards' homes; orphans who slept where they could find a box or a stairway; boys cast out by step-mothers or step-fathers; newsboys, whose incessant answer to the question, "Where do you live?" was "Don't live no-where"; little bootblacks, young pedlers, "canawl-boys," who seem to drift into the city every winter, and live a vagabond life; pickpockets and petty thieves trying to get honest work; child-beggars and flower-sellers growing up to enter courses of crime,— all this motley throng of infantile misery and childish guilt passed through its doors, telling their simple stories of suffering and temptation.

In investigating closely the different parts of the city, with reference to future movements for their benefit, Mr. Brace soon came to know certain centres of crime and misery, until every lane and alley, with its filth and wretchedness and vice, became familiar to him as the lanes of a country homestead to its owner. There was the infamous German "Ragpickers' Den," in Pitt and Willett Streets, double rows of houses flaunting with dirty banners and the yards heaped up with bones and refuse, where cholera raged unchecked in its previous invasion. Here the wild life of the children soon made them outcasts and thieves.

Then came the murderous blocks in Cherry and Water Streets where so many dark crimes were continually committed, and where the little girls who flitted about with baskets and wrapped in old shawls became familiar with vice before they were out of childhood.

There were the thieves' lodging-houses in the lower wards, where the street-boys were trained by older pickpockets and burglars for their nefarious callings, the low immigrant boarding-houses and vile cellars of the First Ward educating a youthful population for courses of guilt, the notorious rogues' den in Laurens Street, and, farther above, the community of young garroters and burglars around Hamersley Street and Cottage Place. And, still more north, the dreadful population of youthful ruffians and degraded men and women in "Poverty Lane," near Sixteenth and Seventeenth Streets and Ninth Avenue, which subsequently ripened into the infamous "Nineteenth Street Gang."

On the east side, again, was "Dutch Hill," near Forty-second Street, the squatters' village, whence issued so many of the little pedlers of the city, and the Eleventh Ward and "Corlear's Hook," where the " copper-pickers " and young wood-stealers and the thieves who beset the ship-yards congregated ; while below, in the Sixth Ward, was the Italian quarter, where houses could be seen crowded with children, monkeys, dogs, and all the appurtenances of the corps of organ-grinders, harpers, and the little Italian street-sweepers, who then, ignorant and untrained, wandered through the down-town streets and alleys.

Near each one of these " fever-nests " and centres of ignorance, crime, and poverty, it was Mr. Brace's hope and aim eventually to place some agency which should be a moral and physical disinfectant, a seed of reform and improvement amid the wilderness of vice and degradation.

It seemed a too enthusiastic hope to be realized, and at times the waves of misery and guilt through these dark places appeared too overwhelming and irresistible for any one effort or association of efforts to be able to stem or oppose.

How the ardent hope was realized, and the plan carried out, will appear hereafter.

The first special effort that was put forth was the providing of work for these children by opening workshops.

These experiments, of which many were made at different times, were not successful. The object was to render the shops self-supporting. But the irregularity of the class attending them, the work spoiled, and the necessity of competing with skilled labor and often with machinery, soon put them behind.

Mr. Brace soon discovered that, if he could train the children of the street to habits of industry and self-control and neatness, and give them the rudiments of moral and mental education, they can easily make an honest living in this country. The only occasional exception is with young girls depending on the needle for support, inasmuch as the competition here is so severe. But these were often provided with instruction in housework or dressmaking ; and, if taught cleanliness and habits of order and punctuality, they had no difficulty in securing places as servants, or they soon married into a better class.

NEWSBOYS' LODGING HOUSES.

The spectacle which earliest and most painfully arrested Mr. Brace's attention in this work were homeless boys in various portions of the city.

There seemed to be a very considerable class of lads in New York who had no settled home and lived on the outskirts of society, their hand against every man's pocket, and every man looking on them as natural enemies, their wits sharpened like those of a savage, and their principles often no better. Their life was of course a painfully hard one. To sleep in boxes or under stairways or in hay-barges on the coldest winter nights for a mere child was hard enough; but often to have no food, to be kicked and cuffed by the older ruffians and shoved about by the police, standing barefooted and in rags under doorways as the winter storm raged, and to know that in all the great city there was not a single door open with welcome to the little rover, — this was harder.

In planning the alleviation of these evils, Mr. Brace saw it was necessary to keep in view one object: not to weaken the best quality of this class,—their sturdy independence,—and at the same time their prejudices and habits were not too suddenly to be assailed. They had a peculiar dread of Sunday-schools and religious exhortations, partly because of the general creed of their older associates, but more for fear that these exercises were a "pious dodge" for trapping them into some place of detention.

The first thing to be aimed at in the plan was to treat the lads as independent little dealers, and give them nothing without payment, but at the same time to offer them much more for their money than they could get anywhere else. Moral, educational, and religious influences were to come in afterward.

Efforts were made by Mr. Brace among our influential citizens, and in various churches public meetings were held by him, articles written, the press interested; and at length sufficient money was pledged to make the experiment. The board of the new society gave its approval, and a loft was secured in the old " Sun Building," and fitted up as a lodging-room; and in March, 1854, the first lodging-house for street-boys or newsboys in this country, and indeed in the world, was opened, and a night school established.

THE BRACE MEMORIAL BOYS' LODGING-HOUSE AND INDUSTRIAL
SCHOOL.

An excellent superintendent was found in the person of a carpenter, Mr. C. C. Tracy, who showed remarkable ingenuity and tact in the management of these wild lads. These little subjects regarded the first arrangements with some suspicion and much contempt. To find a good bed offered them for six cents, with a bath thrown in, and a supper for four cents, was a hard fact, which they could rest upon and understand; but the motive was evidently "gaseous." There was "no money in it," that was clear. The superintendent was probably "a street preacher," and this was a trap to get them to Sunday-school. Still, they might have a lark there; and it could be no worse than "bumming," — that is, sleeping out. They laid their plans for a general scrimmage in the meeting-room, first cutting off the gas, and then a row in the bedroom.

The superintendent, however, in a bland and benevolent way nipped their plans in the bud. The gas-pipes were guarded: the rough ringleaders were politely dismissed to the lower door.

Little sleeping, however, was there among

DORMITORY, BOYS' LODGING-HOUSE.

them that night, but ejaculations sounded out, such as: "I say, Jim, this is rather better 'an bummin', eh?" "My eyes! what soft beds these is!" "Tom! it's 'most as good as a steam gratin', and there ain't no M. P.'s to poke, neither!" "I'm glad I ain't a bummer to-night!"

A good wash and a breakfast sent the lodgers forth in the morning happier and cleaner, if not better, than when they went in. This night's success established its popularity with the newsboys.

Mr. Brace presided over the Sunday evening services, and under his simple and beautiful teaching the conception of a Superior Being, who knew just the sort of privations and temptations that followed them, and who felt especially for the poorer classes, who was always near them, and pleased at true manhood in them, did keep afterward a considerable number of them from lying and stealing and cheating and vile pleasures.

Their singing was generally prepared for by taking off their coats and rolling up their sleeves, and was entered into with gusto.

REACING-ROOM, BOYS' LODGING-HOUSE.

Their especial vice of money-wasting the superintendent broke up by opening a savings-bank. The small daily deposits accumulated to such a degree that at the opening the amounts which they possessed gave them a great surprise; a n d they began to feel thus the "sense of property" and the desire of accumulation, w h i c h, economists tell us, is the base of all civilization. A liberal interest was allowed on deposits, which stimulated the good habit.

In the course of a year the population of a town passes through the five lodging-houses now established, — in 1892 6,000 different boys. Many are put in good homes ; some find places for themselves ; others drift away, no one knows whither. They are an army of orphans, regiments of children who have not a home or friend, a multitude of little street rovers, who have no place to lay their heads. The lodging-house is at once school, church, intelligence-office, and hotel for them. Here they are shaped to be honest and industrious citizens ; here taught economy, good order, cleanliness, and morality ; here religion brings its powerful influence to bear upon them ; and many are sent forth to begin courses of honest livelihood.

THE WEST SIDE BOYS' LODGING-HOUSE AND INDUSTRIAL SCHOOL.

Erected in 1884 by John Jacob Astor.

The Girls' Lodging-house and Training School.

In 1861 William A. Booth, Esq., accepted the position of president of the society. To a rare combination of qualities which form a thorough presiding officer he added the most earnest zeal in all the benevolent objects of the association, and a clear insight into the means by which the objects might be reached.

Mr. Booth's attention was early fixed on the miserable condition of street girls, older than could be reached in the industrial schools, and suggested for them the formation of a lodging-house corresponding with that which had been so successful with the newsboys. Mr. Brace had long been hoping for such a movement, and at once issued an appeal to the public, which is of great interest in view of the complete success of his plan. The circular is as follows: —

It is well known, both to the public and to all engaged in efforts among the poor, that there is a large class of young girls, from fourteen to seventeen years of age, who are either idle or employed in street trades, and are thus exposed to much temptation and danger. They are not trained to any systematic labor. Some of them employ themselves in peddling, while most make an adventurous kind of livelihood in strolling about the city as rag and bone pickers. . . .

These girls are evidently better adapted, if they were once trained, for places as domestic servants than for any other employment; and, if they could get the requisite education, they would almost universally prefer such situations. The plan, then, is to open a school for training young girls as plain cooks and laundresses. Let a floor be hired for a kitchen where the girls can be trained, and a laundry where washing could be taken in for others. The girls should receive wages as an inducement to enter; and then, after a certain time of training, they could be sent forth with a special recommendation sure to procure them a place.

The profits of the house, if carefully managed, might pay the rent and even the salary of the matron, leaving only a small part of the expenses "a pure gift of charity" for this class.

It is our firm conviction, from considerable experience, that the efforts at reform with the class of young women accustomed to an idle and disgraceful livelihood of crime are almost futile and useless. The only mode of meeting this enormous evil in our city is by prevention, and one special means in this direction is by giving industrial employment early to the class of young street-girls who ultimately feed the other unhappy class.

In 1862 enough subscriptions were obtained to make a beginning, and in this way was established the Girls' Lodging-house and Training School, which has accomplished such wonderful results in the reformation and training of wayward girls. This house became a model for many others, both Catholic and Protestant; and, as a result, the streets of New York have been comparatively cleared of vagrant girls.

INDUSTRIAL SCHOOLS.

As a simple, practical measure to save from vice the girls of the poor, nothing has ever been equal to the industrial schools.

Along with his effort for homeless boys, Mr. Brace early attempted to found a comprehensive organization of industrial schools for the needy and ragged little children of the city.

Though the public schools are open to all, experience has taught

ELIZABETH HOME AND TRAINING SCHOOL FOR GIRLS.

Erected in 1892 to the memory of Miss Elizabeth Davenport Wheeler, by her family.

that vast numbers of children are so ill-clothed and destitute that they are ashamed to attend those places of instruction, or their mothers are obliged to employ them during parts of the day, or they are begging or engaged in street occupations, and will not attend, or, if they do, attend very irregularly. Very many are playing about the docks or idling in the streets.

Forty years ago nothing seemed to check this evil. It was estimated that the number of vagrant children was 30,000. The commitments for vagrancy were enormous, reaching in one year (1857) for females alone 3,449; in 1859, 5,778; and, in 1860, 5,880. In these we have not the exact number of children, but it was certainly very large.

Mr. Brace saw that what was needed to check crime and vagrancy among young children was some school of industry and morals adapted for the class.

They needed some help in the way of clothing and food, much direct moral instruction, and training in industry; while their mothers required to be stimulated by earnest appeals to their consciences to induce them to send them to school. Agents must be sent round to gather the children, and to persuade the parents to educate their offspring. It was manifest that the public schools were not adapted to meet all these wants; and, indeed, the mingling of any eleemosynary features in our public educational establishments would have been injudicious. As the infant society had no funds, Mr. Brace's effort was to found something at first by outside help, with the hope subsequently of obtaining a permanent support for the new enterprises, and bringing them under the supervision of the parent society.

The agencies which he founded, with such wonderful results, were the industrial schools.

Each one of these charities has a history of its own — a history known only to the poor — of sacrifice, patience, and labor.

Some of the most gifted women of New York, of high position and fortune, as well as others of remarkable character and education, have poured forth without stint their services of love in connection with these ministrations of charity.

THE ROOKERIES OF THE FOURTH WARD.— A REMEDY.

In visiting from lane to lane and house to house in the poorest quarters, Mr. Brace soon came to know one district which seemed hopelessly given over to vice and misery,—the region radiating out from or near to Franklin Square, especially such streets as Cherry, Water, Dover, Roosevelt, and the neighboring lanes. Here were huge barracks,—one said to contain some 1,500 persons,

underground cellars crowded with people, and old rickety houses always having "a double" on the rear lot, so as more effectually to shut out light and air. Here were as many liquor-shops as houses, and those worse dens of vice, the "dance-saloons," where prostitution was in its most brazen form, and the unfortunate sailors were continually robbed or murdered. Nowhere in the city were so many murders committed, or was every species of crime so rife. Never, however, in this villanous quarter did he experience the slightest an-

THE SIXTH STREET INDUSTRIAL SCHOOL.
Erected in 1889 by Mrs. Wm. Douglas Sloane.

noyance in his visits, nor did any of the ladies who subsequently ransacked every den and hole where a child could shelter itself.

Mr. Brace's attention was early arrested by the number of wild, ragged little girls who were flitting about through these lanes, some with basket and poker gathering rags, some apparently seeking chances of stealing, and others doing errands for the dance-saloons and brothels or hanging about their doors. The police were constantly arresting them as "vagrants," when the mothers would beg them off from the good-natured justices, and promise to train them better in future. They were evidently fast training, however, for the most abandoned life. It seemed to Mr. Brace, if he could only get the refinement, education, and Christian enthusiasm of the better classes fairly to work here among these children, these terrible evils might be corrected, at least for the next generation. He accordingly went about from house to house among ladies whom he knew, and, representing the condition of the ward, induced them to attend a meeting of ladies to be held at the house of a prominent physician, whose wife had kindly offered her rooms.

For some months he prepared the public mind for these labors by incessant writing for the daily papers, by lectures, and by sermons in various pulpits.

Mr. Brace's hope and effort was to connect the two extremes of society in sympathy, and carry the forces of one class down to lift up the other. Nothing but the "enthusiasm of humanity," inspired by Christ, could lead the comfortable and the fastidious to such disagreeable scenes and hard labors as would meet them in this work.

In the meetings, gathered in the house of Dr. Parker, were prominent ladies from all the leading sects.

An address was delivered by Mr. Brace, and then a constitution presented of the simplest nature, and an association organized and officers appointed by the ladies present. This was the foundation of the "Fourth Ward Industrial School."

In the mean while Mr. Brace went forth through the slums of the ward, and let it be widely known that a school to teach work, and where food was given daily, and clothes were bestowed to the well-behaved, was just forming.

The room was in the basement of a church in Roosevelt Street. Hither gathered, on a morning in December, 1853, the ladies, and a flock of the most ill-clad and wildest little street-girls that could be collected anywhere in New York. They flew over the benches, they swore and fought with one another, they bandied vile language, and could hardly be tamed down sufficiently to allow the school to be opened.

The dress and ornaments of the ladies seemed to excite their admiration greatly. It was observed that they soon hid or softened their own worst peculiarities. They evidently could not at first understand the motive which led so many of a far higher and better class to come to help them. The two regular and salaried teachers took the discipline in hand gently and firmly. The ladies soon had their little classes, each gathered quietly about the one instructing. As a general thing, the ladies took upon themselves the industrial branches,-- sewing, knitting, crocheting, and the like: this gave them also excellent opportunities for moral instruction and winning the sympathy of the children. So it continued. Each day the wild little waifs became more disciplined and controlled: they began to like study and industry; they were more anxious to be clean and nicely dressed; they checked their tongues, and, in some degree, their tempers; they showed affection and gratitude to their teachers; their minds awakened; most of all, their moral faculties. The truths of religion or of morals, especially when dramatized in stories and incidents, reached them.

And no words can adequately picture the amount of loving service and patient sacrifice which was poured out by these ladies in this effort among the poor of the Fourth Ward. They never spared themselves or their means. Some came down every day to help in the school, some twice in the week. They were there in all weathers, and never wearied. Three of the number offered up their lives in these labors of humanity, and died in harness.

The effects of this particular school upon the morals of the juvenile population of the Fourth Ward were precisely as Mr. Brace had hoped. These little girls, who grew up in an atmosphere of crime and degradation, scarcely ever, when mature, joined the ranks of their sisters in crime. Trained to industry and familiar with the modest and refined appearance of pure women in the schools, they had no desire for the society of bad girls or to earn their living in an idle and shameful manner. They felt the disgrace of the abandoned life around them, and were soon above it. Though often the children of drunkards, they did not inherit the appetites of their mothers, or, if they did, their new training substituted higher and stronger desires. They were seldom known to have the habit of drinking as they grew up. Situations were continually found for them in the country or they secured places for themselves as servants in respectable families; and, becoming each day more used to better circumstances and more neatly dressed, they had little desire to visit their own wretched homes and remain in their families. Now and then there would be a fall from virtue among them, but the cases were very few indeed. As they grew up, they married young mechanics or farmers, and were soon far above the class from which they sprang. Such were the fruits, in general, of the patient, self-denying labors of these ladies in the Fourth Ward School.

For a more exact account of the results of the work in the Fourth Ward, it is difficult to obtain precise statistics. But, when we know from the prison reports that soon after the opening of this school there were imprisoned in one year 3,449 female vagrants of all ages, and that in 1870, when the little girls who then attended such schools would have matured, there were only 671 ; or when we observe that the prison in that neighborhood enclosed 3,172 female vagrants in 1861, and only 339 in 1871,— we may be assured that the sacrifices made in that ward have not been without their natural fruit.

The Italian School.

This school is the largest of all the industrial schools of the Children's Aid Society, and, owing to the great work it has accomplished among the poor Italian children, requires a brief description of its foundation.

In 1855 Mr. Brace was painfully struck with the sight of large numbers of poor Italian children engaged in street occupations, following the harp and hand-organ, selling newspapers, blackening boots, and the like, who were growing up utterly without education or moral discipline. The Italian tenement houses in the neighborhood of the Five Points were packed and crowded as buildings seldom are, even in this city. Mr. Brace resolved to try, for their improvement, the experiment of an industrial school entirely devoted to their interests. The greatest difficulties were the greed of the parents to get all possible earnings from their children without regard to their education, the bigotry of some of their advisers, and the existence among them of a species of serfdom, known as the "padroni traffic," whereby a child in Italy could be apprenticed to an association, and sent by it roaming over the world with some hard and cruel master. This traffic was the means of degrading a great number of little children every year.

The school was opened in 1855, and, under the constant exertions of Mr. Cerqua, the principal, has gradually attained greater size and solidity. The influence of the school has been to turn ignorant street children into artisans and mechanics of good moral character, who become excellent citizens. Some few have been sent to the West, who have done remarkably well there. With reference to their moral improvement, the Italian school children, as they grow up, are known generally for their industry and sobriety. So far as is known, out of the thousands of children who have been in the school, hardly three individuals have ever been arrested, and not one, so far as is known, for stealing.

During the early years of the school's history great effort was made by Mr. Brace to break up the "padroni traffic." Earnest representations were made of its evils and enormities in the public press, to distinguished individuals in Italy, and to the Italian Parliament. In a report, in the year 1873, of the committee appointed by the Italian Chamber of Deputies to gather facts in regard to this traffic in children, and to frame a bill for its suppression, the following statement was made:—

If the laws have been silent and the authorities indifferent, not so private and public charities. . . . To the Italian Slave Traders' Company the eminently benevolent institution, the Children's Aid Society, opened a school calculated to redeem these children physically and morally. For a time it was a hand-to-hand struggle with avarice, ignorance, and superstition. The little victims had to be followed from place to place, and their masters intimidated or talked into acquiescence; but perseverance, tact, and energy overcame all obstacles, and after twelve years hundreds of these poor little slaves have become honest and industrious young men. If this noble institution has not yet succeeded in completely eradicating the evil, it is because of the fresh supplies continually going forth from here.

This disgraceful traffic was at length broken up by an act passed by the Italian Parliament in 1873, and by similar acts passed in this country, both in State legislatures and in Congress.

At the present time the Children's Aid Society has under its charge twenty-one industrial schools and twelve night schools, and the history of the Fourth Ward and Italian schools is the history of each of these. No work is more important to the future of the city of New York than that of educating and training the children of the ignorant

THE EAST FORTY-FOURTH STREET BOYS' LODGING-HOUSE
AND INDUSTRIAL SCHOOL.

Erected in 1888 by Morris K. Jesup, Esq.

and helpless foreigners who crowd into the tenements in the Russian, Polish, Bohemian, Hungarian, and Italian quarters of our city. They must be taught our language. They must be trained to be clean, obedient to authority, industrious and truthful, and must be instructed in the elements of an English education. The ignorance, dirt, and poverty of thousands of these children prevent their attendance at the public schools of the city; and but for our industrial schools and others similar they would be left neglected. The daily average attendance is 5,100, and during the year over 11,000 children were brought under these reforming influences. In addition to the primary school work required by the Board of Education of the city, much attention is given to industrial training adapted to the needs of these children. Classes in carpentry, wood carving, typesetting, clay modelling, and drawing, have been taught; and in nearly all the schools are kindergartens, kitchen-training and cooking classes, besides sewing and dressmaking classes. The salaries of the instructors in these manual-training classes, and the cost of the school meals, so necessary to these half-starved children, are paid through the contributions of some of the prominent women of our city who are interested in the work. Several of our schools are greatly in need of such help, and of the friendly interest of volunteers and visitors.

Evening schools for older girls have been established in a few of our buildings by benevolent and charitable women who recognize the importance of interesting and training these girls, and the classes have exercised a great influence for good. These girls are occupied during the day in factories or shops, and have only the evening for social pleasure or improvement. By this means they are kept from the streets, and are brought under the ennobling influence of the Christian women who direct these classes.

Twelve of our industrial schools are in handsome and commodious buildings erected for the purpose by generous friends of the society. In these convenient, well-lighted, well-ventilated buildings the schools have permanent homes, and can be carried on much more efficiently than in their former confined and squalid quarters.

THE BEST REMEDY FOR JUVENILE PAUPERISM.

As is stated in the first circular issued by the society, Mr. Brace clearly saw that the children of the outcast poor must be removed from their debasing surroundings. The same course must also be taken with the homeless lads and girls in the lodging-houses. Though without a home, they were often not legally vagrant,— that is, they had some ostensible occupation, some street trade,— and no judge would commit them unless a flagrant case of vagrancy was made out against them. They were unwilling to be sent to asylums, and, indeed, were so numerous that all the asylums of the State could not contain them. Moreover, their care and charge in public institutions would have entailed enormous expenses on the city.

Mr. Brace also felt from the beginning that "asylum life," for any great length of time, is not the best training for outcast children in preparing them for practical life. In large buildings, where a multitude of children are gathered together, the bad corrupt the good, and the good are not educated in the virtues of real life. The machinery, too, which is so necessary in such large institutions, unfits a poor boy or girl for practical handwork. A few weeks' training and discipline is a good thing, but the best of all asylums for the outcast child is the farmer's home.

The United States has the enormous advantage over all other countries, in the treatment of difficult questions of pauperism and reform, that it possesses a practically unlimited area of arable land. The demand for labor on this land was beyond any supply. Moreover, the cultivators of the soil are in America a solid and intelligent class. From the nature of their circumstances, their laborers, or "help," must be members of their families and share in their social tone. It is accordingly of the utmost importance to them to train up children who shall aid in their work, and be associates of their own children.

Seeing the facts clearly, Mr. Brace first inaugurated for the benefit of the unfortunate children in New York a plan of emigration which, during his life, accomplished more in relieving New York of youthful misery than all other charities together.

At the outset, it was feared that the farmers would not want the children for help. And, when the children were placed, how were their interests to be watched over, and acts of oppression or hard dealing prevented or punished? Were they to be indentured or not? If this was the right scheme, why had it not been tried long ago in other cities or in England?

These and innumerable similar difficulties and objections were offered to this projected plan of relieving the city of its youthful pauperism and suffering. They all fell to the ground before the confident efforts to carry out a well-laid scheme.

The effort to place the children of the street in country families revealed a spirit of humanity and kindness throughout the rural districts which was truly delightful to see. People bore with these children of poverty, sometimes, as they did not with their own. Often there was a sublime spirit of patience exhibited toward these unfortunate little creatures which showed how deep a hold the Christian spirit had taken of many of our countrywomen.

The plan of emigration has been followed out successfully during forty years of constant action.

Little companies of emigrants are formed under the care of a competent agent. These children are brought to us from various sources, the majority being orphans placed in our charge by the infant asylums and homes, the House of Refuge, and other institutions. These children have been carefully selected by our agent with reference to their fitness for homes among the kind-hearted people of the West. Orphan boys and girls are frequently found in the lodging-houses who are fitted to accept good homes, thus removing them from the temptations of street life. These are cleaned and neatly clothed, and are kept under the eye of the superintendent until final selection is made.

The little party, together with such poor families as it has been found wise to assist to join friends or relations in the West, are despatched under the charge of an experienced agent, who has already selected a village where there is a call for the children. The agent on his former trip has appointed a committee of three of the leading citizens of the place, which has charge of the selection of the homes for the children, and passes upon the fitness of the proposed foster-parents to take proper care of the child. The committee is responsible, under the direction of the agent, for the proper selections of the homes; and, as they know the neighborhood well, it is rare that a mistake is made. An agreement is made with the farmer who takes a child, but it is not in any way indentured. The children remain in charge of the society, and may be removed at any time as thought best for their welfare, either by the visiting agent or the committee.

The society's system for visiting the children is very complete.

In Nebraska, Kansas, and Missouri are permanent resident agents. who have oversight of their respective districts, and can be sent hastily to investigate any trouble or remove a child, should occasion arise.   These gentlemen are prominent citizens, who have offered their services because of their interest in these charitable labors. The society also employs four agents of long experience, whose duties are to place the children and subsequently to visit them.   Besides these are the office clerks, under the direct supervision of Mr. Holste, the assistant treasurer, who correspond with the children placed out, and keep the records posted.

Under this system these homeless waifs find themselves in comfortable and kind homes, with all the boundless advantages and opportunities of the Western farmer's life about them.

SUMMER CHARITIES.

The Fresh Air Fund of the Children's Aid Society brings immediate and practical benefits to the children of the poor who are crowded in the hot and stifling tenements of the city.   During the summer months the suffering of the poor in New York is intense. and the mortality among the infants and young children is very great. To give these poor children the happiness of knowing the beautiful world beyond the city limits, the sea and sky and the green fields. was early a great wish of Mr. Brace.   Before the New York *Times* came to his aid in 1872, excursions for the children of the industrial schools had been given.   With the help of the *Times* these excursions had been greatly enlarged, but not until 1874 was the first Summer Home established for poor children.   The following extract from Mr. Brace's report of that year is in point: "One of the most beautiful charities ever devised by human compassion was incorporated with the work of our society during the past summer."   This Home was established at first on Staten Island as a summer resort and sanitarium for children.   The principal mover in the matter was a Christian woman whose heartfelt sympathies were aroused for the children of the poor, who were deprived of those blessings which were so much enjoyed by the more fortunate children of the rich. In speaking of the gratifying results of this trial year, Mr. Brace's report has the following reference: "Early in the summer detachments of seventy from our schools began to go down to the Home, each company to spend a week. They came with pale, pinched faces, and the shadow of much poverty and suffering on their young features. A week's sea air, fresh milk, good fare, and play in the fields made a different company of them. Some who had long been invalids were brought back to health, the sad were cheered, the thin and hungry made stout with good food. It was a gospel of good will to the poor and needy."

THE HAXTUN COTTAGE FOR CRIPPLED GIRLS, AT THE SUMMER
HOME, BATH BEACH.

In 1881 our trustee, Mr. A. B. Stone, presented to the society the beautiful Summer Home at Bath Beach, L.I., where thousands of children in a single season are made healthy and happy by their week of fun and frolic in the country.

Cheering as these results were, Mr. Brace longed for an enlargement of the work. He had noticed the wonderful tonic and healing effect of the sea air upon diarrhœal and all kindred diseases of children, and realized what a great blessing a sanitarium would be to the sick and dying children of the tenement-house population of our city. In the report of 1875 he brought before the public this pressing need: "Considering the terrible mortality of children in the city during July, the fearful amount of one hundred per day, no charity seems to us now more needed than a Seaside Hospital for sick children during the summer months."

D. Willis James, Esq., now president of the society, was in hearty sympathy with the work, and devoted $10,000 to this object. After careful search for the most suitable location, a lot was secured near the west end of Coney Island, having 300 feet upon the ocean, and extending back 1,000 feet to the quiet waters of Gravesend Bay. Upon this site a large and commodious building was erected, with all the necessary appointments for carrying on this work. The Seaside Sanitarium or Health Home opened for the reception of patients June 23, 1884, and during that season of eleven weeks there were 1,186 mothers and children who received the benefits of the Home. Enlargement was made from time to time, as the friends of the work saw the need and supplied the means, so that we were last year (1892) able to care for over 3,000 for the week each; and, if we add to this the number entertained for the day only, the total was 7,500.

The Sick Children's Mission, organized in 1873, employs a corps of physicians during the summer, visiting the sick little ones of the tenements, and ameliorating sufferings both with medicines and, when necessary, with nourishing food. Great demands are made upon this mission, and an immense amount of work is accomplished by its physicians and visitors. No aid to the poor is more necessary or more helpful than this.

Results.

It is forty years since Mr. Brace, the founder of the Children's Aid Society, began his work in behalf of the children of the poor and outcast in New York City. The fundamental idea upon which the society was founded, and which has been its governing motive ever since, was that of self-help,— of teaching children how to help themselves. The industrial schools, now numbering twenty-one, have trained and given aid and encouragement during these years to over 100,000 children of the very poor. In the Boys' and Girls' Lodging-houses about 200,000 homeless and vagrant boys and girls have found shelter, instruction, and the kindly advice and admonition of experienced superintendents.

THE EAST SIDE BOYS' LODGING-HOUSE AND INDUSTRIAL SCHOOL; ALSO OFFICE OF THE SICK CHILDREN'S MISSION AND FLOWER MISSION.

Erected in 1880 by Catherine L. Wolfe.

But, of all the efforts of the society to redeem juvenile humanity from the misery and suffering incident to a homeless life in a great city, the most inspiring is in connection with our system of placing homeless children in permanent homes in the West.

The following schedule shows the number of persons sent to each State by the Children's Aid Society since its formation in 1853. Homes were found for the younger of these children, employment for the older in New York and neighboring States, and poor families with children were assisted to points in the West where employment had been obtained for them by friends : —

Alabama,	24	Montana,	30
Arkansas,	57	Nebraska,	2,343
British America,	8	Nevada,	54
California,	254	New Hampshire,	56
Canada,	296	New Jersey,	4,149
Colorado,	739	New York,	38,719
Connecticut,	1,159	North Carolina,	73
Dakota,	469	Nova Scotia,	2
Delaware,	353	Ohio,	4,418
District of Columbia,	27	Oklahoma Territory,	12
Europe,	63	Oregon,	26
Florida,	258	Pennsylvania,	1,839
Georgia,	235	Rhode Island,	267
Idaho,	11	South Carolina,	136
Illinois,	7,366	Tennessee,	117
Indiana,	3,782	Texas,	318
Indian Territory,	16	South America,	1
Iowa,	4,852	Utah,	7
Kansas,	3,310	Vermont,	173
Kentucky,	152	Virginia,	1,448
Louisiana,	28	Washington,	114
Maine,	64	West Indies,	1
Manitoba,	15	West Virginia,	7
Maryland,	315	Wisconsin,	2,135
Massachusetts,	876	Wyoming,	6
Michigan,	2,900	To Sea,	3
Minnesota,	2,448	Returned to Parents,	4,722
Mississippi,	181	To Institutions,	1,480
Missouri,	4,835		
Total,			**97,738**

Of this whole number, 84,318 were children, 51,427 being boys and 32,891 girls. 39,406 were orphans; 17,383 had both parents living; 5,892, a father only; 11,954, a mother only; and of 9,680 the parental relations were unknown.

The younger of these children were placed in homes in the West and South, and the records of their careers have been carefully kept. They are visited to see that they are well cared for by their adoptive parents, and are corresponded with, from time to time, from the Society's office, and encouraged to do their best. The vast majority of the children so placed have turned out well, and many expressions of heartfelt gratitude come to us from them. Our labors in this field have been well rewarded, our records showing that 85 per cent. of those placed in homes are known to have turned out well, and but 2 per cent. badly. Many of these little ones, originally brought to us orphaned and destitute, have developed into useful men and women, with homes of their own; many are in the professions and ministry; and several hold positions of trust and great responsibility; and one has risen to the highest honor within the gift of his State, having been elected governor. When we contrast their present lives with what they might be but for the help of this society, we are enabled to realize the vast benefit to humanity accomplished by the plan so clearly set forth in Mr. Brace's first circular in 1853, and consistently followed to this day.

Mr. Brace, with wonderful foresight, saw clearly the great results to be reached by following the simple methods he pointed out; and the enlightened public opinion supported him. He resolutely eschewed all "sensations," "raffles," "fairs," or pathetic exhibitions of abandoned children; but by keeping the movements of the society before the public, through the pulpit and the daily press, Mr. Brace was able to interest people of influence, to obtain aid from the State legislature for the industrial schools, and the donations of all interested in humane work among the unfortunate and destitute.

In the annual report of the treasurer, George S. Coe, Esq., there appears an interesting table of receipts and expenditures from 1853 to this time, showing clearly the growth of the society from year to year, together with the total amount expended during the forty years.

TABLE OF RECEIPTS AND PAYMENTS TO NOV. 1, 1892.

	Received.	Paid.	Balance.
From Mar. 2, 1853, to Feb. 1, 1854	$4,732 77	$4,191.55	$541.22
From Feb. 1, 1854, to Feb. 1, 1855	10,399.85	9,939.88	459.98
From Feb. 1, 1855, to Feb. 1, 1856	10,524.06	10,027.09	496.97
From Feb. 1, 1856, to Feb. 1, 1857	12,148.67	11,532.75	615.92
From Feb. 1, 1857, to Feb. 1, 1858	15,662.39	15,566.42	95.07
From Feb. 1, 1858, to Feb. 1, 1859	17,399.29	17,072.40	326.89
From Feb. 1, 1859, to Feb. 1, 1860	12,634.92	12,210.11	435.81
From Feb. 1, 1860, to Feb. 1, 1861	21,241.17	19,762.92	478.25
From Feb. 1, 1861, to Feb. 1, 1862	17,186.00	16,613.98	572.72
From Feb. 1, 1862, to Feb. 1, 1863	22,926.69	22,803.88	684.93
From Feb. 1, 1863, to Feb. 1, 1864	38,065.65	38,743.90	933.68
From Feb. 1, 1864, to Feb. 1, 1865	54,935.72	53,682.46	1,253 26
From Feb. 1, 1865, to Feb. 1, 1866	74,249.73	72,043.65	2,206.08
From Feb. 1, 1866, to Feb. 1, 1867	93,377.07	92,408.37	1,167.90
From Feb. 1, 1867, to Feb. 1. 1868	115,017.48	113,643.99	1,373.49
From Feb. 1, 1868, to Feb. 1, 1869	162,963.56	159,793.21	3,170.53
From Feb. 1, 1869, to Nov. 1, 1869	98,084.54	96,978.59	1,105.95
From Nov. 1, 1869, to Nov. 1, 1870	175,935.33	173,166.78	2,768.55
From Nov. 1, 1870, to Nov. 1, 1871	156,427.99	153,471.55	2,686.44
From Nov. 1, 1871, to Nov. 1, 1872	162,459.39	159,064.71	3,394.68
From Nov. 1, 1872, to Nov. 1, 1873	172,325.70	171,058.11	1,267.59
From Nov. 1, 1873, to Nov. 1, 1874	225,747 92	224,690.90	1,057.22
From Nov. 1, 1874, to Nov. 1, 1875	230,664.46	228,832.65	1,771.81
From Nov. 1, 1875, to Nov. 1, 1876	214,489.53	213,438.16	1,051.27
From Nov. 1, 1876, to Nov. 1, 1877	233,911.40	229,396.26	6,515.13
From Nov. 1, 1877, to Nov. 1, 1878	229,697.01	125,197.44	4,499.57
From Nov. 1, 1878, to Nov. 1, 1879	205,583.25	204,340.26	1,242.99
From Nov. 1, 1879, to Nov. 1, 1880	215,473.61	211,007.25	4,446.26
From Nov. 1, 1880, to Nov. 1, 1881	234,892.25	230,919.17	3,973.08
From Nov. 1, 1881, to Nov. 1, 1882	237,583.25	236,069.93	1,554.32
From Nov. 1, 1882, to Nov. 1, 1883	251,713.94	253,865.00	
From Nov. 1, 1883, to Nov. 1, 1884	283,485.70	280,702.36	2,783.34
From Nov. 1, 1884, to Nov. 1, 1885	257,713.84	280,713.84	
From Nov. 1, 1885, to Nov. 1, 1886	277,072.04	276,916.03	156 01
From Nov 1, 1886, to Nov. 1, 1887	353,716.02	351,739.26	1,976.76
From Nov. 1, 1887, to Nov. 1, 1888	478,480.13	477,365.28	1,114 85
From Nov. 1, 1888, to Nov. 1, 1889	410,974.52	409,561.69	1,412.83
From Nov. 1, 1889, to Nov. 1, 1890	366 998.26	362.007.56	4,990.70
From Nov. 1, 1890, to Nov. 1, 1891	342,311.25	339,700.36	2,610 89
From Nov. 1, 1891, to Nov. 1, 1892	368,934.87	366,323.01	2,611.86

Total amount paid for whole term of years, ... $6,801,932.51

The following-named buildings and land are owned by the Children's Aid Society, viz.: —

1. Brace Memorial Lodging-house on Duane, William, and New Chambers Streets.
2. Italian School, 156 Leonard Street.
3. East Side Lodging-house, 287 East Broadway.
4. West Side Lodging-house, 201 West 32d Street.
5. Children's Summer Home, Bath Beach, L.I.
6. Health Home, West End, Coney Island.
7. Tompkins Square Lodging-house, 295 East 8th Street.
8. East 44th Street Lodging-house, 247 East 44th Street.
9. Astor Memorial School, 256 Mott Street.
10. 6th Street School, 632 6th Street.
11. Jones Memorial School, 407 East 73d Street.
12. Henrietta School, 215 East 21st Street.
13. Rhinelander School, 350 East 88th Street.
14. Elizabeth Home for Girls, 307 East 12th Street.
15. Sullivan Street School, 219 Sullivan Street.
16. Pike Street School, 28 Pike Street.
17. Avenue B School, 533 East 16th Street.
18. Lord Memorial School, 173 Rivington Street.
19. Farm School, Westchester County.

The following-named schools are located in buildings rented by the society: —

1. Fifth Ward School, 36 Beach Street.
2. Phelps School, 314 East 35th Street.
3. German School, 272 Second Street.
4. West Side Italian School, 24 Sullivan Street.
5. 52d Street School, 573 West 52d Street.
6. 64th Street School, 207 West 64th Street.

Calling attention to the list of buildings now owned by this society, and also those which are rented for its uses, Mr. Coe well says: "They show how this great city, by voluntary offerings alone, has been dotted over with convenient structures, which light it up in every direction with intelligent purpose and with kindly desire to promote the best interests and to relieve the distresses of that portion of the community most in need. These buildings have silently grown in such numbers and proportions as to be reckoned among the substantial and permanent elements of our Christian civilization. They can never be dispensed with; but, on the contrary, they stand conspicuously forward, craving continual increase and still more liberal support. . . .

"If wealth has increased, poverty has also kept pace with it, and this association stands between the two, offering invaluable service to both, while quietly soliciting of the benevolent their thoughtful charity."

CHAS. LORING BRACE,
Secretary.

CHILDREN'S AID SOCIETY, UNITED CHARITIES BUILDING,
Cor. 22d St. and 4th Ave., New York City,
March, 1893.

TRUSTEES AND OFFICERS

OF THE

CHILDREN'S AID SOCIETY.

☞ Subscriptions will be gladly received by the Treasurer, GEORGE S. COE, in the American Exchange National Bank, 128 Broadway, by either of the above Trustees, or by the Secretary at the Office.

Donations of clothing, shoes, stockings, etc., are very much needed, and may be sent to the Office, United Charities Building, 4th Avenue and 22d Street, or will be called for if the address be sent. Also old toys, children's books, etc., will be gladly received for distribution among the poor children at Christmas.

INDUSTRIAL SCHOOLS.

Astor Memorial School,	256 Mott Street.	Miss H. E. Stevens, Principal.
Avenue B "	533 East 16th Street.	Miss J. A. Andrews, "
Duane Street "	9 Duane Street.	Mrs. S. A. Seymour, "
East River "	247 East 44th Street.	Mrs. L. B. Briant, "
East Side "	287 East Broadway.	Miss A. Johnson, "
Fifth Ward "	36 Beach Street.	Miss M. G. Satterlee, "
52D Street "	573 West 52d Street.	Miss E. B. Bishop, "
German "	272 2d Street.	Miss E. Robertson, "
Henrietta "	215 East 21st Street.	Miss A. W. Strathern, "
Italian "	156 Leonard Street.	Mrs. A. Van Rhyn, "
Jones Memorial "	407 East 73d Street.	Miss E. Wells, "
Lord Memorial . "	173 Rivington Street.	Miss A. Hill, "
Phelps "	314 East 35th Street.	Miss B. M. Schlegel, "
Pike Street "	28 Pike Street.	Miss I K. Hook, "
Rhinelander "	350 East 88th Street.	Miss M. P. Pascal, "
6th Street "	630 6th Street.	Miss K. A. Hook, "
64th Street "	207 West 64th Street.	Mrs. E. O. Meeker, "
Sullivan Street "	219 Sullivan Street.	Mrs. C. A. Forman, "
Tompkins Square "	295 8th Street.	Miss I. Alburtus, "
West Side "	201 West 32d Street.	Miss E. Haight, "
West Side Italian "	24 Sullivan Street.	Mrs. E. T. Alleyn, "

NIGHT SCHOOLS.

East Side, 287 East Broadway.
Tompkins Square, 295 East 8th Street.
52D Street, 573 West 52d Street.
German, 272 2d Street.
44th Street, 247 East 44th Street.
Elizabeth Home for Girls, 507 East 12th Street.
Sullivan Street, 219 Sullivan Street.

Henrietta, 215 East 21st Street.
Italian, 156 Leonard Street.
Jones Memorial, 407 East 73d Street.
West Side, 201 West 32d Street.
Newsboys', 9 Duane Street.
West 64th Street, 207 West 64th Street.
6th Street, 630 6th Street.

LODGING-HOUSES.

Brace Memorial Lodging-house,	9 Duane Street.
East Side Lodging-house,	287 East Broadway.
44th Street Lodging-house,	247 East 44th Street.
Elizabeth Home,	307 East 12th Street.
Tompkins Square Lodging-house,	295 8th Street.
West Side Lodging-house,	201 West 32d Street.

SUMMER CHARITIES.

Children's Summer Home,	Bath Beach, L.I.
Cottage for Crippled Girls,	Summer Home, Bath Beach, L.I.
Health Home,	West Coney Island.
Sick Children's Mission,	287 East Broadway.

DRESSMAKING, SEWING-MACHINE, TYPE-WRITING SCHOOL, AND LAUNDRY, 807 East 12th Street.

FREE READING-ROOMS.

219 Sullivan Street.   247 East 44th Street.
AND AT ALL THE LODGING-HOUSES.

BOYS' JOB PRINTING OFFICE AND PUBLISHING HOUSE,
201 West 32nd Street.

FAMILY LIFE *VERSUS* INSTITUTION LIFE.

BY MISS SOPHIE E. MINTON,

CHAIRMAN COMMITTEE ON CHILDREN, STATE CHARITIES AID ASSOCIATION,
NEW YORK.

" He had once enjoyed the comforts of a Home with a capital ' H,' but it was the cosey one with the little ' h ' that he so much desired for her. Not that he had any ill-treatment to remember in the excellent institution of which he was for several years an inmate. The matron was an amiable and hard-working woman, who wished to do her duty to all the children under her care; but it would be an inspired being, indeed, who could give 150 motherless and fatherless children all the education and care and training they needed, to say nothing of the love they missed and craved. What wonder, then, that an occasional hungry little soul starved for want of something not provided by the management? — say, a morning cuddle in father's bed or a ride on father's knee,— in short, the sweet daily jumble of lap-trotting, gentle caressing, endearing words, twilight stories, motherly tucks-in-bed, good-night kisses,— all the dear, simple, every-day accompaniments of the home with the little ' h.' "

To any one who has read Mrs. Wiggin's charming story, and who recalls the quest of little Timothy, accompanied by the clothes-basket, the dog, and the baby, for a mother and a home, and his subsequent capture of the two old maids in the country village, the application of this story to our heading will be obvious.

In fact, here the key-note of the family system has been struck, and from it arise the harmony of natural law and the God-given command " to set the solitary in families." " Find out a law of nature, and work along its lines for the improvement of man, and success will crown your efforts," said a social economist to the writer not long since; and we who advocate the " placing out " of children believe that we have found in it that natural law. It seems strange that this cause should require advocating in this country, when the system is an accomplished fact all over Europe; and it lays the United States open to the charge of ignorance as regards progressive thought in "child-saving." There is no one of the monarchies which our crude young judgment terms "effete" that does not carry out the boarding-out plan largely to the exclusion of every other, even such countries as Spain and Italy; and we still cling to the old system of what might be called "child factories," manufactories in as true a sense as any others that work up material by the dozen.

When we look at England and France, what do we find? Such careful consideration of the environment in which the child is best acclimated, and where it could attain its most vigorous and healthy development, such close examination into cause and effect, such nice comparison of the results of various experiments, that we are filled with admiration for the painstaking study. What we do not find is a bequest of so much money, an architectural monument raised, so many children placed in it, and the same old regimental discipline continued that has been going on blindly for the last one hundred years. We take it as a foregone conclusion that here there has been no investigation of the modes of other countries, nor study of the progress made by the thinkers and workers of the day, else such obsolete systems could not be carried on in the face of the enlightenment of the nineteenth century. The Local Government Board of England has indorsed boarding out. France pursues it as its government system. We owe our best thanks for this to both countries.

Boarding-out, in Ireland termed "fosterage," dates back to immemorial times. After the abolishment of the Protestant Charter Schools in 1828, three Protestant workingmen determined to care for the orphan children of a friend from whose funeral they were returning; and "a penny a week" subscription was started, which was the origin of the Protestant Orphan Society. The children are boarded with respectable laborers or small farmers of their own faith. The character of the foster-mother is attested by the parish minister and the nearest resident magistrate. Inspectors appointed by the society visit and report. Nurses and their wards are required to present themselves at the annual meetings with a certificate that the children attend church, Sunday-school, and day-school. The society numbers 193 children in its care, and has started 2,781 young people on a useful career. While apprenticed, they are visited semi-annually by inspectors. A similarly conducted society, St. Bridget's, was started by a Roman Catholic lady in Dublin thirty years ago, with like good results. June, 1888, 105 of the 163 Irish unions had adopted boarding out. The Local Government Board issued an order in 1876, but unfortunately did not encourage voluntary visiting committees, essential safeguards to any placing-out system.

Scotland had no poorhouses before 1846 : the children were consequently cared for in families, but on an outdoor relief plan. Boarding out has now attained a success "that is proverbial." The foster-mother is termed "nurse," and belongs to the cottage, farm-laborer, or trades class ; and the homes are in the country. Children are visited by the assistant inspector once a month, and by the inspector annually. There is an effort made to find places for them in the neighborhood of the Home, so that they may continue to visit the nurse, and that she may exercise something of a mother's care over them. A liberal reading of the Scotch law allows the guardians to remove a child from the neighborhood of its parents, where they are notorious evil livers. In 1888 the whole number boarded out was 5,082. The career of 541 out of 624 was traced, and only 9 found unsatisfactory. "The crucial test of the system is the decrease of pauperism," which has become marked in Scotland. In 1859 the ratio of persons receiving parochial aid was 4 per cent. In 1888, and for the three preceding years, the percentage of pauperism to population was 2 to 4. The same year in England and Wales it was about 3 per cent.[*]

Leaving England and France, with which we wish to deal in detail, let us glance at some more remote countries.

Reaching our furthest points, we find in Spain, in Sweden, in the Netherlands, in Italy, depot asylums for the first reception of children, from which they are boarded in peasant families. Austria makes the mistake of placing them with their mothers or relatives, thus degrading the system to that of outdoor relief. Vast institutions were established at Moscow and St. Petersburg. The mortality in the latter was in the first fifteen months after its opening two-thirds of the whole. This fact, added to the increased desertion by mothers, occasioned by the opportunity offered them, led to the reform of this institution. In 1797 the number of children received was limited, and they were boarded out with "agricultural laborers." Central stations, which serve also as schools and infirmaries, are erected through the country.

Much study has been given in Germany to child-saving problems ;

[*] "Children of State," Florence Davenport Hill.

and we owe to her the best reformatory system known, that of Wichern's Rauhe Haus, near Hamburg, denominated the cottage system, and closely followed by Demetz's colony at Mettray, France. Owing to want of proper supervision, boarding out fell into disfavor. At one time asylums and orphanages were built; but their short-comings soon became apparent, and recourse was had to the old sys- tem under better safeguards. In 1845 Pastor Braun established a society in Rhenish Prussia, which distributes its children through a "clearing-house." Hamburg boards out its wards, and more than half the Berlin children find the same outcome. Here the system has been extended to include delinquent cases, discretion being ex- ercised as to which children shall be put in a family, which sent to a reformatory school. The celebrated orphanage at Rummelsburg, thirty years old, has five houses for fifty boys each, two houses for girls, one hundred each, a nursery for children under seven, hospital departments, etc.,— in all, 480 children. The opinion is expressed that "for girls individual treatment is decidedly better than keeping them in orphanages"; and the result seems to have been that the report for 1884 speaks only "of boys born in wedlock, except in the invalid house."

Berlin claims a mixed system of boarding out and orphanages.

The history of dependent children is nowhere more interesting than in France, where from very early times the custom has existed of putting out children to nurse in the country. As long ago as the reign of King John, in 1450, an ordinance existed regulating the en- gagement and payment of nurses. So many children were found "exposed" on the highways by their parents that Louis XIV. es- tablished the Hospice des Enfants Trouvés. From here the children were sent to country nurses; but as no regular surveillance was had, and at the age of five or six payment for them ceased, and they were returned to the hospice, the accumulation became great, overrunning not only the St. Antoine, but the Pitié and the Salpétrière. Happily for the children, the remedy was found in allowing them to continue with their nurses until the age of thirteen; and this grew into the family method, the present State system of France. "Assisted children" comprise all children abandoned by their parents, orphans in fact or through circumstance; and, as there exists great facility for such abandonments, the class is very large. Their system in this respect seems open to criticism; but, as we have to do with the final disposal of children, and not with their reception, we will pass by this phase of the situation. Suffice it to say that the Foundling Asylum in London had but five hundred children in a population of four millions, and the annual abandonments in the department of the Seine amount to 3,200.*

To the "assisted" was added the care of the "morally abandoned" in 1881, the class cared for by our Societies for Prevention of Cruelty. In this service we note some striking and progressive features, but let us first examine the system of the "enfants assistés."

This provides for the child "a guardian to watch over its rights, a family to supply that which he has lost, a calling, which later will assure his support." The Minister of the Interior appoints the resident inspector for each department. The larger divisions — that of the Seine has twenty-eight thousand children — are divided into districts, each with a resident agent; and these are again subdivided by medical inspectors. These latter visit small children once a month, and older ones at least four times a year, which visits are noted. The inspector also visits. Almost all the nurses belong to the agricultural class. The child becomes a laborer, marries, raises a family, and thus somewhat counterbalances the depletion of the Provinces, so largely drawn upon by Paris. Now, children are often kept at the hospice only over night, and a consequent reduction of the death-rate has ensued. In 1870 for those under twelve it was 8.88. It reached its lowest point in ten years, in 1878, when it was 4.47. In 1887 the number of children under the department of the Seine was 27,982: the number of deaths in the asylum, 78; in the country, 752.† Expenses are shared between the departments and the State.

The striking features in the service of the morally abandoned are not only the extension of the placing-out system to the reformatory cases, but the novel idea of placing such cases in groups in manufacturing establishments. Children under ten are placed like "assisted" children in families. "A child is rarely born vicious; he becomes so." The results for these young children have been excellent. Children over ten are placed sometimes singly as apprentices, but largely in groups of twenty, forty, fifty, in industrial establishments and factories, great success being claimed for the latter

* L. Brueyre, "Cercle de St. Simon," 1886.
† De Thulié, "Enfants assistés de la Seine."

experiment.   Large industrial houses make a contract with the Administration, receiving the children as apprentices.   The head of the establishment undertakes to give them separate lodgings, to feed and clothe them, to give them primary instruction in the calling, by special teacher.   They receive a salary proportioned to their services. The Administration pays their general expenses, their instruction and medical care, and also allows small sums in prizes, etc.   Each account is hung on the walls of the building,— a powerful incentive to exertion.   A debit and credit account is kept, and it frequently happens that on his majority a well-conducted pupil has eight hundred to one thousand francs : the sum has been known to amount to two thousand.*   There remain the schools of agriculture at Villefranche. of cabinet-making at Montevrain, and two schools of printing and artificial flower-making, the latter for girls, for a selected class.   In the placing of groups in factories, we find the application of another natural law, interest awakened in a career and self-respect gained. by teaching the pupil that he can be " the artificer of his own fortunes."

We have dealt so at length with France because nowhere has the family system been more thoroughly and triumphantly carried out. It will be seen that, except for special cases, institutions have been absolutely laid aside, and that the admirable power of analysis of the French mind has divined the natural, and therefore the best, solution of the pauper problem.

The care of children on the Continent is much simplified by the absence of the workhouse and its consequent hereditary pauperism. and by the non-existence of large pauper schools supported by legal taxation, which means contribute to form an artificial system and to perpetuate the very pauperism they are designed to correct.

When we come to England, we have the complicated machinery of poor-laws with which to deal, from which our own system, though less rigid, seems to have been drawn.

There are the workhouse schools, which we need not describe, because in nearly all our States the evils of poorhouse contamination have been recognized and the children removed from its influence.

Then come the separate or district schools.   These greatly resemble our large institutions. drawing their resources from public funds, except for being theoretically a part of the workhouse.   It is

* L. Brueyre, 1890.

required that children sent into employment should return to the workhouse to get their discharges. These are managed by a board of guardians, "representatives of contributory unions," who employ an adequate staff of paid officers and servants. The objections urged against them are the setting apart of the children as a separate class, the wearing of uniform, the want of classification, the mixing of so-called "ins and outs," temporary with permanent children, and the herding together of large numbers, treated not individually, but in the mass. Even here our larger institutions do not compare favorably, because 500 inmates is set as too large a number; and it is regretted that there "still exist three schools of over 500 children, one over 600, two over 700, and another over 1,000." *

To any one acquainted with the figures of our large institutions, the comparison is to their detriment. In the city and State of New York in October, 1889, various institutions held respectively 2,255, 1,497, 1,927, 1,464, 1,023, 864, 779, 715, 672, 802, 633, 591, 543, 864, 556, 401 ; and a number contained between 100 and 200.†

Some of the best of these separate schools are thus described : Quatt School began with forty children, boys and girls. The number is now one hundred and sixty-three. There are a chaplain, seven resident officers, besides servants. The boys do the rough housework and cultivate the farm, which produces milk, butter, and vegetables. Pigs and calves are raised. The girls do the lighter housework, besides sewing and knitting for themselves and the boys. The bigger children have their own gardens. There are a savings-bank and a library. The success in after-life of the boys much exceeded that of the girls, but 80 per cent. were known to do well. The *Cottage Home* at Swansea ‡ consists of six cottages, built for twelve children each, boys and girls being brought up in association, thus allowing brothers and sisters to remain together. All the children are half-timers, the boys working on the land, the girls in the house. The demand for children for places in homes exceeds the supply, and their after-careers are said to be very satisfactory. At the Forest Gate Homes the girls before leaving are sent to a small class for special training in housework, buy the food they require at the neighboring shops, and keep their own accounts. In another instance, girls have their own rooms and bureaus before leaving.

* Children of the State.   † Report of New York State Board of Charities, 1890.
‡ This is the system at the Presbyterian Orphanage, Philadelphia.

Of homes supported entirely by private charity, we find one at Brockham, Surrey, consisting of two departments, a nursery and children's home, the limit in the latter thirty-eight girls. One at Bath for twelve to fifteen children. Another supported by the West Derby Union for twenty or twenty-five. That of the Countess of Devon, twenty-four girls. The Howard Home, accounted too large, accommodates forty. That of the Sisters of the Orphanage of Mercy, Kilburn, three hundred and fifty, mainly girls; and it is regretted that its excellent management has recently enlarged the admission.

It will be seen that the success of these schools is considered to be in exact ratio to the smallness of their capacity. Comparing them with even the best of our own institutions, we must admit our inferiority. Where shall we find such a Home as the Quatt School? Where Homes for such little groups of children, and where such attention paid to individuality, as at Forest Gate? If, then, holding this superiority, boarding out is acknowledged by the best practical theorists to be attended with the greater success, how much more effective would be the system with us, with our larger facilities for placing in family homes!

But we have not yet stated our boarding-out case for England. An examination into Eton Union apprentices in 1861, for two years back, showed that 40 per cent. had turned out ill. The children were subsequently boarded out, with a success which has continued ever since. Charlton, Kings Norton, Clifton, Bethnal Green, Calverton, the Association for the Advancement of Boarding Out, the Church of England Society, all place out children with markedly successful results; and in 1870 the Poor Law Board of London issued an order sanctioning the boarding out of children beyond their union, under the charge of certified committees.

Such is the experience and present practice of the Old World. Let us see what testimony meets us from the newest of civilizations.

South Australia had a "barrack school" at Magill, where the tendency of a congregate mass of children to become institutionized soon showed itself. An outbreak of ophthalmia was added to the evil effects already recognized, with the result of breaking up the school except as a temporary depot. A State Children's Council was created, and all children "destitute, neglected or convicted," are now placed in families. Local Visiting Committees of ladies were formed, forty-two in one year. June 30, 1892, the Council had 858 children in charge. 514 were boarded out, 214 licensed to service, 63 placed with relatives on approbation, 42 were adopted. The total number under supervision was 878. The report of the Council for 1892 says, "The boarding-out system is undoubtedly the best plan for successfully dealing with State children."

Victoria closed its Infant, Industrial, and Royal Park Schools in 1879. There are now only two receiving depots in Melbourne, one for boys and one for girls. A few small probationary schools, for not more than eighteen each, have been opened, simply as "feeders" of boarding out.

New South Wales, on the same system, proves a diminishing number of State children. "As in Victoria, the family system has not been accepted half-heartedly: the children have not been left in large institutions, because they were already built, and it was a pity not to use them."

We have chosen to draw these examples from the experience of other nationalities (and we here wish to express our indebtedness to Miss Davenport Hill's "Children of the State") rather than from our own, because to most students of "child saving" the admirable work of Coldwater, Mich., with its one child to every 10,000 of population, the Massachusetts system with its like percentage of one to every 1,500, of Ohio with one to every 1,000,* the story of the Children's Aid of New York, and the effective enterprise of the Children's Aid of Philadelphia are well known, or can readily be known by reference to the reports of these societies.

Such, then, are our authorities for urging placing out. In some of our own States, as at Coldwater or in Ohio, Connecticut, etc., temporary homes are in requisition; but these are strictly used as "clearing-houses," first steps to placing out. And now what plea do we use for the substitution of this system for institution life? It seems to us this is easily deduced from the examples we have had before us.

Children brought up in a well-systematized institution must be made to conform to certain discipline and machinery of government essential to its good management. The same drill which makes a good soldier annihilates the individuality of the child. He is taught to dress, to act, to repeat a lesson in a uniform manner and in a set

* Report of Coldwater School, Michigan, 1888.

way. He is not a unit, but a fraction of a whole. His wants are all provided for without care or responsibility on his part : he cannot realize that on his own frugality, his own industry, his own integrity. depend the future he may expect. How can boys who have not had manual training or been taught practical agriculture work readily at a trade, at the hard labor of a field, or undertake the care of cattle? It will be urged that in an occasional institution manual training is given; but is not this usually the teaching part of, and not a whole trade, merely the "rudiments of work"? How can girls prepare for cooking in a plain home in a building where large ranges are used? how learn to wash and iron in huge laundries, where the entire wash of a large establishment is done? What chances have they for practice in domestic housework, their natural and proper outcome? Will not children used to the comfort of steam-heated halls and to being waited on, find it a hardship to break ice for water to drink or wash in, to bring water from a well, to chop wood, bring coals from a cellar, make fires at dawn,— all experiences likely to come to them in a hard-working after-life? In a word, does such treatment toughen a child, and give him strength to fight his way in the world? Does it not rather weaken him? But more serious than all this is the want of fathering and mothering, "the ride on father's knee or the cuddle in mother's arms," impossible even to the best-intentioned matron, except in the very smallest of institutions, say for eight or ten. We have known families in the uppermost class where there were ten or twelve children, and one pretty generally took care of the other. How shall they attain the development of character gained in the rough-and-tumble of every-day life, with its petty annoyances, small disciplines, little pleasures? No shut-in existence can fit a person for the battle of life; and these children are born to such a combat as surely "as the sparks fly upward." They need primarily the home life,— cuffs and caresses, sympathy and reproof, self-restraint and self-reliance. These are not on the curriculum of any institution: even the little English Homes are but a substitute for a reality, and they come twice as dear. The matron at Magill said: "I would never have a lot of young children together: they never develop. They only grow up into half-idiotic men and women. We have only five now, and they are as bright again as when we had twenty." Children massed in large institutions are "singularly backward and stupid, showing a want of pluck, dependence on others, inability to shift for themselves,— characteristics which develop into the grown pauper." Again, "there are many girls who are immoral from the barrack system, hardly any from foster-homes." * They are " ignorant of money, the rights and duties of property, the necessity for providence and economy." † " Sent out to service, they are called stupid because they have never seen the articles they are called on to use." Permanent children are subjected to the influence of casuals, and to association with " corrupted " children,— a class recognized in all institutions. Lastly, however good the institution, the children are still a class apart, looking naturally to the public for support.

On the other hand, when we place a child in a home by a small payment, with its share in the household work, it gives something for what it gets; and we place it in its natural surroundings. "Children should be placed as nearly as possible in the same material conditions as those in which they were born. Rough conditions are nothing, if the influence is good, morally and physically." We expect from the foster-mother " the same care she would give one of her own children "; and we have ascertained that that care is good by earnest inquiry, and continue to insure it by careful visitation. That such affection cannot be expected from a foster-mother is disproved by universal testimony. Instance after instance, in many lands and in many tongues, is given of the attachment between foster-parent and child, to the extent of retaining the child without payment, and final adoption. One little fellow shouted out to the neighbors, " I've got a father now." " Living the same life as his nurse, sharing the family joys and sorrows, brought up in the same cottage and without other treatment than that of his foster-brothers and sisters, the assisted child becomes an integral part of the family." ‡

The only advantage we can concede to an institution is that of a possible " higher education "; but this is purchased at a loss of more vital considerations, such as the freedom from the contamination of " corrupted " children, the safety from ophthalmia,— " rarely known in boarded-out cases,"— the superior robustness of mind and body, the development of individuality, and the removal from a pauper classification.

The question of a sufficient supply of good homes has been abundantly answered in the experience of our great " boarding-out and placing-out " societies. The doubt of this, we think, has arisen

* Children of the State. † M. Peyron. ‡ M. Brueyre.

from the wish to place the child on a higher social scale than that in which it was born. This we believe to be a mistake. We have already quoted Miss Hill. Mr. Henly, the English Poor Law Inspector, says, " So long as the essential requirements of health are considered, the rougher and homelier they [the homes] are, the better." And we all know Mrs. Lowell's " A good home, however poor, is better than the best institution." " When we are to provide for the education of any body of men, we ought seriously to consider the particular functions they are to perform in life." *

Now, we doubt the desirability of raising these children from the laboring classes to that of factory girls, of petty clerks, perhaps the most doubtful moral outcome in our community.

Moreover, why should not the French principle apply here? Why should not the depletion of our rural districts be made up by a return supply of city children to the country? Be it understood we are not speaking of abnormal or defective children who require special treatment. Neither do we claim this method as an easy one, nor free from dangers and difficulties. Much care must be had in choosing of homes, much discretion and fidelity must be observed in visiting. " Supervision must be quiet, not regarded as a court of appeal from the family."

English study endows us with many useful lessons. An advantage cited is that, when a child is old enough to go out to a situation, he has a home to return to temporarily, and he does not lose his family ties. Instances are given where children found work in their neighborhood, and the foster-mother continued to wash for them and mend their clothes. We are warned that payment for the child should not be given in his presence, every effort should be made to obliterate the artificial connection. Payment should be " a fair remuneration, but not a source of profit"; and in no case should a child be placed where his board is a sole source of revenue. The younger children are sent the better, the more easily are they absorbed in the family, and they escape the well-known mortality of babies' hospitals. Objection is made to boarding children with relatives or their parents, as the money becomes " outdoor relief," and is open to the evils of that system. Care must be taken not to relieve parents of their children too easily,— an evil which leads to a great abuse of institutions, and which is greatly lessened by the

* Herbert Spencer.

boarding-out system. The excellent means taken in Pennsylvania and Massachusetts to stem the tide of abandoned children, by placing out mothers with children in families, will be treated in other papers, so that we need not touch on it here.

Mrs. Cobb's interesting treatise on the "Responsibility of States to their Dependent Children" insists strongly on the non-separation of mother and child; but we find in it definite statements which call for a reply.

She refers to the common plea against institutional homes: that the treatment of children is hard and unloving, that the matrons, teachers, etc., do not care for the children, but are only parts of the huge machinery, that the discipline is too strict, that the children have all work and no play. And she then proceeds to use as an argument against these statements that visiting boards prevent cruelty and provide pleasure; that children are no more institution-ized than at public schools or at Girard College; that children are ont readily surrendered to institutions on "account of the agony of a desolate creature who gives up the child she has long striven to sup-port"; and that nearly one-tenth of the expenses of an institution are paid by the so-termed "pauperized parents." * And she winds up with the usual charge against theorists.

Now, we have never heard the reasons she assigns urged as charges against institutions. The "manufactured" children that are their products do not come from any deficiency in the kind hearts or good heads of the managers or the matrons, but simply from the unwieldy bulk of the machine. Children living in their own homes attend-ing public schools, or the older and better class attending Girard College, are working to prepare themselves for their future support, have their home influence, and cannot in any way be compared with the class known as "destitute" children. We believe that Mrs. Cobb's broken-hearted mother exists; but, surely, our conclusions are proved by the statistics of asylums, which show how readily chil-dren are surrendered by parents or relatives. The fact is that these children are sent to an asylum as to a free boarding-school; and, when the working age is attained, they are withdrawn with equal freedom. We do not know how much parents pay for children in Rhode Island, but we know that tax-payers and private benevolence pay for them in New York; and, if these so-called pauperized parents do pay in

* Responsibility of States to their Dependent Children.

part for them at an asylum, had they not infinitely better be caring for them at home? The term "theorists" can hardly be applied to persons who have been placing children in families from time immemorial to the present day. We are surprised that Mrs. Cobb. who so wisely urges the preservation of the family tie, should not see how the institution system loosens it.

To the family system she objects that the only home admissible is the "ideal home." This idea, as we have before stated, arises, we think, from a mistaken desire to elevate the child in the social scale. and the not being content with rough, if good and honest, surroundings. She considers that persons capable of selecting and supervising homes must have "superhuman qualifications." Now, no system is perfect, largely owing to the imperfect tools to be employed. and mistakes have been and always will be made; but the after-results of placing out, as shown by examination all over the world. justify the statement that here is found "the greatest good to the greatest number," and this presupposes some efficiency in the ordinary run of human beings. The "desire for cheap help" is a danger, but one that can be guarded against; and the "unfitness between child and place" can also be guarded by the power of transfer lodged in the committees, and by the establishment of a most simple temporary home as a clearing-house.

It is also true that boarding out in France is rendered easy by the placing of Catholic children in Catholic families, and in Scotland by placing Protestant children in Protestant families; but this difficulty has been met in England and Ireland by the establishment of committees respectively of the two faiths, and we presume the same plan would work in this country in the same way.

The "crucial test," after all, as Miss Hill has wisely said, "lies in the diminution of pauperism": and this proof will be found on the side of placing out.

Granted, then, that we do not consider institution life a good provision for dependent children, we find one of the strongest arguments against it, and one of the strongest pleas for boarding out. in the immense accumulation which has taken place in New York City institutions. We have already cited some of the largest figures, and we now draw others from Mrs. Lowell's strong report to the State Board of Charities. Before the passage of Chapter 173. 1875. the city was supporting 9,363 children in private institutions and on

Randall's Island, at a cost of $757,858. In 1888 it supported 15,697 children in the same way, at a cost of $1,632,891. This is an increase of 6,334 children, $875,033 in cost. New York State supported 1 to every 251 of the population, Michigan 1 to every 10,000, Massachusetts 1 to every 995,— a strong showing of the different systems. The investigation and control assumed by the Brooklyn officials over the children drawing support from the public fund had the effect of reducing this number from 1,479 children in 1880 to 1,180 in 1889.* A comparison of the systems of New York and Pennsylvania in 1890 gives the following figures: New York City, with a population of 1,500,000, appropriated in the year 1890 $1,840,292, for the support in private institutions and on Randall's Island, of an average of not less than 15,000 children; and Philadelphia, with a population of 1,000,000, appropriated during the same period $28,724.82 for the support of an average of less than 250 children, including those of the Philadelphia Hospital and Training School for Feeble-minded. A sum of money in bulk from the State treasury was divided at the same time among three institutions, thus bringing up the total cost of Philadelphia children for that year to $40,224.82.† The enormous contrast in these figures emphasizes strongly the relative merits of the systems in the two cities.

There is no question that the New York system of a per capita sum drawn from the public funds is a direct bid for the accumulation of children in asylums. The danger to a board of managers lies in the temptation to make a pet of the establishment, to allow the prosperity of the institution to take the place in their minds of the good of the individual. To this weakness, common to human nature, the system is an exact appeal. It is easier and cheaper to provide for a number than a few. How convenient to swell the treasury by an additional per capita child! To the superficial glance, how much better to do a little good to a great number than an effective good to a few! "How many children have you under your care?" is the test question of the unthinking, instead of, "How many can you prove to have turned out well in after-life?" which is the only absolute test question. On the other hand, looking at it from the point of view of the poor parent, how convenient is a free boarding-school, where he has confidence in the manage-

* Report of New York State Board of Charities, 1890.
† State Charities Record, New York, December, 1891.

ment, where his child is taught his own faith, where all care and responsibility are lifted from his shoulder, and whence he can withdraw his child at will! How easy it is for him to shift his burden upon the public!

We have said why this is not good for the child. Is it good for the parent? Does it not break one of the most sacred of ties? Does it not make both willing dependants on public support? Does it not encourage laziness and self-indulgence? How many a poor woman has to surrender a child to an institution because the drunken father does not provide for it! We cannot sacrifice the child to the father's vice, but we must not make it too easy for him to continue in evil living. Is it just that honest tax-payers should be forced to support his vices? On the mother's side of the question, any system that leads to the easy abandonment of a child leads to subsequent immorality on the mother's part, and degrades the parent to the animal species. We have seen the results of this in the foundling system of Paris, and we hope that the key to the enigma has been found by Pennsylvania and Massachusetts in their placing out of mothers with children.

Now, we believe boarding out to be a simple remedy for all this accumulation. It is a fact that many poor people, who would readily place their child in an institution for the above-mentioned reasons, would strenuously object to have him boarded out. They have not the same confidence in the management, and their pride is hurt and their jealousy excited by handing over the care of their child to some other woman, while these same emotions are not excited by the impersonality of a board of managers. Hence they will make every effort, both of hard-working and decent living, to keep the child, or at least to get him back as soon as possible. We are presupposing love for the child; for, alas! it is well known that with some unfortunate women there is little more tenderness than with an animal for its offspring. And, surely, in this latter case the way to cultivate the maternal instinct is not to separate the child from the mother, but to use every means to urge her to care for it.

It is true that almost all institutions claim ultimate placing out, but state that obstacles lie in the way of it, such as parental claims or the defective nature of children under their care; their inefficiency in this regard is proved by the average number of the children still remaining in the institutions annually.

For defective cases ultimate placing out can be reached only by the preliminary watchful care accorded to groups of four or five children, and such care is not attainable in our institutions.

Summing up the case for boarding out, let us conclude with these words from "Children of the State": "When we find nations differing in origin, living under various forms of government, and educated in divergent religious beliefs, seeking to solve a difficult social problem, and all of them without preconcerted action or special communication lighting on one and the same solution, we may safely conclude that that solution must be the best, based in the universal needs of our common human nature, asserting themselves above all temporary and external differences of creed and politics, country and race."

THE MASSACHUSETTS SYSTEM OF CARING FOR STATE MINOR WARDS.

BY MRS. ANNE B. RICHARDSON,

MEMBER STATE BOARD OF LUNACY AND CHARITY, LOWELL, MASS.

The plan for the work of child saving — preventive work, or, as it is termed in Massachusetts, "Care of the minor wards of the State" — includes three classes of children, — "neglected children," "dependent children," and "juvenile offenders."

Dependent children are those who are deprived of natural support by reason of the poverty, illness, death, or criminality of their parents, such parents having no "settlement" in any town of the State, and thus becoming a State charge. The meaning of "neglected children" is not quite so obvious, because it is not apparent why they are not included in the "dependent" class. The distinction is this: neglected children are the offspring of parents who *can*, but *do not*, provide suitably for them, and whose vicious lives render them unfit to have the care of them. The term "juvenile offenders" conveys its own meaning.

In the cases of the first two named, "dependent" and "neglected" children, all necessary facts being established, they are placed by the courts in the care of overseers of the poor in the towns where they live, who, if they are found to be of "unsettled" parentage, turn them over to the custody of the State Board of Lunacy and Charity. Any citizen may make complaint in the cases of "neglected" children to the proper court or magistrate. This placing of these two classes of children, exclusive of infants (whose care will be described later), usually results in putting them in the State Primary School. Of the older children, such as are classed as "juvenile offenders," other means are employed and other disposition made of them. "Complaint having been made before court or magistrate, a summons is issued to the parents or legal guardians of the boy or girl; and, if there is no such person, the court or magistrate appoints some suitable person to act in behalf of such boy or girl, requiring

NEGLECTED CHILDREN, TAKEN JUST AFTER COMMITMENT TO CUSTODY OF STATE BOARD OF LUNACY AND CHARITY. (CARE OF DEPARTMENT OF INDOOR POOR.)

him or her to appear at a time and place stated in the summons,
and show cause why such boy or girl shall not be committed to the
Lyman School for Boys or the Industrial School for Girls, respectively." Written notice is sent to "the Board of Lunacy and
Charity of the pending of such complaint." An agent of the Board
is sent to attend the trial, whose business it is to find all the facts
in the case, and with whom the magistrate consults as to the final
disposition of the child. In the cases of young children convicted
of petty offences, a commitment is made to the "custody of the
Board," as it is called, by which body the child is placed in the
Primary School, and who, though remaining there under precisely
the same conditions as the "dependent" and "neglected" children,
has a legal status somewhat differing from that of the latter classes.

In the cases of the juvenile delinquents, commitment is made, if
a boy under fifteen years of age, to the Lyman School at Westborough; if a girl under seventeen, to the State Industrial School at
Lancaster. They are so placed "during minority." They may,
however, instead of being sent to either of these institutions, be
placed in the "custody of the Board of Lunacy and Charity," as
has been stated of the younger offenders; may be placed "on probation" in their own homes or elsewhere; or "otherwise disposed of,
at the discretion of the court or magistrate, in accordance with law."

From the neglected and dependent classes there are taken the
infants or children under three years of age, technically known as
"foundlings and destitute infants," who receive entirely different
care, such as their helpless age requires. All foundlings and all
destitute, motherless infants who have no settlements in the cities
and towns are cared for directly by the State. Until within fifteen
years these infants were, like the older pauper children, sent to the
State Almshouse. In 1876 the trustees, in consequence of the great
mortality in that institution among these children, and by the advice of the State Board of Lunacy and Charity, refused to receive
any infants without their mothers. In 1880 a law was passed by
the legislature, providing that all such children should be cared for
directly by the State Board. It should be stated here that this high
rate of mortality was not in excess of that of any institution where
infants are congregated under like conditions. Since 1880 these
infants have been boarded in families, with the best results. This
course had an effect to reduce the percentage of deaths from 97 to

50 the first year. The next year this percentage was still further
reduced to 30, and since that time has not averaged more than from
14 to 20 per cent.

The present method of providing for these children is as
follows; and here I copy an extract from a paper by Mr. Shurt-
leff, Superintendent of Outdoor Poor, who has these infants in
charge : —

An infant, upon its commitment by the overseers of the poor
of a city or town, and its reception by the State Board, is examined by a medical officer of the Board's Department of Outdoor Poor, who makes a record of its condition. It is then sent
to a temporary nursery provided for the purpose, and as soon
as possible is placed at board in a good home in the country,
under the constant supervision of the Board and its medical officers. Every effort is at once made to find the parents of deserted children, with frequent success. In such case, the parent
is compelled to provide for the child. There is always a large
number of applications on file of persons who desire to take the
children to board, so that there is no lack of good homes in the
country towns near Boston readily reached by rail. Every home is
visited and investigated before being accepted. This visit is a sanitary inspection. The number and arrangement of sleeping-rooms
are noted, as well as the ventilation, sunlight, drainage, supply of
water and of milk, number of children in the family, and all other important matters, especially the character of the woman and her natural disposition and aptitude for caring for the child. In general,
not more than one or two children are placed in one home. Material
for clothing is bought in quantity at wholesale prices, of good quality,
plain, but varying in pattern, so as to avoid the appearance of uniformity. Most of the foster-mothers prefer to make up the clothing
themselves, and this disposition is encouraged. Part of the clothing
is supplied ready made. All material and clothing are stored at the
State House, and given out on a requisition. A record is kept of
everything given out or returned.

Some of the infants, when received, are hopelessly diseased ; while
others are moribund from drugging, starvation, and exposure. All
that can be done with these is to relieve them by proper nursing and
comfortable surroundings during their short lives. Some are maras-
mic, rachitic, syphilitic, or deformed ; and constant watchfulness and
attendance are required to bring them to a fair degree of health.
Others are fairly well, but feeble, and much more liable to disease
than other children ; while a few are robust, and seem to do well
from the outset. Whenever a child is placed at board, the woman
who takes it is instructed to telegraph at once to the medical officer

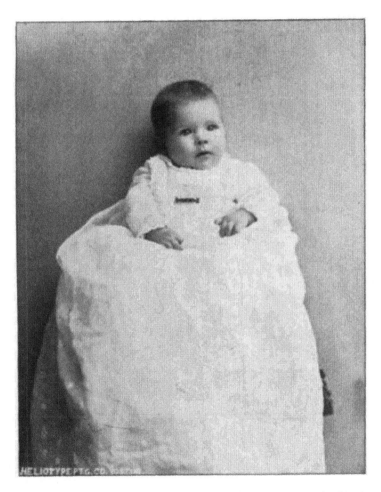

INFANT IN CARE OF DEPARTMENT OF OUTDOOR POOR TAKEN WHILE ON
TRIAL FOR ADOPTION. SINCE ADOPTED

having the child in charge at the first appearance of real illness ; and the physician responds at once. Sometimes the woman is directed by telegraph to employ her family physician temporarily, until it is possible for the medical visitor to attend. She is also cautioned to notify whenever in doubt about the illness of a child. Of course there can be no stated time of visiting a sick child by night or day, especially in the acute diseases to which these children are particularly liable in certain seasons. In summer a child with cholera infantum might require three visits a day; and the same would be true in cases of croup, diphtheria, or pneumonia. The medical officers are consequently never off duty. Their labor in summer is largely increased by the fact that all the young children are at that time in the country or at the seashore. It is a rule of the department that every child shall be visited as often as once a month for observation and as a preventive measure. Surgical appliances for mechanical support are often needed and supplied for ruptured or rachitic children, or for broken bones, club feet, etc.; and these cases require more time than ordinary medical cases in adjustment and after-treatment. As a rule, the necessary medicine is dispensed by the medical officers; but sometimes prescriptions are filled at a trustworthy pharmacy, and paid for by the woman, who sends her bill to the department for reimbursement. In such cases, the medical officer indorses the bill before it is approved. Supplies of medicine are furnished to the medical officer by a Boston druggist, who sends his bill to the department monthly. A careful record of each child is kept at the department, giving the name, age, date of commitment, physical condition, history, result of investigations, location, name of person boarding, visitation, course and treatment of disease, transfer, discharge, or death. When a child is considered eligible for adoption, its photograph is frequently added to the record.

These children are under the supervision of the Department of Outdoor Poor until they are three years old, or until discharged for adoption, to the town of settlement, or to the care of relatives, or by death. At the age of three years they are transferred to the charge of another department, but in many instances are not removed from their foster-mothers, or from the care of the same medical officers as before the transfer. In recent years the opportunities for obtaining homes by legal adoption into good families have been so great that it is rarely that a child reaches the age of three years without being thus permanently and satisfactorily provided for. No pains are spared to give these charges of the State the best possible start in their physical life; and closer medical oversight is unquestionably received by these children than by those of average families in the Commonwealth. The success of this work is distinctly the result of growth, of experience, of daily observation and scrutiny into the needs of each individual child. Adoption does not necessarily place the child beyond the knowledge of the department and its medical visitors.

and frequently the adoptive parents bring in the children to show their growth and improvement or to ask advice.

The method of procedure in cases of adoption is as follows : —

On receipt of an application for a child the names and locations of eligible children are given to the applicant. The children are visited ; and, if a satisfactory one is found, the home of the applicant is visited, and references are required and investigated. If everything seems satisfactory, the child is placed on trial with the family. If, after a certain length of time, all parties are satisfied and all legal conditions have been complied with, application is made to the Probate Court for legal adoption of the child.

In the case of a child's death occurring in Boston, the city undertaker is notified, the body is buried in Mt. Hope Cemetery, and the grave is numbered, so that the remains can be identified. In out-of-town cases, the child's body is usually buried by the undertaker of the town where the death occurred. In some instances, the persons who boarded the children bury them in their own lots and at their own expense. The spot is always marked. Funeral services are held over the remains of every deceased child of those boarded out under the charge of the department. Where the death has occurred from a contagious disease, as scarlet fever, the services are held at the house after the burial.

There can be no doubt regarding the very great advantages of the system of boarding out the infant children of the State as compared with the old method of caring for large numbers of them in an institution.

Thus, in a general way, I have stated how Massachusetts takes the initiatory steps in child-saving: that the State has cognizance of the "dependent," the "neglected" child, the "juvenile offender," the "foundling or destitute infant," from the time attention has been called to the "dependent" and "neglected" by the citizen or overseer of the poor, to the "juvenile offender" by his or her arraignment before a court or magistrate, or to an illegitimate or orphaned child, and to an abandoned baby, until all such have been placed in institution or family, in nursery or at board. It will be seen that no interest of these helpless ones has been neglected. They have had a defence in court, and have been finally placed according to the best judgment of magistrate and agent of the Board.

Of the institutions, the three schools to which these children are sent when not allowed to remain "on probation" (and this latter condition is exceptional), it is necessary that something should be said. The first in point of time is the one formerly known as the

FOUNDLING. TAKEN WHILE ON TRIAL FOR ADOPTION. ADOPTED SINCE.

Reform School, now the Lyman School at Westborough. In this
connection it may be proper to state that preventive work for children *by the State* really began with the establishment of this school,
which is certainly the first in this country, and probably the first in
the world, provided and maintained by the State alone ; for the New
York House of Refuge, established in 1824, the Boston House of
Reformation, in 1826, the Philadelphia House of Refuge, in 1826,
the Boston Farm School, in 1833, with the two European models,
Herr Wichern's Rauhe Haus at Hamburg (in 1833) and the famous
Mettray institution under the charge of M. Demetz at Tours (in
1839), were all private institutions. It was reserved for Massachusetts to inaugurate a *State* system of preventive work; for though inspired by the success of these private enterprises, and enriched by
the generosity of a private individual, Mr. Theodore Lyman, the
burden of maintenance and support was assumed from the first, and
has been continued to this time, by the Commonwealth. Mr. Lyman
had been interested in the subject of the reformation of juvenile offenders, because of his connection with the management of the above-
named Farm School. Some years before the final accomplishment
of the project of the State Reform School, so important was the
project considered that a petition was presented to the legislature,
signed by Chief Justice Shaw and many of Massachusetts' most
prominent citizens, asking for the creation of "a State institution for
the reformation of juvenile offenders." It was, however, not till
1847, and after Mr. Lyman had given $20,000 toward the object,
that an appropriation was made by the legislature, which was supplemented by still another in a few months (in all $66,000). The
buildings were erected, and the school opened Nov. 1, 1848.

It was the opinion of Mr. Lyman, and of others best fitted to give
such an opinion, that not more than three hundred boys should be
received. The numbers increased rapidly, and ten years from its
opening were more than doubled ; and the original accommodations
had been doubled also. More land was added, until the farm included nearly three hundred acres. A fire destroyed all the new
structure, and a part of the original one in 1859, when it was decided
that the main building should be remodelled, and should be arranged
for not more than two hundred boys, and that the family system
should be partially tried by the occupation of two or three detached
houses by families not to exceed thirty boys, and that the number of

families should not exceed five. In fact, only three such families were formed, two occupying old buildings originally on the place, and one a new building near the main structure.

This institution was intended for a reformatory, but from the beginning the main building was to all intents and purposes a prison. The doors were bolted, the windows barred, and the dormitories were practically cells, while places of confinement were provided not unlike the ordinary prison "solitary." Schools were organized, and the boys were taught four hours daily. Five and a half hours were devoted to devotional exercises, incidental duties, and recreation, six were spent in work, leaving eight and a half hours for sleep. The boys, who were expected by Mr. Lyman to be employed mainly on the land in agriculture, were (those in the main house were thus wholly employed in locked workshops) superintended by task-masters. The earnings of the boys were considerable, and contributed largely to the support of the institution. This was a wide departure from the original plan of Mr. Lyman, who said, "The general business of the school will be agriculture; but in the winter months more time will be given to the boys in the common branches of education, and it may be in some instruction in some of the mechanical trades." It was soon found that the boys, some of whom at the time of commitment were often fully sixteen years of age, were totally unfit subjects for a school, and that, when the fire of 1859 necessitated reconstruction, what was considered as a misfortune proved an opportunity for the first step towards the best system,— that of the family. Another evil had had much to do with a want of success, and this was that the sentence committing to it was an alternate one. In place of a commitment to the jail or house of correction, boys were sent to the Reform School for a period longer than the sentence to the first-named institutions would have been, so they often committed offences in the hope that they would be transferred to the House of Correction or jail for a shorter period than that of the school. After the fire of 1859 the legislature abolished this alternative sentence, and lowered the maximum age of commitment, which has fluctuated till 1884, when it was fixed at fifteen years. At this time the buildings were taken, with the farm, by the State for a lunatic hospital, a new site was purchased, and the school established strictly on the family system.

When the opportunity came with the sale of the old buildings in

1884 for entire reconstruction, the hope sprung up that something might be realized of the original intent ; and such has been the case. The fact had been demonstrated that a large congregate prison could not be the place best fitted for the reform of boys of ages varying from ten to sixteen. The present system of seven or eight families, each in charge of a master and mistress, each employed in domestic work of the houses, on the farm, in the barn, — in any way required by the occasions arising,— building, digging, etc., each family having regular school training for three or four hours daily, regular instruction in the Sloyd system of wood-working, in military drill, with necessary recreation,— this system is as satisfactory as that of any institution can be. The school is not perfect; and no claim is made that it is; but it is on the right road, and, as a preparation for life outside, is doing its work, on the whole, as well as can be expected. The numbers, though far less than in the old days, because boys then sent to the school are now often sent to the Reformatory Prison, which did not exist at that time, are still increasing ; and the buildings are still inadequate. It is a question whether the colony should be enlarged or a new one started. Other steps in the work of reform for which this school was instituted will be considered under the head of visitation.

THE STATE INDUSTRIAL SCHOOL AT LANCASTER.

The next step of Massachusetts in preventive work was the establishment of the Industrial School at Lancaster, for girls. The subject was somewhat agitated at the time the act establishing the Westborough School was brought before the legislature. It was felt that it was inopportune to introduce anything which might delay, perhaps prevent altogether, the passage of the Reform School Act ; and, it being finally decided that the two schools should have no connection with each other, the matter of the Industrial School was deferred until 1854, when the first appropriation was made, a commission appointed to select site, present plans, and finally to erect the buildings. The family system was from the first decided upon. On the present site buildings were erected suitable to carry out this system, and the school was opened August, 1856. The houses were intended to accommodate families of thirty, but have proved inadequate properly to contain so many ; and from time to time others have been provided.   No division by fences has ever existed between the houses, no means for restraint.   They have the look of common dwelling-houses, and the institution appearance is almost entirely avoided.   The family system has been strictly adhered to from the first.   Each house is governed by a matron, assisted by a teacher. who gives instruction at stated hours for a stated time, and a house-keeper who superintends and instructs the girls in cooking and other domestic duties.   The superintendent has general charge of the whole.   A farm of two hundred and thirty-five acres surrounds the buildings, and, besides contributing towards the food of the establishment, has added something in the way of income.   At one time there were five families; but since 1876 there have been but four, one house, having been burned, has never been rebuilt.   The numbers have been kept within the capacity of the remaining four houses by the constant placing of girls in families outside for domestic service.   This was always done to a considerable extent, either by indenture or otherwise; but the practice has grown very largely in the last few years, so that the numbers outside, who are still subject to the control of the trustees, nearly double those remaining in the school.   The maximum age of commitment has always been seventeen, and no desire has been expressed of late years to lower that age.   Girls of the minimum age, seven years, are no longer received, though permitted by the statute, because the trustees and others concerned disapprove of such a course, and because children requiring the discipline of an institution can be more suitably committed to the Primary School at Monson.   The school has had from its organization till 1883 male superintendents.   Since that time a woman has been its superintendent, to the great satisfaction of the trustees and of the Board of Lunacy and Charity.

For many years an attempt was made to introduce an industry which, while employing the girls, should also be remunerative.   It was always difficult, and of late years no such attempt has been made.   The girls are employed in domestic affairs, cooking, laundry work, general housework, on the farm in sowing, weeding, gathering crops, making hay, keeping walks in order, and in a variety of occupations, always superintended by a female attendant.   They also make repairs in the buildings in the way of papering, painting, oiling floors, whitewashing,— all inside repairs.   For several years no mechanics have been employed except on the outside of the

NEGLECTED CHILD, AT BOARD TAKEN JUST AFTER COMMITMENT TO
CUSTODY OF STATE BOARD OF LUNACY AND CHARITY. (CARE
OF DEPARTMENT OF INDOOR POOR.)

buildings or in plumbing or repair of heating apparatus. Their efficiency is most remarkable, and needs no other commentary than the statement that the demand for their services outside far exceeds the supply. No "modern improvements" have been permitted in the houses. They wash in tubs, which they must fill and empty themselves. They have no mangles run by steam. They iron in the old-fashioned way, and polish with the efforts of their own muscles. They have no steam-heated apartments in which to sleep. It is the intention of the superintendent and trustees to accustom them to the usual conditions of the farm-houses of New England, in which their services are most in demand, and which are their best homes. It is not intended to furnish the institution with such appliances as shall discontent them with those they will find in these farm-houses or in the homes they have left or in those which they will have perhaps some day of their own.

It is not necessary to state to those who will read this history of the school that these methods, this constant occupation, this variety of employment, this work hard and engrossing in itself, are agencies towards reform, leaving little time for reminiscences of a past which has been bad, and little room for thoughts which turn inward or downward rather than outward and upward.

Recreation is not forgotten. Schools have their share of time. Good reading is provided, and lives as healthy and happy as they can be are substituted for those which have been depraved, impure, and unhealthy.

THE STATE PRIMARY SCHOOL.

It has been shown at the beginning of this paper that the State Primary School receives children from Tewksbury, "juvenile offenders" from the courts when placed in the custody of the Board, and such "neglected" and "dependent" ones as are sent by the Board from the courts or directly from places of residence.

The school was established in 1866, in the buildings erected and used for a State Almshouse. The statute forbids their being classed as paupers; and, though for a time it seemed necessary to retain adult paupers here, the children were allowed no association with them. Graded schools are maintained, beginning with a kindergarten. To those who have seen the developing process of Froebel's system for the average child, and who have marvelled at its rapid progress, it would be still more of a marvel to witness the unfolding of these little *animals*, as they seem when admitted, into bright, active human beings. Whatever this system may be for the cultured and intelligent, there can be no question of its beneficent effect upon these untrained and untaught little ones.

The school is congregate, the arrangement of these old buildings admitting of no other system; but much has been done by judicious classification and by intelligent supervision, and less injury results from this system because it is really only a place of temporary detention during the process of fitting the children for outside life. This being done, the children are at once placed in families. Those too young to work are boarded until they are old enough to compensate for such board by the little they can do. After ten years of age, all, both boys and girls, are expected thus to earn their living.

In the history of these schools I have purposely omitted all reference to the undesirability of keeping children from any of the classes in institutions longer than is absolutely necessary for proper preparation to live outside. Family life is the only natural life; and, the sooner a boy or girl can be restored to it, the sooner will he or she be on the way toward development and usefulness.

The experiment of boarding children under ten years from the State Primary School in families, begun in 1882, has been considered a successful one; and at that date until 1886 45 per cent. of the average population of the school was so placed. In another year this percentage increased to 65 per cent. With some variation it advanced to 84 in 1891, while during the last year it has risen to 142 per cent. This sudden increase has been accomplished by the appointment of a special officer for the purpose of finding suitable homes. The statute originally provided for this policy of placing out; and it is the unanimous sentiment of the Board, with which the whole power rests of placing at board, with or without compensation, as also the power of discharge.

In Massachusetts, and indeed, as is believed, among the most enlightened thinkers elsewhere, there prevails the opinion that almost any healthful life with good moral influences is better than institution life, and that the real benefit to be derived from institutions is accomplished in a short time, if at all. Temporary detention is essential as preliminary preparation for family life, but except in

NEGLECTED CHILD. TAKEN WHILE IN A PRIVATE FAMILY, AFTER HAVING
BEEN AT BOARD. SINCE INDENTURED.

the cases of defective children — mentally or physically defective ones — it has little value after it has served the purpose named. Although reformatory institutions were once hoped to be the cure for many of the ills of society, such hopes have been dispelled by the experience of the last half-century; and, as has been stated, there is a growing distrust of their efficiency as the prime means to the desired end. It is felt that institution life must be unnatural, that long continuance in it handicaps the boy or girl for outside life. What a child needs in an institution is provided for it. It has a vague idea of some power which provides; but nothing is required of him or her,— no sacrifice, no effort. Life in an institution means crippling powers intended to be used: life in a family means using and developing these powers. To live in an institution, subject to rule and routine, at the State's expense, means stunted mental and moral faculties, means irresponsibility and inefficiency; to live in a family, development and growth of these faculties. A child may be obedient to all the rules of an institution, may even be conscientious in his obedience; but it cannot be fortified against outside temptations, for he meets there nothing akin to these temptations. Theories of conduct can be taught; but they fail, as all theories fail without an opportunity for practice. There is little opportunity to try mental or moral strength. If these children can, after the needed instruction in decency, and after reaching a fair physical condition, be sent out to meet the "rough-and-tumble" that other boys and girls born in humble circumstances are liable to meet, they are far more liable to emerge from the struggle strong and well equipped for life's work than if sheltered, fed, and clothed for years at public or private expense. No child should stay so long in an institution that there is begotten a helplessness, a spirit of dependence, than which nothing is more ignoble in itself or more deplorable in its consequences.

The experience of Massachusetts has proved that homes, and good ones, may be found for all classes of its dependent or delinquent ones,— for the infants of a few months, for the children of the State Primary School, for the boys of the Lyman School, and for the girls from the Industrial School. It will be questioned by those not familiar with this system if the rights of these helpless ones can be protected, if cognizance of their condition can be obtained when once outside the pale of institution life. To this end a system of visitation is most efficiently and thoroughly carried out by what is known as the Department of Indoor Poor, under the general direction of the Board of Lunacy and Charity. These visitors to boys consist of six men. The duty of one is mostly confined to the Lyman School boys, placing, visiting, advising, and returning these boys when necessary. The others attend courts in the interest of "juvenile offenders," investigate homes to ascertain if they are suitable ones, and visit boys placed in them.

A woman has the charge of children placed at board, and visits all such at their several boarding places. She procures adoption when it is advisable (afterward sanctioned by the Board), makes all bills for the children's board, and registers an account of the same in the ledger kept for that purpose. A special salaried visitor assists and advises in the placing of the older female wards, is ready for emergencies, exercises constant watchfulness over such as need this watchfulness, with such other duties as require good judgment and superior ability. The deputy-superintendent,— a woman,— assisted by two other women, attends to the correspondence concerning "juvenile offenders," "neglected," "dependent," or pauper children, with other matters pertaining to them, prepares reports on all applications for release or discharge of children from the custody of the Board, writes up the history of each child who is from any cause in the care of the State.

Since the organization of the Board of Lunacy and Charity there has been attendance at court in the interest of offenders in twenty-four thousand cases, thirteen thousand five hundred investigations of homes, and twenty-eight thousand visits to wards of the State.

In addition to these paid visitors there are nearly one hundred women known as Auxiliary Visitors, who visit the girls over twelve years of age (those under that age being visited by salaried visitors) placed out from the State Primary and Industrial Schools. These auxiliary visitors give gratuitous service, having only money paid out for actual expenses refunded. They are appointed by the Board of Lunacy and Charity after careful inquiry and receipt of information as to their fitness for the position. They advise the girls under their charge, stand between them and their employers, secure justice to both, see to it that the girls are protected from wrong, outside as well as inside, by their rules laid down for employers, and by all means in their power promote their best interest, prove to them that

NEGLECTED CHILD. TAKEN JUST AFTER RETURN TO HIS HOME BY STATE
BOARD OF LUNACY AND CHARITY.

they have a friend in need, and that the State stands to them *in loco parentis* in reality as well as in form.

The success of this organization has been most gratifying; and, though there have been failures and mistakes, it is the opinion of the Board that it could ill afford to dispense with the visitors' services. They report regularly to the Superintendent of Indoor Poor, and their reports are recorded in books kept for the purpose. These reports, together with the other information obtained from the mittimus at the time of commitment to the schools, and from the superintendents of the schools, form an almost unbroken record of these words of the State until they attain majority.

Thus it will be seen that, though Massachusetts, through its official representatives, disapproves of continuous and protracted institution life, it has provided for still better preventive methods of reform than such life, or for what it believes to be better. No system can claim perfection; but, surely, no system can claim progress which does not look constantly at results, and judge by them as to its value. Unsatisfactory as results must still be to those constantly raising the standard, it must be allowed that these results are better than those under the old *régime* of long-continued institution life of restraint, rule, and routine.

It is not claimed that the Massachusetts system of caring for State wards is as economical pecuniarily as would be that which mainly confines them to institutions; but it is claimed that the gain in good citizenship in the future of these children warrants the investment.

NON–SECTARIAN ENDOWED CHILD–SAVING INSTITUTIONS.

BY LYMAN P. ALDEN, TERRE HAUTE, IND.,

SUPERINTENDENT FOR EIGHT YEARS OF THE MICHIGAN STATE PUBLIC SCHOOL AND FOR NINE YEARS OF THE ROSE ORPHAN HOME, TERRE HAUTE.

The aphorism, "Prevention is better than cure," is an old one; but it is only in recent times that the truth embodied in it has been practically applied.   Formerly physicians directed their best energies to the *curing* of disease.   They fought plague, small-pox, typhoid fever, and cholera with drugs only, and were generally worsted in the encounter.   But the battle with these fell destroyers is now fought with different weapons on a different field.   Not *disease* itself so much as the *cause* of disease now receives the closest attention of medical men.   On this field the science of medicine has achieved splendid victories.   Vaccination, strict quarantine regulations, and attention to cleanliness, ventilation, good food, and pure water have brought these diseases largely under human control.

And so with respect to the treatment of crime and pauperism. While heroic efforts are still being made to reform criminals, and occasionally with some degree of success, it is true, yet all will agree that it would have been easier and cheaper in the first place to have prevented the crime than it has been to rehabilitate the criminal. And so, as never before, throughout all the civilized world the attention of philanthropists and social scientists, during the past forty years has been turned to the prevention of social evils by caring for and properly training that large class of destitute and neglected children from which the pauper and criminal classes largely spring.   In this country and Europe, to say nothing of the free kindergartens, aid societies, and other agencies, thousands of orphan homes, homes for destitute children, State public schools, industrial schools, and other institutions for saving the children have already been established; and the children cared for by them would make a grand army.

In this country the results of this work are a little disappointing at first sight. Crime is still slightly increasing. The census statistics for 1890 show that it has increased, during the past decade, in the United States, three and one-half per cent. faster than population. But much of this growth is clearly attributable to foreign immigration. It is well known that for many years our country has been the dumping-ground for the criminal, insane, pauper, and other defective classes of all the nations of Europe. Doubtless this increase of crime would have been vastly greater than it is, had it not been for these child-saving agencies. When our immigration laws have been revised and this indiscriminate immigration has been stopped and a longer time has been given to show the full effects of this work, we shall see crime steadily decreasing.

In Great Britain, where this work has been conducted for a longer period and more persistently and systematically, and where the government annually contributes large sums to supplement the gifts of the benevolent, the results are all that could be expected. Recent statistics show that, while population is increasing in Great Britain, crime has steadily decreased until it is now about thirty per cent. lower than it was thirty years ago. While various things may have aided in bringing about this gratifying result, it is believed that it has been largely accomplished through these preventive agencies. The directors of convict prisons, in one of their reports, after stating that the "development of the criminal classes appears to have received a permanent check," say, "The directors infer from these figures that the means which have been adopted in recent times for preventing crime by cutting it off at its source have begun to take effect on all but a comparatively small portion who are incorrigible."

The institutions for children in the United States are supported both by taxation and by the contributions of the benevolent. The census statistics for 1890 relating to children's homes are not yet published, and it is not known how many of them are sustained by taxation and how many by voluntary giving. The proportion supported by taxation is evidently on the increase. State after State is falling into line in assuming the support of its dependent wards. As all citizens are equally benefited, it is fair that all should share the expense; and, could our institutions be kept away from the blighting influence of politics, this would be the best way in some respects. But, unfortunately, this is not the case. The civil service reform has not yet reached even our benevolent State institutions.

Of those institutions supported by private charity, some are under the control of various associations and orders, others are under the fostering care of religious sects, while others still, independent of State, sect, association, or order, are either endowed or receive their support from the contributions of all classes of benevolent people. There are many such institutions in the United States which are doing a noble work, and their number is annually increasing. It is one of the compensations for the evils arising often from the accumulation of large fortunes in the hands of the few that so much of it is finally given to educational and charitable institutions, making it possible to accomplish, in this regard, in a year what would have required generations, had wealth been more evenly distributed. And for no purpose have our large-hearted wealthy citizens given their money more cheerfully than for the founding of homes for destitute children.

In response to the request of the Chairman of the Committee on the "History of the Child-saving Work," appointed by the last National Conference of Charities, I herewith present sketches of a few of our non-sectarian institutions which are either partially or fully endowed. As their methods of working, as well as their systems and aims, are unlike, they will serve to illustrate, in a general way, what many other similar institutions in the United States are now accomplishing.

GIRARD COLLEGE OF PHILADELPHIA, PENN.

The largest orphan asylum — indeed, the greatest private charity in the world — is Girard College, located at Philadelphia, Penn., founded in 1831 by the man whose name it bears.

Stephen Girard was born May 20, 1750, near Bordeaux, France. His father was a sea-captain, and a man of some means; but, owing to a disagreement with his stepmother and his love for the sea, Stephen left home at the early age of fourteen years, and shipped on board a merchant ship as a cabin boy, his father advancing him a small sum of money, with which he purchased some goods to trade with. At the early age of twenty-three, we find him the captain of a merchant ship, trading also on his own account. With about $3,000 worth of goods "he started on his first mercantile adventure," and this proved to be the foundation of his subsequent great fortune. In

1776, we find him located at Philadelphia, having given up the profession of a sailor, and become a merchant, for which profession his experience as trader and captain of a merchant vessel had fitted him. Subsequently his trade extended to Canton, Calcutta, and the East; and at one time he owned a fleet of fourteen merchant vessels, six of which were the finest merchantmen of that day. In 1812 he became a banker, and continued in that business through the rest of his life. In 1814, when our government was in great distress for want of money, Mr. Girard loaned it $5,000,000, and saved the credit of the country. When he died in 1831, at the age of eighty-one years, his fortune was estimated at $8,000,000.

Mr. Girard was once married, and had one child that died in infancy. His wife, to whom he was devotedly attached, eight years after their marriage began to show signs of insanity, and five years later, became hopelessly insane; and it was necessary to confine her to a hospital, where she remained until her death, twenty-five years later, or in 1815. Her husband survived her sixteen years. Mr. Girard was not a member of any church, though he believed in the general principles of religion. His religion consisted in being moral, honest, and just, and in relieving the wants of the sick, poor, and needy. In 1793, when yellow fever raged all summer in Philadelphia, and one-fifth of the people remaining in the city were swept away, when doctors were dead and there were no nurses left to care for the sick, Stephen Girard spent his entire time, for two months, in caring for and nursing the sick. After the pestilence had abated, he cared for two hundred orphan children who had no means nor friends.

It is not at all surprising, therefore, that at his death he should have left the bulk of his great fortune to objects of benevolence. After providing for his near relatives, leaving $116,000 to be divided among eight different city charities, giving $500,000 to the city of Philadelphia for certain improvements, $300,000 to the State of Pennsylvania for her canals, certain valuable property to the city of New Orleans, the remainder of his estate, worth then $6,000,000, he left for the erection of buildings and endowment of a college for orphans.

The work of construction on the first five buildings commenced in 1834; but they were not completed until 1847, in order that the accumulating interest might aid in meeting the expense, and so avoid drawing on the fund set aside for endowment.   These buildings were all constructed of white marble, at a cost of $2,966,237.   The central, or main, building is the finest specimen of pure Greek architecture in America.   It is a three-story building, 110 feet wide by 160 feet long and 97 feet high, covered by a massive marble roof.   A portico, 21 feet wide, supported by a peristyle of 34 Corinthian columns, 56 feet high, costing $13,000 each, surrounds the building, making the dimensions of the entire edifice, on the ground, 152 feet wide and 202 feet long.   Since then, at various times, seven additional buildings have been erected.   All are built of white marble: and some of them are very large and handsome, one being 400 feet long.   Several of the finest of these were designed by James H. Windrim, who was a former pupil of the college.

Notwithstanding this vast expenditure for buildings and the support of the college during the past forty-five years, the endowment fund has steadily increased, until it is now considerably over $15,000,-000, yielding a gross annual revenue of about $1,500,000.

Mr. Girard specified in his will that "as many poor white male orphans, between the ages of six and ten years, as the said income shall be adequate to maintain, shall be introduced into the college as soon as possible ; and from time to time, as there may be vacancies, or as increased ability from income may warrant, others shall be introduced."   Preference was to be given, first, to orphans born in Philadelphia ; secondly, to those born in any other part of Pennsylvania ; thirdly, to those born in the city of New York ; and, lastly, to those born in the city of New Orleans."   Children must be legally surrendered to the college before they can be admitted.   Those admitted are fed, clothed, cared for, and instructed at the expense of the college so long as they remain in it.   His will provides that "they shall be instructed in the various branches of a sound education, comprehending reading, writing, grammar, arithmetic, geography, navigation, surveying, practical mathematics, astronomy, natural, chemical, and experimental philosophy, the French and Spanish languages, and such other learning and science as the capacities of the several scholars may merit or warrant."   Mr. Girard especially desired that a pure attachment to our republican institutions and to the sacred rights of conscience should be formed in the minds of the scholars, and that great pains should be taken to instil into them a love for truth, sobriety, industry, and benevolence towards their fellow-creatures. No minister of any sect was ever to be admitted within the premises, as he wished to "keep the tender minds of the orphans, who are to derive advantage from this bequest, free from the excitement which clashing doctrines and sectarian controversy are apt to produce." But the college has an elegant chapel and moral and religious instruction is given on all suitable occasions. The officers and pupils attend worship daily in the chapel, before the opening of the schools and after their close. "The exercises consist of singing, reading the Scriptures, and prayer. On Sundays religious instruction is given by lectures or addresses delivered by the president of the college or some layman who may be invited, morning and afternoon, in addition to the daily worship." Boys who prove to be incorrigible under the mild means of reformation resorted to are summarily dismissed, as they should be, in order that they may not prove a source of contamination to better boys and injure the discipline and good name of the institution. All who have visited this noble institution have observed the courtesy and politeness of all the pupils. The other scholars "are discharged by binding them out," or by returning them to friends, where they have any, or by allowing them to do for themselves when they have completed their education. Mr. Girard desired that those who were proper subjects should remain until after they were fourteen years old, and not longer than till they should reach the age of eighteen years. With regard to binding children out, the president of the college, A. H. Fetterolf, LL.D., says: "Our experience with farmers has not been satisfactory. They are not considerate for the child's welfare, caring only to use him for their profit. We send our boys out between the ages of fourteen and eighteen. ... While I have no statistics on hand, judging from what I see of our graduates, I am inclined to think that they do better in life than the same number of boys picked from the public schools. If you can give children industrial training as well as a good English education, you will undoubtedly do better by them by keeping them until they are able to earn their own living. This is what a judicious parent would do: and why not those who stand in a parent's stead?"

The number leaving the college annually is about one hundred and fifty. Those who are bound out are looked after by an officer from the college, to see that they are well cared for. If not well treated, the child is taken back to the college.

The college was first opened for the reception of orphan boys Jan. 1, 1848, with one hundred pupils. From year to year the number has increased until there are now nearly 1,600 in attendance, the highest number being 1,585. The total number admitted up to the present time from the beginning is 4,844. The average annual expense of caring for and instructing each boy is $300.

The boys are from poor but respectable families, and, in this regard, are superior to the children found in most institutions for poor children. This partly explains the remarkable results attained by this institution. Of those annually dismissed from the college, about one hundred and fifty, or, on an average, not more than six, or four per cent., were dismissed for incorrigibility. Of four hundred and eight boys sent out in 1888, 1889, and 1890, only fifteen were reported as "doing badly," thirty as doing "fairly well," while the rest were all "doing well."

The practice of binding out boys has almost ceased. Only seventeen boys have been bound out in the last six years; though for many years, in the early history of the college, large numbers were so placed out in families. But it was found that after a boy had received his education, and had passed through the school of manual training,— a five years' course,— he could take better care of himself than the average family would give him. About fifty-seven per cent. of the four hundred and eight reported above as sent out in 1888, 1889, and 1890, engaged in "mechanical or kindred pursuits." The remainder engaged in commercial or clerical pursuits. The average age of the boys on leaving the college is sixteen years, though many remain until eighteen years old.

Mr. Girard left his property "in trust to the mayor, aldermen, and citizens of Philadelphia," and their successors forever. The city has since created a board called "Directors of City Trusts," and to this board is confided the management of the college. This board, composed of twelve citizens, is appointed by the judges of the Supreme Court of Pennsylvania, the judges of the District Court, and the Court of Common Pleas of the city and county of Philadelphia; which form a Board of Appointment, the members of the board serving during good behavior. The Board of Directors is composed of gentlemen who, by culture, social position, and otherwise, are eminently fitted for discharging the duties of their great trust.

The very successful management of the college and its funds dur-

INDUSTRIAL SCHOOL BUILDINGS, CHILDREN'S AID SOCIETY.

ing the past fifty-nine years, gives assurance that the management will
be equally good in the years to come ; and that this great charity will
remain a grand monument to the memory of Stephen Girard so long
as our country and any of its institutions shall exist.

CHILDREN'S INDUSTRIAL SCHOOL AND HOME OF CLEVELAND, OHIO.

In marked contrast with Girard College and its methods stands
the "Children's Industrial School and Home" of Cleveland, Ohio.
Girard College started with a large endowment. This institution
opened with no visible means of support. Girard College believes
in giving its graduates a thorough intellectual and manual training before sending them into the world, continued through a term
of from four to twelve years. This institution retains its children long enough, only, to thoroughly clean them up, correct a few
habits, start them in school, become somewhat acquainted with
their dispositions, and then returns them to friends or places them in
families. It maintains that no institution can take the place of a
family home, no matter how humble it may be. Says the Hon.
Harvey Rice, in his sketch of the Home, "So rapid is the transfer of
the children to homes that very few remain for a year in the institution. There is no purer or holier influence on earth than that which
surrounds the family altar."

This institution is the outgrowth of the Children's Aid Society
of Cleveland to rescue the destitute children of that city. Many
years ago the Rev. Dillon Prosser, a well-known Christian philan-
thropist of that city, opened a school for these children, every Sunday afternoon, in the front room of an old, unoccupied house on
Canal Street. A few old chairs and a flour barrel, bottom end up,
for a pulpit, constituted the only furniture. The school was known
as the "Ragged School," and soon grew and attracted public attention. In 1854 this school united with another benevolent enterprise,
known as the City Industrial School, which had been sustained by
an organization of charity workers named the "Children's Aid Society." This school was located on Champlain Street, and was partly
supported by the city and partly by benevolent contributions of its
citizens, but was under the control of the Children's Aid Society.
The average daily attendance was about seventy-five. But little permanent good was accomplished for the reason that the scholars were

mere day scholars, irregular in attendance, coming and going as the fancy took them; and, while at home, counter influences neutralized the moral instruction given in the school. But six or eight, who had no homes, were lodged, fed, and clothed in the rear part of the school building. These were surrendered to the exclusive control of the society, and for some of them homes were found. This feature of the work increased in importance; and the results were so much more satisfactory that the day scholars were all dismissed, and only those were received and instructed who had been fully surrendered to the society. About this time Mrs. Eliza Jennings gave to the society ten acres of land on Detroit Street with its farm buildings, and later, a liberal sum of money. To this the society added fifty acres by purchase, making sixty acres in all; and thither the home department was removed. Since then the late Amasa Stone, of Cleveland, has erected an elegant stone building for the children, costing $40,000: and Mrs. E. G. Leffingwell of that city has given a beautiful stone chapel, costing about $11,000. Various legacies have been left the institution from time to time, until it now has an endowment fund of over $64,000. So strong is its hold on the public that, ere many years, the endowment fund will doubtless be ample for its entire support. At present, the expenses are partly met by the annual contributions of benevolent people.

The children admitted to this Home come largely from Cleveland or from Cuyahoga County, and no charge is made for caring for these. But some children are also received from other counties, in Northern Ohio, for which a reasonable charge is made. Babies and children over sixteen years of age are not admitted, and all children must be sound in body and mind. If, after receiving them, they become incurably diseased, they are returned to their friends, as it is not the intention to make a hospital or reform school of the Home. After the children are legally surrendered and admitted to the Home, under the laws of Ohio, the natural parents are deprived of all right to interfere in any way with the care or management of them. In order to protect foster parents, who have taken children to raise, from the annoyance of visits from the natural parents, it has been found indispensably necessary that they shall not be told where their children are placed. It has the appearance of cruelty sometimes to withhold this information, but it is found by all institutions to lie at the foundation of success in placing out children. If informed, notwithstand-

ing the most solemn pledges to do nothing to make the children discontented, in almost every instance they succeed in breaking up the new home.

While in the institution, the children are provided with books and teachers, and such of them as are old enough are taught to do light work. While the Home is so conducted as to avoid all sectarian as well as political influences, it is pervaded with a deeply religious spirit; and the fundamental principles of Christianity that aid in moulding the lives of the children, so that they shall develop into noble Christian men and women, are daily taught. While there are accommodations in this institution for only fifty children, and the average attendance is less than that number, during the past year one hundred and thirty-seven children were admitted, and one hundred and forty-one were dismissed. Of those dismissed, eighty-six were placed in homes, fifty-four were returned to parents and friends, and one was sent to the Reform Farm. That is, about two-fifths were returned again to friends after a few weeks' or months' detention; and three-fifths were placed in families.

Children who are placed in families are occasionally visited, but how often is not stated in their last report. Great care is taken in selecting places for them. Of the 2,300 children and more that have been admitted to the institution from the beginning, over 1,200 have been placed in homes, generally in the country. Of those placed in homes, it is claimed that ninety-five per cent. are doing well. This is quite a remarkable showing, better than farmers can claim for their own children. It is possible that this estimate is based on reports received from children a few months after going out into families, and before there has been time for the child to show all its weak points, or before differences between guardian and child have occurred, which are apt to arise a little later on. During the first six months or so good reports are apt to come from almost every child. A year or two later, frictions have arisen which entirely change the complexion of the reports, repecting the same children, and at the end of a term of five or ten years, the percentage of those who have turned out well is apt to be greatly lowered.

Much of the great success of this institution is attributed by the trustees to the superintendent, Rev. William Sampson, who has had charge of it since 1876.

THE CLEVELAND PROTESTANT ORPHAN ASYLUM.

Another beautiful institution in Cleveland, Ohio, closely resembling the "Industrial School and Home" of the same city, is the "Cleveland Protestant Orphan Asylum." It, like the other, is the outgrowth of a society started in 1852 for the care of orphan children. Its work, however, at the present time, is not confined to orphan children alone. All homeless, neglected, and destitute children, who are sound in body and mind, and are not incorrigible, and who are of a suitable age, are admitted. To receive diseased, idiotic, insane, or incorrigible children would soon fill up such an institution with a class for whom no homes in families could be found, and shut out a hopeful class that could soon be placed in families and make room for others.

The children come from the city, county, and State, and must be surrendered by natural or legal guardians. Under the laws of Ohio children who are legally surrendered to any children's institution become its wards until they are twenty-one years old, and the control of the parent forever ceases. The institution may, however, surrender them again to the parent or parents when their circumstances have so improved that they are capable of suitably providing for them, and give them good mental and moral training; and, of the 3,496 children already admitted to this Home, a large percentage has been so returned. The others have been placed mostly in country homes, generally by adoption. This institution does not indenture its children. While some of their children do not do well continuously, and it is found necessary to place many of them out several times before they find just the home adapted to them, the large majority remain where first placed; and the superintendent, A. H. Shunk, thinks that, after a ten years' probation, ninety per cent. of them become at least fair, law-abiding citizens.

This institution, however, is extremely careful about placing its children. On an average, eight letters of inquiry are written regarding the standing of each applicant, and a "carefully kept record shows the percentage of homes accepted, after this rigid investigation, is one out of ten; or ten per cent. only of the homes offered are accepted by the committee." Mr. Douglas Perkins, who is president of the board, says: "We feel a great injury is done by promiscuous placing out,— not only to the child, whose life may be a wreck in consequence,

THE CLEVELAND PROTESTANT
ORPHAN ASYLUM.
1460 ST CLAIR ST

THE CLEVELAND BOOK...

but to the community into which the child is taken; and the cause of homeless children throughout the land suffers thereby." In one of the reports of this institution the following language is used:—

"Prior to the placing of nearly all our children, a careful preparatory work must be done, untidy, thriftless habits must be broken up, obedience to authority must become a habit, listless, contented idleness must be driven out by an ambition to excel in school and work, lax notions of integrity and truth must be supplanted by that self-respect and fear of God which are the basis of all future improvement in character."

The managers of this institution fully believe that as soon as the child is fitted for a home it should be placed in one. In another address Mr. Perkins says: "Experience, however, testifies that the institution, with its enforced habits of neatness and regularity and obedience, is useful for a short time for those taken from neglect and squalor. But even for this class this training is to be relied on only as a preparation for the free, higher life of the home and family. There it is that special individual care can train the heart to responsive, generous love, the hands to skilful work, and the head to thoughtful, varied care. But it is a serious thing to place a child in a home subject to the rule of that home. If it is kind and wise, it is an incalculable blessing; but, if a child is taken as a farm is rented, for the most that can be got out of it for the time being, at least cost, it is a cruel and wicked thing. So this system is like liberty, safe only with eternal vigilance."

The children that are placed out are regularly visited. During the past year the agents of the home spent 208 days, and travelled 31,145 miles in visiting them.

While this institution is non-sectarian, it is pervaded by a deeply religious spirit. The various religious organizations of the city are represented on its Board of Managers, without distinction of sect or sex, and have all contributed to its support and the endowment fund. In the past it was for some time dependent for its income upon the annual contributions of the benevolent; but its endowment fund has now reached $300,000, and it is entirely self-supporting. Still, it has such a warm hold on the affections of the charitably disposed in Cleveland that it is constantly the recipient of many generous donations in the line of clothing, pictures, books, games, toys, fruits, candies, etc.

For many years the acommodations for the children were very limited. But on the 19th of June, 1880, the asylum family was moved into one of the most elegant buildings belonging to any American institution for children. This building, which has accommodations for from ninety to one hundred children, on the congregate plan, cost $78,285.24, and was the gift of Mr. J. H. Wade. In addition to this Dr. Maynard erected a hospital department at a cost of $4,566,99; and the board expended a further sum of $12,487,81 for wash-house, flagging, fencing, etc. These sums do not cover any portion of the furnishing, which was donated, and is elegant. Mr. Leonard Case also gave four and one-half acres of land, on which the buildings stand, worth now $100,000.

The average number of children at the asylum is about eighty-five. During the past year one hundred and fifty-four were admitted. One hundred were adopted into homes, sixty-seven were returned to friends, and one died. The very able superintendent, Mr. A. H. Shunk, has been in charge many years.

THE WASHBURN MEMORIAL ORPHAN ASYLUM.

About four miles distant from the heart of Minneapolis,—that city of grassy lawns and beautiful homes,—in the midst of a grove of natural forest trees, and on an eminence overlooking the city, is a large and lofty red brick building, whose spire and chimneys can be seen from afar. This is one of the lions of Minneapolis, and to no place in the city do the citizens conduct strangers with greater pride and pleasure. This is the Washburn Orphan Home. The building was erected and the home was endowed with funds left for this purpose by the late ex-Governor Cadwallader C. Washburn as a memorial to his mother, whom he greatly loved and revered, and to whose moulding influences much that was great and noble in him was due.

Mr. Washburn was born about seventy-five years ago, at Livermore. Maine, where his boyhood and youth were spent. Later he went West; and the remainder of his life was spent in the States of Illinois, Wisconsin, and Minnesota, where he acquired both honors and a large fortune. There is in America no family name more illustrious or widely known than that of the Washburn family. Divided among the five brothers are the titles of Congressman, United States senator, judge, general, foreign minister, and governor. Three of the five

C. C. Washburn

brothers were governors of three different States, and all were eminent. Cadwallader C. Washburn at different times filled the positions of Congressman, general, and governor of Wisconsin.

His great fortune was largely acquired in Minneapolis by milling. He and his brother were proprietors of the great flour mills there which bear his family name, and which are known in business circles all over this country and Europe.

Mr. Washburn was no sectarian, and probably not a church member. But he thoroughly believed in applied Christianity. He may have been uncertain regarding many theological questions, important as many of them are; but he believed heartily in that practical religion that pays one hundred cents on the dollar, that makes men temperate, frugal, and industrious, that provides clothes for the naked, food for the hungry, medicine and nurses for the sick, shelter for orphans, and that visits the widow in her affliction. The best evidence we have that he loved his God is that he loved his fellow-men. To better their condition and lighten the burdens which so many must wearily carry all through life, he made many munificent bequests. Among these he left $375,000 for founding and endowing this asylum for orphans. In his will he says: "It is my intention during my life to found and endow an orphan asylum ... for the benefit of orphans and half-orphans having a legal residence in Minnesota, and in memory of my beloved mother, to be called The Washburn Memorial Asylum. But, if I shall fail to accomplish my intention during my lifetime, then I appoint the seven persons below named my trustees to carry my intentions into effect." These trustees included one of his brothers, William D. Washburn, and a sister, Mrs. Caroline Holmes. His life was cut short before he had the pleasure of seeing his plans materialize, but his trustees have faithfully carried out his intentions; and for several years quite a number of dependent orphan children have enjoyed the benefits of his munificence and kind provision for their wants.

The beautiful site, consisting of twenty acres, was given by his brother, W. D. Washburn. Since then fifteen acres have been added by purchase, making thirty-five acres in all. Excluding the value of the site, the sum of $136,353.18 has been expended in the erection of the building, grading of the grounds, planting of trees, furnishing and general equipment. The permanent endowment fund has increased; and on June 1, 1892, it amounted to $464,544.19.

The capacity of the present building, which is a large four-story edifice (the institution being conducted on the congregate plan), is for one hundred children ; and it is probable that in the near future another building will be added.

The Home was opened Nov. 16, 1886, with eight boys and one girl.   Year by year the number has been growing.   Up to last June one hundred and twenty children had been received since the opening of the Home.   Of these, two had died, fifteen have been returned to friends, eight have been placed in families, three were returned as incorrigible, one ran away, leaving ninety-one children in the Home at that date, of whom fifty-eight were boys and thirty-three were girls.

While in the Home, the children are instructed in the elements of an English education, and are trained to do the same kind of work that the boys and girls on the average farm are expected to perform. Trades are not taught.

Mr. Washburn specified very minutely what class of children should be admitted, and how they should be dismissed.   His will provided that " any child under fourteen years of age " (having a legal residence in Minnesota), "whether orphan or half-orphan, shall be received without any question or distinction as to age, sex, color, or religion, and shall be discharged at the age of fifteen, or as near that age as may be consistent with the terms into which the year may be divided.   In no case except sickness shall any one remain beyond the age of fifteen and one-half years, and then no longer than may be necessary for removal with safety, as it is not my intention that the asylum shall be used as a hospital. . . . My trustees are authorized to exclude or remove insane, idiotic, and imbecile children, and to exclude or remove children whose vicious habits would be a source of contamination and danger to the well-disposed."

Evidently, Mr. Washburn's idea was to retain all children who were suitable in body, mind, and character until they should secure a respectable English education, which never could be taken from them, and then return them to friends or place them in families. He recognized the possibility that children sent out to country homes, before the elements of an education were secured, might grow up to citizenship in almost entire ignorance, notwithstanding the ordinary contract that secures indentured children three or four months' schooling each year ; for many country schools are almost worthless, and many guardians cut a little off the prescribed school term at both

ends, and sometimes in the middle. His ideas in this regard resembled those of Mr. Girard, though the latter allowed those susceptible of receiving a higher education to remain in his institution until eighteen years of age.

The Washburn Home is so well endowed and has such a solid foundation that there are no fears that it will not be permanent.

THE ROSE ORPHAN HOME OF TERRE HAUTE, IND.

Another institution for children endowed by the beneficence of one individual, resembling the Washburn Asylum in some respects, yet sharply contrasted with it in others, is the Rose Orphan Home of Terre Haute, Ind. Both were endowed by men who had made their own fortunes, and at about the same time. Both receive orphans and half-orphans, and each has accommodations for nearly one hundred children. But the Rose Home limits its beneficence to the children of the county where it is located. The other admits children from the entire State of Minnesota. Children in the Rose Home may be retained, if it is thought advisable, until they reach the age of sixteen years, but, as a fact, are placed in families as soon as good homes can be found, and the children are prepared to go out. The Washburn Asylum does not dismiss its children till they are fifteen years old, and, except in case of sickness, may not retain them any longer. The former has the cottage, while the latter has the congregate system.

This institution was established and endowed by the late Chauncey Rose, who was born in Wethersfield, Conn., Dec. 24, 1794. His father was a farmer of small means, with eight children to support, all of whom died childless, and three of them quite wealthy. He came to Terre Haute in 1818, a few years after the town was laid out, but soon afterwards engaged in milling for five years in an adjoining county, and did not permanently establish himself in Terre Haute till 1824. From that time he was a resident of this city until he died in 1877, at the age of eighty-one years. During these years, by successful merchandising and judicious investments in real estate and railroad enterprises, he acquired a princely fortune, every dollar of which was earned by the most rigid honesty. He was strictly just in all his dealings with others, but insisted on others dealing exactly with him. He was the chief promoter of three of the most prominent railroads centering in Terre Haute, and for a time was president of one of them. His name was identified for many years with every enterprise connected with the development of the city. He was no miser, hoarding his wealth till death overtook him, and he could keep it no longer. During his life he gave freely to churches and every charity that commended itself to his judgment. Between the years 1863 and 1869 he gave at different times, in sums ranging from $1,000 to $200,000, to each of over seventy different charities in New York City alone, amounting to over $1,400,000. He gave also, while living, quite a sum to the charities of Charleston, S.C., where a brother once lived, $18,500 to his native town, $85,000 to Wabash College, and about $100,000 to some other college, the name of which is forgotten. These gifts all went outside Terre Haute. When he died, having outlived every member of his immediate family, and having never married, after making a generous provision for his servants and some distant connections, he left the remainder of his property to educational and benevolent institutions in that city. These gifts amounted to over $1,000,000. To the Rose Dispensary he left $80,000, to the Ladies' Aid Society of Terre Haute $100,000, and to the Providence Hospital and to St. Ann's Orphan Asylum he gave a generous sum. Before his death he established and endowed the Rose Polytechnic Institute of Terre Haute, now one of the best schools of technology in the United States. The property left that institution is variously estimated to be now worth from $500,000 to $800,000. The buildings were erected while he was living, but the school was not opened until after his death. And, last, he gave a building site and $300,000 to endow the Rose Orphan Home. During his life and at his death his total benefactions must have approximated $3,000,000. With the exception of Stephen Girard and two or three others, no one man in America had, at that time, given away to public purposes such a princely sum. Like Girard and Washburn, he was not a member of any church, but was kind-hearted toward the poor and needy, and ready at all times to relieve the suffering. Of each one of the great institutions and benevolences he founded, he could well have said, "I have reared a monument more lasting than brass." The name of Jay Gould will in a few years perish, but that of Chauncey Rose will be remembered for centuries to come.

Dying in 1877, Mr. Rose did not live to see his plans for the Rose Orphan Home realized. He left the execution of them to a

board of thirteen members, composed of his personal acquaintances, who have the power to fill all vacancies in their number. The president is the venerable Colonel W. R. Thompson, ex-Secretary of the Navy, and the vice-president is W. R. McKeen, president of the Vandalia Railroad. All are prominent business men of Terre Haute.

This board, thinking it wiser to let the interest of the fund accumulate until they would have the means to erect the buildings and equip the institution without touching the principal, did not commence operations till 1883; and the Home was not opened until Sept. 3, 1884. In the mean time the fund has been constantly increasing: and it is thought that it will be large enough in coming years to provide for all the destitute orphan children that may be thrown upon their hands, even though the city and county should become much more populous than it is at present. About $110,000 has been spent on buildings, grading of grounds, trees, furnishing, and general equipment, including sewerage, water supply, machinery, and steam-heating plant.

The Home is situated at the intersection of Wabash Avenue with Twenty-fifth Street, about one and one-half miles east from its business centre. The Terre Haute Electric Street Railway passes it.

The grounds comprise twenty acres of very valuable land, bounded on four sides by streets, about eight acres of which are devoted to lawns and building purposes. The remainder is cultivated.

The well-graded and closely shaven lawns are ornamented with a fountain, flowers, winding walks and drives, and a great variety of shade-trees. The buildings number at present nine, and consist of an administration building, a chapel, a school-house, three cottages, an engine-house, with laundry overhead, a barn, and ice-house. All are built of brick, except the ice-house, are roofed with slate, furnished with gas, and are warmed by steam. The chapel and school-house are connected with the administration building by corridors: and all three of these buildings are constructed of Zanesville red pressed brick, richly ornamented with cut stone from Indiana quarries. The style of architecture of the whole group may be called "Queen Anne," though the buildings are really a modern rendering of the "Queen Anne" of the latter part of the seventeenth century. The architect was Mr. Samuel Hanaford, of Cincinnati, who has designed many of the finest buildings in Cincinnati as well as in this city.

They are supplied with most of the modern improvements suggested by the latest experience in institutional life, and are probably not surpassed in this respect by any child's institution in the world.

The system is that of the family and congregate combined. The children live in the cottages, over each of which is a house-mother, styled " cottage manager " ; but they attend school together, take their meals in a common dining-room. And the laundry work, sewing, and cooking are all done in separate buildings, leaving the manager her full time and strength to look after the order of the cottage and clothing and the moral and religious training of the children, while the mental training is left to teachers in the school-house.

All orphan and half-orphan children who have had a residence of at least six months in Vigo County, who are over three and under fourteen years of age, who are not criminal nor vicious, and who are sound in body and mind, are admissible to the Home, when there is room.

Before deciding upon what system they would adopt, a competent committee visited all the leading institutions of the Eastern and Middle States. The board, after listening to their carefully prepared and elaborate report, and comparing the merits of the congregate and cottage systems, unanimously chose the latter for the following reasons: In case of fire the children can be more easily rescued ; and, if the buildings are sufficiently separated, the destruction of property would be much less. Cottages are easier to ventilate and flood with sunlight than a massive four-story structure. They are cheaper of construction. If it is necessary to enlarge the institution, one or more additional cottages can be erected without tearing anything down or marring the symmetry of other buildings. But, principally, because the cottage system makes it easier to classify the children, and is more like that of the ordinary family, affording better opportunities for the development of the domestic virtues. Excellent results, however, may be secured on the congregate plan if properly managed, and very poor work may be done on the cottage plan if the superintendent is inefficient.

Children must be legally surrendered to the Home by the nearest relative or guardian before they can be admitted, with full authority to place them in families until they are twenty-one years of age. While in the Home, their surroundings are like those of a well-ordered Christian family, except that the cottage mother has a group of from twenty to thirty children to look after, while the ordinary family rarely numbers more than eight or ten individuals. They have the same recreations and sports, the same books and papers, the same employments indoors and out, and as good schools and teachers as have children of the ordinary family. Religious exercises, consisting of singing, Scripture recitations, readings, and prayer, are held every evening in each cottage. The Sunday-school lessons are thoroughly taught, and an interesting Sunday-school is held in the chapel on Sunday afternoons. The older children frequently attend the city churches on pleasant Sunday mornings, and quite a number of them have at various times connected themselves with different city churches.

No effort is made to hurry them into families, unless the institution is full and the applications for admission exceed the accommodations: but, whenever a first-class home can be found and there is a child adapted to it, it is placed out, possibly within a few weeks after its admission. About forty are dismissed each year, some being returned to friends whenever they are in circumstances to care for them, and are suitable persons. Some remain six or seven years in the Home for the reason that, if sent out too soon, they would be returned in a few weeks. This has often been demonstrated in the work of this institution. Many of these children come from the slums of Terre Haute, and have habits that at first unfit them to go into families. Lying, petty thieving, disobedience, carelessness, sauciness, and vulgarity do not at all surprise the workers of this Home. They are expecting such traits of character, and quietly go to work to correct them. But few families will patiently bear with such children. They will take and keep the pretty, refined, obedient, good children, whose Sunday-school lessons are already learned: and the bad children are returned. Some institutions keep passing them around from place to place, three months here, six months there, until they are sixteen or eighteen years old, and then let them drift. But it would seem wiser to retain them in the institution, unless they are incorrigibly bad, until their faults are corrected. Many of these children, tossed about thus, are not at all difficult to control in the institution; and a residence there of from three to seven years often fits them for good citizenship and happy lives. The average residence of children in the Rose Home is about three years.

Great care is taken in selecting places for the children before send ing them out. Not more than fifteen per cent. of the applicants for children are found, upon a close, private investigation, to be suitable people to take children, even when they come indorsed by leading county officials and others. And, even after this investigation, some of the homes found for the children prove very disappointing. Incorrigible children, after a thorough trial, are returned to their nearest relatives, who have, in a number of cases, found it necessary to send them to the Reform School.

The children sent out to homes (mostly in the country) are visited or heard from at least once each year, and as much oftener as may be necessary.

The children are placed out by adoption, or by a simple agreement on the part of the persons taking them that they will kindly treat them, give them four months' schooling each year, and comfortably provide for them in sickness and health, and allow them Sabbath privileges, until they are eighteen years old, when they are allowed to remain where they are or select another home for themselves. No law but the law of love and self-interest will hold a child in a home after it is sixteen years old even: and a simple agreement has the same moral restraint on the guardian and child that an indenture has. as has been repeatedly demonstrated. No *money* compensation for the child's services is required, for the reason that the guardians are tempted to scrimp the children in clothing, schooling, and reasonable recreations, and to work them too hard in order to make enough out of them, over the cost of their keeping, to provide for this payment. Besides, every guardian who has taken a child under twelve years of age, and has generously schooled, clothed and otherwise provided for it, in sickness and health, until it is eighteen years old, has done all that should be demanded of him. If he chooses to do more. it should be a free, not compulsory gift. Some generous souls, out of pure regard for the children, voluntarily do much more than this.

Since the opening of the Home, Sept. 3, 1884, till Feb. 1, 1893. there have been received three hundred and nine children, of whom ninety-four remained in the institution. Of the others, three absconded. thirteen were returned for disease or incorrigibility, six were dismissed as capable of self-support, three died, and the rest were placed in families or with relatives able to care for them. Most of them promise well, but it will take ten years yet to show what the final result will be.

THE KINDERGARTEN IN ITS BEARINGS UPON CRIME, PAUPERISM, AND INSANITY.

BY MRS. SARAH B. COOPER, OF SAN FRANCISCO.

My theme is one in which bright-eyed Hope must clasp the hand of blind Despair, and lead the way to better things.

To start from the very foundation of things, we are compelled to admit that a large proportion of the unfortunate children that go to make up the great army of criminals, paupers, and lunatics, are not born right. They come into the world freighted down with evil propensities and vicious tendencies. They start out handicapped in the race of life. I should like to devote the whole time allotted to me to the consideration of this great, divine, inexorable law of heredity, through which the sins of the fathers are visited upon the children unto the third and fourth generation, and through which, also, mercy is shown to thousands who live in conformity to divine love and law. This is not the subject assigned to me; but I trust it *will* be discussed, on this occasion, by the most learned and experienced in professional lines, who will be able to do the subject the justice which its importance demands. We are apt to deal too exclusively with the stem and branches, and pay little or no heed to the root life of the human plant. There are little children -- Heaven pity them! — who come into the world with three or four generations of crime or pauperism or lunacy in their poor little bodies and brains. This is a mighty injustice to childhood. It deserves the best thought and work of the world. The emphasis of the pulpit, the energy of the public lecture, the influence of the social *conversazione*, the counsel of the medical adviser, the pleading earnestness of the press, the trenchant pen of the writer, should all be directed against this corroding curse. Every lover of humanity should "fight with gentle words till time lends friends."

But I am to talk about what can be done for these little waifs after they are born. By what process of education and development are they to be made valuable members of society? The doctrine that the hereditary defectiveness of the masses must be corrected by education and hereditary culture is the true doctrine. Any system of education that does not contemplate these results does not deserve the name of education. What the world most needs to-day is character,— genuine character. In order to this, we must get hold of the little waifs that grow up to form the criminal element just as early in life as possible. Hunt up the children of poverty, of crime, and of brutality, just as soon as they can be reached,— the children that flock in the tenement houses, on the narrow, dirty streets; the children that have no one to call them by dear names; children that are buffeted hither and thither,— " flotsam and jetsam on the wild, mad sea of life." This is the element out of which criminals are made. It was Juvenal who said, " The man's character is made at seven: what he is then he will always be." This seems a sweeping assertion; but Plato, Aristotle, Plutarch, Bacon, Locke, Lord Brougham, and Lycurgus, all emphasize the same idea. Leading educators of a modern day are all united upon this point. The pliable period of early childhood is the time most favorable to the eradication of vicious tendencies, and to the development of the latent possibilities for good. The foundations for national prosperity and perpetuity are to be laid deep down in our infant schools. And the infant school, to be most successful, must be organized and carried forward on the kindergarten plan. The kindergarten has rightfully been termed the "paradise of childhood." It is the gate through which many a little outcast has re-entered Eden.

Froebel, that great and beloved apostle of childhood, has founded a system that is destined to revolutionize all former methods of developing little children. His battle-cry was, "Come! let us live with our children!"

The simple salient fact is, we do not get hold of the little children of vice and of crime *soon enough*. An unfortunate childhood is the sure prophecy of an unfortunate life. Implant lessons of virtue and well-doing in earliest childhood, says Plato. Give me the child, says Lord Bacon, and the State shall have the man. Let the very playthings of your children have a bearing upon the life and work of the coming man, says Aristotle. It is early training that makes the master, says the great German poet. Train up a child in the way he should go: and, when he is old, he will not depart from it, says the

Revealed Word. Let us take heed to these entreaties, and work with the children. Work with little children will always pay handsome dividends to the family, to the community, to the State, and to the world.

It is Ruskin who says, "The true history of a nation is not of its wars, but of its households"; and he holds it to be the duty of a State to see that every child born therein shall be well housed, clothed, fed, and educated, till it attain years of discretion. But he admits that, in order to the effecting of this, the government must have an authority over the people of which we do not now so much as dream.

Whether such a view be practical or not, one thing is certain: nothing but virtue and intelligence can save a republic from ending in despotism, corruption, and anarchy. There must be genuine character.

And, since virtue is secured by early training and habit, the children of a republic must be trained in ways of honesty, industry, and self-control. It matters not who they are nor where they are, the State cannot afford to allow them to grow up in ignorance and crime. The great conspirator, when he aimed to overthrow Rome, corrupted the young men. When our fathers would conserve liberty for their children and for mankind, they "fed the lambs": they looked to the proper training of the young. We have a vast number of humane institutions for the reclamation and recovery of the wayward and the erring. We have reformatory institutions, asylums, prisons, jails, and houses of correction; but all these are only repair shops. Their work is secondary, not primal. It is vastly more economical to build new houses than to overhaul and remodel old ones. It is a great deal better to manufacture new wagons than to be forever patching up the creaking, shambling old vehicles.

The prevention of crime is the duty of society. But society has no right to punish crime at one end, if it does nothing to prevent it at the other end. Society's chief concern should be to remove the causes from which crime springs. It is as much a duty to prevent crime as it is to punish crime. The father who whips his boy for swearing should look well after his own speech.

Parents must be what they would have their children to be. Parentage and society are very clumsy in their management of the children. We have our duties to one another; and we may be sure of one thing: that any one, however flippant or however scornful, who asks, like Cain, "Am I my brother's keeper?" like Cain, has somehow lost his brother; like Cain, has somehow slain him. It seems to me that two great ministrant forces engird this universe,— love and law. We need them both in the education and development of human beings,— of little children. The mother love should bind the child to home and duty: the father power should construct order and administer government. Society should have both these elements in its government.

As factors in society, what are we doing to prevent crime? We may be very eloquent in pleading that punishments may be quick, sharp, and decisive, that the gallows may have every victim that it claims by law, and that eternal vigilance may be kept on evil-doers. But all this will not avail. As has been truly said: "Crime cannot be hindered by punishment. It will always find some shape and outlet unpunishable and unclosed. Crime can only be truly hindered by letting no man grow up a criminal, by taking away the will to commit sin,— not by mere punishment of its commission. Crime, small and great, can only be truly stayed by education,— not the education of the intellect only, which is on some men wasted and for others mischievous, but education of the heart, which is alike good and necessary for all." We want that sort of education which has in it more of the element of character-building.

The end of all culture must be character, and its outcome in conduct. "Conduct," says Matthew Arnold, "is three-fourths of life." The State's concern in education is to rear virtuous, law-abiding, self-governing citizens.

I repeat it, the doctrine that the hereditary defectiveness of the masses must be corrected, both by hereditary culture and by education, is the true doctrine. Virtue, integrity, and well-doing are not sufficiently aimed at in earliest childhood. The head, and not the heart, comes in for the maximum of training. And yet right action is far more important than rare scholarship. The foundations of national prosperity and perpetuity are laid deep down in the bed-rock of individual character. Let the plodding, the thriftless, and the unaspiring of any country have the monopoly of peopling that country, and the race will become gradually deteriorated, until finally the whole social fabric gives way, and the nation reverts back to barbarism or is blotted from the earth. When a nation exceeds more in quantity than in quality, it is in a bad plight. Ignorance and lack of character in the masses will never breed wisdom so long as ignorance and lack of character in the individual breed folly. The intelligent tradesman, the thrifty mechanic, and the sturdy yeomanry constitute the bulwarks of a nation,— the proud assurance of her perpetuity, her prosperity, and her strength.

> " Ill fares the land, to hastening ills a prey,
> Where wealth accumulates and men decay;
> Princes and lords may flourish or may fade;
> A breath can make them, as a breath has made;
> But a bold peasantry, their country's pride,
> When once destroyed, can never be supplied."

I tell you, friends, we do not half comprehend the importance of looking after the unfortunate children of our streets. What said the great and good Teacher on this subject? " Take heed that ye despise not one of these little ones; for I say unto you, That in heaven their angels do always behold the face of my Father who is in heaven." And when I see the neglected, sad-faced, prematurely old, weary-eyed little ones, in the purlieus of vice and crime, there is just one thought, that comes like a ray of sunlight through the rifts of cloud, and it is this: There is not one of these uncombed, unwashed, untaught little pensioners of care that has not some kind angel heart that is pitying it in the heavens above. Parents may be harsh and brutal, communities may be cold and neglectful; but the angels must ever regard them with eyes luminous with tender pity.

What shall we do with these children? Good people everywhere should combine to care for them and teach them. Churches should make it an important part of their work to look after them. The law of self-preservation, if no higher law, demands that they should be looked after. How shall they be looked after? By establishing free kindergartens in every destitute part of large cities.

Said a wealthy tax-payer to me recently, as he paid me his monthly kindergarten subscription: " Mrs. Cooper, this work among the children is the best work that can be done. I give you this aid most gladly. I consider it an investment for my children. I would rather give five dollars a month to educate these children than to have my own taxed ten times that amount by and by to sustain prisons and penitentiaries." This was the practical view of a practical business man,— a man of wise forethought and of generous, genial impulses. Many needy children have been turned back into the street, to learn all its vice and crime, who could not find accommodation in the different charity kindergartens. I tell you this is a fact of momentous import to any community. Remember that from a single neglected child in a wealthy county in the State of New York there has come a notorious stock of criminals, vagabonds, and paupers, imperilling every dollars' worth of property and every individual in the community. Not less than twelve hundred persons have been traced as the lineage of six children who were born of this one perverted and depraved woman, who was once a pure, sweet, dimpled little child, and who, with proper influences thrown about her at a tender age, might have given to the world twelve hundred progeny, who would have blest their day and generation. Look at the tremendous fact involved! In neglecting to train this one child to ways of virtue and well-doing, the descendants of the respectable neighbors of that child have been compelled to endure the depredations, and support in almshouses and prisons, scores of her descendants for six generations! If the people of this country would protect the virtue of their children, their persons from murder, their property from theft, or their wealth from consuming tax to support paupers and criminals, they must provide a scheme of education that will not allow a single youth to escape its influence. And, to effect the surest and best results, these children must be reached just as early in life as possible. The design of the kindergarten system is to prevent criminals. And what estimate shall be placed upon an instrumentality which saves the child from becoming a criminal, and thus not only saves the State from the care and expense incident to such reform, but also secures to the State all that which the life of a good citizen brings to it? Think of the vast difference in results, had there been twelve hundred useful, well-equipped men and women at work in that county in New York, building it up in productive industries, instead of twelve hundred paupers and criminals tearing down and defiling the fair heritage! We have but to look at this significant fact to estimate the value of a single child to the commonwealth.

The true kindergartner proceeds upon the principle asserted by Froebel, that every child is a child of nature, a child of man and a child of God, and that education can only fulfil its mission when it views the human being in this threefold relation, and takes each into account. In other words, the true kindergartner regards with scrupulous care the physical, the intellectual, and the moral. "You cannot," says Froebel, "do heroic deeds in words, or by talking about them; but you can educate a child to self-activity and to well-doing, and through these to a faith which will not be dead." The child in the kindergarten is not only *told* to be good, but inspired by help and sympathy to *be* good. The kindergarten child is taught to manifest his love in deeds rather than in words; and a child thus taught never knows lip-service, but is led forward to that higher form of service where their good works glorify the Father, thus proving Froebel's assertion to be true, where he says, "I have based my education on religion, and it must lead to religion." The little child, after all, is the important factor in this universe.

When the old king demanded of the Spartans fifty of their children as hostages, they replied, "We would prefer to give you a hundred of our most distinguished men." This was but a fair testimony to the everlasting value of the child to any commonwealth and to any age. The hope of the world lies in the children. The hope of this nation lies in the little children that throng the streets to-day. Is it a small question, then, "What shall we do with our children?" It seems to me that the very best work that can be done for the world is work with the children. We talk a vast deal about the work of reclamation and restoration, reformatory institutions and the like; and all this is well, but far better is it to begin at the beginning. The best physicians are not those who follow disease alone, but those who, as far as possible, go ahead and prevent it. They seek to teach the community the laws of health,— how not to get sick.

We too often start out on the principle that actuated the medical tyro who was working, might and main, over a patient burning up with fever. When gently entreated to know what he was doing, he snappishly replied: "Doing? Why, I'm trying to throw this man into a fit. I don't know much about curing fevers, but I'm death on fits. Just let me get him into a fit, and I'll fetch him!" It seems to me we often go on the same principle: we work harder in laying plans to redeem those who have fallen than to save others from falling. We seem to take it for granted that a certain condition of declension must be reached before we can work to advantage. I repeat again what I have said before,— *we do not begin soon enough with the children*. It seems to me that both Church and State have yet to learn the vast import of those matchless words of the great Teacher himself, where he said, pointing to a little child, "he that receiveth him in my name receiveth me." He said it because, with omniscient vision, he saw the wondrous, folded away possibilities imprisoned within the little child.

Now, I do not propose to go into the *rationale* of the kindergarten system at all on this occasion; but I do wish to emphasize a few salient points. And, first, the kindergarten aims at the cultivation of the heart. As its great founder himself declared, its regnant aim is to guide the heart and soul in the right direction, and lead them to the Creator of all life, and to personal union with him. As we before said, the kindergarten is the paradise of childhood, the gate through which the little children may re-enter Eden. The law of duty is recognized by the little ones as the law of love. Froebel recognized the divine spirit as the true developing power. His theory was that the human heart can only be satisfied with the consciousness of the love of a personal God and Father, to whom we can pray and speak. He said religious *education* was *more* than religious *instruction*. It was his aim to lead the little ones to their heavenly Friend. He taught them to love one another, to help one another, to be kind to one another, to care for one another. No one can love God who does not love his fellows. Froebel grieved over the criminal classes. We say again, the design of the kindergarten is to PREVENT criminals. And what estimate shall be placed upon an instrumentality which saves the child from becoming a criminal, and so saves the State from the care and expense incident to such reform, and secures to the State all that which the life of a good citizen brings to it?

The State begins *too late* when it permits the child to enter the public school at six years of age. It is locking the stable door after the horse is stolen.

One of the most distinguished writers on the law of heredity, Dr. Maudsley, says: "It is certain that lunatics and criminals are as much manufactured articles as are steam-engines and calico printing machines, only the processes of the organic manufactory are so complex that we are not able to follow them. They are neither accidents nor anomalies in the universe, but come by law and testify to causality; and it is the business of science to find out what the causes are, and by what laws they work." A republic that expects to survive, and to increase in power and greatness, must see to it that she does not carry within her the seeds of her own dissolution. It remains forever true of nations, as of individuals, that ignorance and crime breed dissolution and death.

I want to say that the men and women who indorse, sustain, and advocate kindergarten work in San Francisco are among its most thoughtful, philanthropic, and far-seeing citizens,— men who seek to crown with ceaseless blessing the destinies of this western world, men and women whose better nature is always within call,— and who, with a rich and mellow spirit of humanity, determine to leave the world better than they found it, happier and nobler for the legacy of their fruitful lives; men and women who are always devising generous things, and who go through life like a band of music; men and women who live to develop the resources of a great State,— citizens of the world made by the time to make a new time. Such are the men and women who, by their generous gifts and pleading earnestness, help on this great work in San Francisco. Noble, far-seeing men and women! I love and honor them, every one.

Dear friends, I believe with all my soul that the shortest cut to permanent victory in the great and glorious cause of temperance is through the training of very little children in ways of virtue, self-government, and self-control, by the proper cultivation of the heart, as well as the head and hand, in the kindergarten. Only such schools as these, moulding and shaping character by careful habit and training, will ever build up a vigorous, healthful, virtuous national life. Only such schools as these will make poorhouses, insane asylums, penitentiaries, and like institutions unnecessary. Do they cost too much? Think of it! $50,000,000 invested for asylums, poorhouses, hospitals, blind, deaf-mute, and insane asylums in the State of New York alone, with an annual outlay of $10,000,000; and this does not include houses of correction, penitentiaries, prisons, jails, and the like. Even a portion of this money expended in kindergarten schools would make these penal and corrective institutions unnecessary in a few years.

If the civil authorities cannot and do not attend to the needy, neglected children that go to swell the great lists of crime, pauperism, and insanity, then Christian philanthropy should do it. Christianity, thank God, is coming to be more and more practical in its aspect and work. We are coming to feel more and more that a religion that has everything for a future world, and nothing for this world, has nothing for either. A religion that neglects this present life is a mother who neglects her infant, with the expectation that manhood will set everything right. There is a class of persons who spend their lives in trying to *be* good. There is another class who spend their lives in trying to *do* good. Genuine goodness is something more than a mere self-seeking for eternity. It is something more than that sort of pious living which means little else than a safe and sagacious investment in the skies. It is a working together with God in this world for the uplifting and advancement of the human race. It is a seeking to lessen the pains and burdens of life among the toilers and the strugglers. It is a reaching out after the little children of poverty and want,— the hapless little ones who have been hurled prematurely against the life-wrecking problems of existence. Help that can run to help the helpless, and comfort the comfortless, always keeps closest by the side of God. Intensity of life is intensity of helpfulness. The great waiting world understands good actions far more readily than abstract doctrines.

Perhaps we shall find at last, in the day of final disclosure, that the deepest and most far-reaching influence that we ever exerted was the influence that we exerted over the helpless and neglected little children of the streets. Perhaps we shall find it to be the best work we ever accomplished. At all events, it is well to live well. And he lives the longest who lives the best. He is great who confers most of blessing on mankind.

SAVING THE CHILDREN:

SIXTEEN YEARS' WORK AMONG THE DEPENDENT YOUTH OF CHICAGO.

BY OSCAR L. DUDLEY,

SECRETARY AND GENERAL MANAGER OF THE ILLINOIS SCHOOL OF AGRICULT-
URE AND MANUAL TRAINING FOR BOYS.

In presenting this brief historical sketch of the work of rescuing the dependent boys of Chicago from misery, indigence, and a life of crime, the writer will attempt only to speak from his own experience and observation, extending over sixteen years of active work in this field of labor.

Prior to the year 1877 the city of Chicago, and indeed the great State of Illinois, had no organized protection for the dependent children, and no provision of an official character for the prosecution of parents or others who ill-used and brutally treated the young and defenceless. Of course, the laws of the State provided for the protection of children against wanton brutality or neglect on the part of their natural guardians; but what is everybody's business is nobody's business, and the machinery for putting into effect the laws dealing with such offenders was wanting.

Not but what there existed orphan asylums, homes for the friendless, the House of the Good Shepherd (a reformatory institution), and other asylums and homes, now increased in number and usefulness. But Chicago had grown in population with great rapidity, and the provisions for the care of the dependent children had by no means kept pace with the increase in their number. A city like Chicago, receiving yearly vast accretions in numbers and constantly extending its limits, must of course expect to find a certain portion of undesirable, cruel, neglectful, drunken, and criminal people. There must be, even in the most flourishing of cities, in every aggregation of large bodies, a percentage of indigence and crime.

SOCIETY FOR THE PREVENTION OF CRUELTY TO ANIMALS.

We had in Chicago at the time spoken of a worthy Society for the Prevention of Cruelty to Animals, which did good and effective service in protecting the brute creation from brutality and starvation. But up to 1877 we had no institution charged with the special duty of caring for and protecting the neglected children, and no means were provided for affording them an opportunity to improve their condition and to become good and useful citizens.

It fell to the lot of the present writer, then in the employ of the Society for the Prevention of Cruelty to Animals, to arrest the offender and to prosecute the first case of cruelty to children ever tried in the State of Illinois. Unhappily, we know that the neglect of and cruelty to children was far too common before that time; but, public attention being directed to the existence of this form of crime, energetic measures were taken for its suppression and punishment. In July, 1877, the Illinois Humane Society came into existence, the name being changed from that of the old Society for the Prevention of Cruelty to Animals and its scope of usefulness enlarged. Since that time it has performed a noble work.

STATE INSTITUTIONS.

Before describing the results of the movement for the protection of indigent and dependent children, and the magnitude of the results which have been obtained, a brief statement of the provisions made by the city of Chicago and the State of Illinois for the care of the dependent and unfortunate classes may be given.

The State provides four large and well-conducted asylums for the insane, situated at Kankakee, Elgin, Jacksonville, and Anna, with a total of 4,489 inmates in January, 1893. The total cost of these institutions for the land and buildings has been almost $4,000,000; and during the fiscal year ending June 30, 1892, the cost for maintenance and repairs amounted to $1,037,422. More than one thousand insane are provided for by Cook County in its asylum at Dunning, where there is also a poor farm and infirmary, with from 800 to 1,000 inmates, according to the season. The criminal insane have an asylum at Chester. The criminals convicted of penitentiary offences are confined in the State prisons at Joliet and at Chester, the first named containing 1,434 and the last 613 convicts. At Pontiac is located the State Reform School, to which boys between ten and twenty-one years, convicted of crime in courts of record, are sent. They are taught useful trades, and by being separated from the more hardened criminals in the penitentiaries have a chance to reform. In December, 1892, there were 339 inmates of this school.

The State also maintains an Asylum for Feeble-minded Children at Lincoln, which cost $250,000 for the land and buildings, and is conducted at an annual expense of $125,000. This is a most useful institution, its objects being "to promote the intellectual, moral, and physical culture of the feeble-minded children, and to fit them as far as possible for earning their own living and for future usefulness in society."

The Illinois Institution for the Education of the Blind is situated at Jacksonville, and occupies land and buildings which cost $250,000. At the same city is a like institution for the deaf and dumb, with land and buildings worth $500,000. In Chicago is an Eye and Ear Infirmary, occupying a fine building costing $80,000.

The Soldiers' and Sailors' Home at Quincy is a State institution, but the United States contributes half the expenses. At Normal is the Soldiers' Orphans' Home, possessing land and buildings valued at $250,000. The estimated appropriations for all State charitable institutions for 1893–94 (excluding the prisons) is $2,735,175. It will thus be seen that Illinois has provided nobly and amply for the insane and the afflicted of its people.

But the State has done practically nothing for one class of dependants, and that the most helpless of all. Although an Industrial School law was passed some years ago, permitting private corporations to establish and maintain Manual and Training Schools for dependent children, the legislature appropriates nothing for their support. The State maintains a Reform School at Pontiac; but, in order to qualify for this, a boy must have been indicted and convicted of a crime, which, if he had been a few years older, would have landed him in the penitentiary. And not even this provision is made for the corresponding class of girls, although a Reform School for them is much needed.

ILLINOIS INDUSTRIAL SCHOOL FOR GIRLS.

A useful institution for dependent girls was, however, provided in the Girls' Industrial Home at South Evanston, which affords shelter and instruction to a number of young females who would otherwise be left at the mercy of the world. This occupies the building which was at one time used as a Soldiers' Home, and to which additions have recently been made. Girls are sent here by the county court, and are instructed in household duties, as well as being trained in the principles of morality and religion. The institution is managed by a board of lady managers, including some of the best known workers in the charitable field; and it is doing a good and useful work.

The Chicago Industrial School for Girls has a Home on Forty-ninth Street and Indiana Avenue, and there are other institutions under denominational control, to which juvenile offenders can be sent by the police magistrates; but nothing of the kind is provided by the State, nor does the latter furnish any aid to the industrial training schools already established by private enterprise and the assistance of charitable persons and supported by voluntary contributions. Yet the absolute necessity for some means of taking care of the neglected offspring of the streets and the abused children of brutal parents existed for years, and with the phenomenal growth of Chicago its quota of dependent children increased rapidly. It was evident that something had to be done; and by the exertions of a few good citizens, who appreciated the extent of the evil and desired to do something to remedy it, a beginning was made.

A brief reference to the special cases of ill-treatment and neglect of children which led to the inauguration of a systematized and organized movement for their protection, may be made at this point.

During the year 1877 complaint was made to the Illinois Society for the Prevention of Cruelty to Animals that a woman residing at No. 171 Randolph Street had beaten a six-year-old boy nearly to death, and that she was in the habit of practising all manner of cruelties upon him. The evidence of the neighbors pointed to so serious a state of affairs that the writer, who represented the Society for the Prevention of Cruelty to Animals at that time, seeing no reason that a child should not be entitled to as much protection under the law as a dumb animal, concluded to investigate the charges, with a view to taking action if they could be substantiated. He found that the woman had for a long time been in the practice of inflicting the most barbarous treatment upon her six-year-old stepson, Harry. The boy was bright and intelligent, but very delicate in health. On examination it was found that his back was one mass of bruised flesh, while on the left shoulder were deep red scars, evidently inflicted with some pointed instrument, although the frightened little fellow, when questioned, said, "The cat did it." His hips were black and blue, the coagulated blood being visible beneath the skin. Both eyes were blackened; and the face, legs, and arms were covered with burns and contusions. The neighbors had heard the woman frequently beating the child, and he had told them that his mother held his hands on the stove until they were blistered. The woman was sent to jail, and the child was taken care of by the Society.

Through the publicity given to this shocking case by the press a great many other cases of cruelty and neglect were brought to the notice of the Society, but for a time only the most aggravated instances were taken cognizance of by its officers. But, among those prosecuted within the next year or two, a few specimens may be noted, as demonstrating the imperative necessity of the Society's action.

Henry Sass and a woman living with him were complained of for cruelly beating the ten-year-old daughter of Sass. It was found on investigation that the couple were in the habit of locking the child up in a cold, damp basement, used by the man for storing the soap which he peddled, and of keeping her there all night with nothing but an old soap-box for a bed, while he and the woman were enjoying comfortable quarters at a lodging-house. The rats which infested the place so terrified the child that she became a maniac. She was immediately taken charge of by the representative of the Society, while the man and woman were arrested, subsequently indicted, tried, and sentenced to a term of imprisonment. The poor child was tenderly cared for at the writer's own home, to which she was taken, and after a time partially recovered her reason; but her constitution had been ruined by the hardships to which she was subjected. She was finally placed in charge of her dead mother's sister, who had lost trace of her after the mother's death; but she lingered only a year or two, and then passed away.

Two more typical cases occurring shortly after the attention of the society had been called to this work were those of Millie Harris, a housekeeper, who beat her employer's daughter with a riding whip, having stripped her naked, and then rubbed salt and water into the bruises. This child was sent to the Sisters' School. The other case was that of a drunken beer-pedler named Shea, who took his little son away from the Half-orphan Asylum, drove him around all day in the cold, and beat him with a whip because the lad was unable to lift the beer-kegs which the brute himself was too drunk to load.

ILLINOIS HUMANE SOCIETY.

The work grew on our hands until two-thirds of our time was taken up with the investigation of charges of cruelty to children and the prosecution of offenders. Finally, it became necessary to improve the machinery of operations ; and the Board of Directors of the Society for the Prevention of Cruelty to Animals met on Jan. 23, 1881, and adopted the following resolutions, subsequently changing the name of the Society to the Illinois Humane Society. The resolutions read : —

We report that the protection of children of tender years from cruelty, abuse, and criminal neglect, and their rescue from immoral surroundings and influences, is, in our opinion, a work not exceeded in importance by any other benevolence among us. . . . That it seems at present naturally and legitimately to belong to the work of the Society, aside from which we know of no organization in the State prepared to engage in it. That its prosecution thus far has not lessened nor impaired the efficiency of our animal protection service. That, without our seeking it, the work has come to us, we are now performing it, and the public sentiment demands that we continue to do so. That the creation of a separate branch for this service does not now appear to be necessary. That Chicago has never yet failed to give a generous support to all forms of benevolent work for which a real necessity exists, when honestly and efficiently performed and plainly and fairly presented for support. Therefore.

Resolved, That we will continue to prosecute this work of protecting children, as well as dumb animals, from cruelty, abuse, and criminal neglect, appealing to and relying upon the liberality of all who are in sympathy with our purposes and aims, for the means with which to meet the increased expenses of the work, that it may be carried on efficiently and without embarrassment.

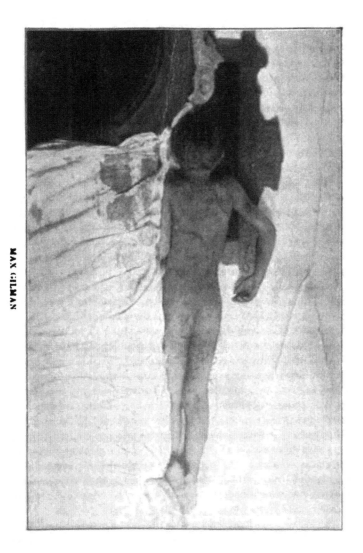

MAX GILMAN

Public opinion having become aroused to the existence in our midst of these evils, the society was called upon to investigate every conceivable kind of case of ill-treatment and neglect of children. Good work was done in breaking up the padrone system, and the similar arrangement under which Belgian and other foreign children were forced to beg for the support of their so-called guardians, who thrashed them unmercifully and half-starved them if they failed to bring in a certain sum every night. We had to find asylums for all of these victims of man's inhumanity, and this we were enabled to do; but for a long time no provision was made for the street waifs and truant boys who had not offended against the law sufficiently to qualify them for the jail or the bridewell.

In the year 1881 a man named Nicholas Ohr was arrested and held to the criminal court for brutally ill-treating his children, aged seven and nine years respectively. He beat them every day with a broomstick, knocked them down with a club which he had fitted with a string to his wrist, and even the two-year-old child received similar treatment. His defence was that the children were liars, and that he had a right to chastise them.

Another case was that of Thomas and Ellen Burns, a drunken couple living in a tenement house, who starved and kicked their twelve-year-old child. On one occasion the mother threw a kettle of boiling water over the girl, scalding her terribly. We took away from Frank Linderhoot and his wife five small children, four of whom were placed in the Home for the Friendless. But the worst case of all with which the writer ever had to do was that of Max Gilman, an eleven-year-old boy, who was beaten to death by his step-father, August Hetzke, in February, 1888. The boy's mother died in June, 1887; and from that time the brutal parent beat and starved the unhappy boy. A witness named Haartze heard sounds of a whipping and plaintive cries of " papa " at eleven o'clock at night, and then a heavy fall as of a body hurled on the floor. At seven in the morning the beating was renewed, and then, with a refinement of hypocrisy, the wretch bade the boy to " get his Bible and read the Commandments." In the afternoon he was dead.

The county physician, who made the post-mortem examination, found the body covered with new scars from the knees to the neck. The back and the backs of the legs and arms were one mass of bruises. Thirty-six of these had been made with one instrument, the iron buckle of a strap. All the internal organs were healthy. The boy was simply beaten to death as Russian prisoners are under the knout. It was shown that the father had continued his brutal conduct for months. The man was sentenced to be hanged, but applied for a new trial on a technicality. A new trial was granted, conditioned on his pleading guilty, as the jury had coupled a recommendation to mercy with their verdict; and he was then sentenced to imprisonment for life. But it is needless to multiply instances of cruelty and crime to impress upon the public the necessity of supporting institutions of a remedial character. It is sufficient to state that the records of the society show that since May, 1881, over twelve thousand children have been rescued. This good work was carried on for years,—all classes of children rescued from every conceivable form of cruelty. The younger of these unfortunate children were readily received at the already existing institutions, but there seemed to be no place for dependent street waifs or the boys rescued who had not yet committed an offence that would gain their admittance to the State Reform School.

Illinois School of Agriculture and Manual Training for Boys.

Under these conditions, the State, being delinquent in the matter of caring for dependent boys, the writer took up the matter; and the Illinois School of Agriculture and Manual Training for Boys was established in June, 1887, a charter being obtained under the new State law for the establishment of industrial training schools. A building with four acres of ground was rented in a Chicago suburb; and, although the institution had but limited means, it was decided to make a beginning. Ten dependent boys, picked up on the streets, neglected waifs with nothing to live on in the present and no hope for the future, were sent to the Home by order of the county judge. Before the end of the year there were over a hundred boys in the Home. They were instructed in the ordinary branches of education, and were taught to make brooms, shoes, etc., and to do wood carving. Soon we outgrew our Home, for it became overcrowded within a year. We needed more land for cultivation, for it was realized that the best way of fitting these boys for getting their own living and removing them from the temptations of overcrowded cities was to render them adapted for agricultural pursuits.

ILLINOIS SCHOOL OF AGRICULTURE AND MANUAL TRAINING FOR BOYS.

With this object in view, a special effort was made; and three hundred acres of fertile land, situated on a railroad line, twenty-three miles south of the business centre of Chicago, in the village of Glenwood, were donated. A fund was raised for constructive purposes, but not without an immense amount of labor; for the number of our charges continued to increase, and the current expenses were heavy. Finally, in June, 1890, three years from the date of our initial effort, we moved into our new Home.

Aside from the barns and other buildings devoted to agricultural purposes which were already on the farm, eight new structures were erected for the school. These buildings are of uniform height, two stories and a basement, and built of brick on stone foundations, and are ranged in a semicircle. The Administration building, in the centre, contains the offices, reception-rooms, library, parlors, officers' living-rooms, kitchen, laundry, bakery, officers' and employees' dining-room, and the main dining-room in which all the children eat. Near by stands the armory, of which the main floor is devoted to the gymnasium, and the upper floor to the training school in wood-work. Here the boys are instructed in wood carving and general carpentry, some fifty to sixty being thus employed. There is also a machine-shop and a shoe-shop in which all the repairing for the institution is done.

The school-house stands at the north end of the semicircle, and contains four large school-rooms for as many grades of scholars. It is thoroughly equipped with every modern appliance.

For the housing of the boys we adopted the cottage plan. The five cottages each cost about $7,000 to build, and are of uniform design. Each contains on the main floor a parlor, care-taker's room, boys' wardrobe and lavatory, reading-room and library and a sewing-room. The upper floor contains seven sleeping-rooms, one for the teacher and six for the boys, each of the latter accommodating five pupils, making room for thirty boys in each cottage. The basements are used for play-rooms; and the cottages are furnished neatly and comfortably, and made as homelike as possible. There is a fine lawn in front, and the gardens and flower-beds render the place attractive and beautiful. Altogether, the Home offers a new life under totally different surroundings to those who come under its care.

Our boys, of whom we have already received and cared for more

WILLIE CUNNINGHAM AS HE WAS RECEIVED AT THE SCHOOL.

than a thousand, do not remain in the institution longer than it is necessary to fit them for obtaining a living outside. More than six hundred have been placed in private families in the North-west, where they are well treated, well fed, and are enabled to continue their schooling while assisting in farm or household duties, as boys born on the farm do. An agent is sent every year to visit them. There are two hundred boys now in the Home, and new recruits are constantly received. More cottages are needed; for in a city of a million and a half of people, and growing so rapidly as Chicago is, the field of our usefulness is a large one.

A considerable contribution to our work is made by the products of the farm, which is cultivated by the pupils under the direction of a farmer. Potatoes, vegetables, and fruits are raised, and considerable live stock. Our system of government and instruction is based upon the principles adopted by the founder of the great school at Mettray, near Tours, France, the parent of all institutions intended not to punish, but to reform juvenile delinquents, and to restore them to society with the capacity to become good and useful citizens. The fundamental principles upon which Mettray was founded, and to which we have closely adhered, were: first, that the school should be located in a fertile agricultural region; second, that the children should be separated into small groups and brought up as much as possible as a family; third, that great attention should be paid to moral and religious training (while avoiding all sectarianism); fourth, that instruction in agriculture and manual training should form a special feature; and, lastly, that the interests of the children should be watched over after they have passed into the outer world, and that the Home should be always their nursing mother and guardian.

In order to gain admission to our school, a petition to establish dependency under the State law is presented to the county court, the section governing this proceeding being as follows:—

79 — PETITION TO ESTABLISH DEPENDENCY.

PARTIES. SECTION 3. Any responsible person, a resident of any county in this State, may petition the county court, or any court of record in said county, to inquire into the alleged dependency of any boy then within the county, and every boy who shall come within the following description shall be considered a dependent boy:

WILLIE CUNNINGHAM SIX MONTHS AFTER ENTERING THE SCHOOL.

namely, every boy who frequents any street, alley, or other place for the purpose of begging or receiving alms; every boy who shall have no permanent place of abode, proper parental care or guardianship; every boy who shall not have sufficient means of subsistence, or who from other cause shall be a wanderer through streets and alleys or other public places; and every boy who shall live with, or frequent the company of, or consort with reputed thieves or other vicious persons. The petitioner shall also state the name of the father and mother of the boy, if living and if known, or, if either be dead, the name of the survivor, if known; and if neither the father nor mother of the boy be living or to be found in the county, or their names to be ascertained, then the name of the guardian, if there be one. If there be a parent living, whose name can be ascertained, or a guardian, the petition shall set forth not only the dependency of the boy, but shall also show either that the parents or parent or guardian are or is not fit persons or person to have the custody of such boy, or that, if fit, the father, mother, or guardian consents or consent to the boy being found dependent. Such petition shall be verified by oath upon the belief of the petitioner, and, upon being filed, the judge of the court shall have the boy named in the petition brought before him for the purpose of determining the application in said petition contained, and for the hearing of such petition the county court shall be considered always open.

The trial of the alleged dependent boy is by a jury of twelve. If they find the boy to be dependent, the court orders his commitment to the Training School, and appoints one of its officers as his guardian. He is at once admitted to the school, where in most cases the influences of cleanliness, decency, and home surroundings, transform him in a few weeks from a homeless, dirty waif, ragged, hungry, and hopeless, into a bright, well-clad, well-fed lad, with the opportunity before him of receiving a good education and learning a trade which will give him an object in life. The Training School is in no sense a prison, and has neither bolts nor bars nor corporal punishments. The boys are governed by love and kindness; and, although they are taken from the street and the gutter, it is surprising as it is gratifying to find how short a time produces an entire change in their appearance, manners, and conduct.

Under the family system emulation in well-doing and a feeling of esprit de corps are fostered among the boys. Each one gets to feel that the credit of his own family home depends in a measure upon himself. Susceptible as the young are to the influence of their surroundings, our boys, when brought to us, are more often the victims

FIVE BROTHERS RESCUED BY THE WRITER, AND AFTER A YEAR IN THE SCHOOL ALL WERE PLACED IN GOOD HOMES IN ONE TOWN IN IOWA.

of evil associations than of inherent vice or criminal instinct.   Experience has demonstrated that they are as capable and intelligent as the average of more fortunate children, for their wits have been sharpened by rough contact with the world.   Never having known kindness in their former life, they respond readily to its influence in the school ; and the new associations with which they are surrounded work even more powerfully upon them than did the evil ones of old. Habits of industry, truth-telling, cleanliness, decency, and self-respect, thus acquired, go to form characters perhaps more stable and self-reliant than some which have never known the test of adversity.

In conclusion, it is unnecessary to add anything as to the value of our work.   We believe that prevention is better than cure, that neither the bridewell nor the Reform School is the proper place to reclaim boys who have taken the first step in wrong-doing, and that, by supplying our dependent youth with better facilities for learning a trade and giving them the advantages of moral training, a great work can be done.   Philanthropic citizens who seek a means to benefit their fellows have done much by founding great universities, hospitals, libraries, art institutes, and other institutions ; but we submit that the indigent children of our great cities have a precedent claim, and that in no way could more good be effected than by a generous support of such an institution as I have described.   Let us save the children.

THE HISTORY OF CHILD-SAVING WORK IN CONNECTICUT.

BY MRS. VIRGINIA T. SMITH, OF HARTFORD, CONN.

The work of prevention for neglected children began in Connecticut a little more than sixty years ago.   Before that time the poorhouse sheltered all children friendless and homeless, except as boys were "bound out" on farms or as apprentices to trades, and girls to housework.   Poorhouses have kept their hold on children, in spite of the multiplying preventive measures of the State, until within the last ten years, since which time it has been forbidden by law that they should remain in them after they were two years of age.

Back in those years, for the children of the poorhouse, for those "bound out," and, in fact, for all children of ordinary grades, the maxim that "children should be seen, and not heard," was well adhered to; for beyond being instructed to repeat the Catechism, to read aloud in the New Testament, write, and study 'rithmetic, to tell one's name and age in a clear voice, and to "curtsey" by the roadside to carriages passing, there seems to have been little education to anticipate.

The earliest preventive and protective agency for neglected children was the Female Beneficent Society of Hartford, founded in 1819 for friendless and indigent little girls, which was soon merged into the Hartford Orphan Asylum, and we will let the records of that noble and undiminished charity tell its own story to the present day: "The Hartford Orphan Asylum traces its origin to an event which occurred in this city just sixty-four years ago. In February of 1829 a poor woman, bearing the name of Aldrich, whose husband had forsaken her, leaving her destitute of any means of support, died at the house of Mrs. Savage on State Street, leaving an infant four days old.   This child was subsequently baptized by the Rev. N. S. Wheaton, rector of Christ Church, by the name of Joseph Waite.   Miss Elizabeth Bull, the benevolence of whose character will long be remembered in this city, became interested in this destitute orphan child, and obtained means for his support.   He was cherished and protected, and in July of the same year was placed under the care of Mrs. Knox, where he remained until Oct. 4, 1832.

" In the mean time, attention having been directed to other indigent and friendless boys, a temporary asylum was secured for them and for the little Joseph, then three years old, in a private family in the city. A meeting of citizens had already been held, at which resolutions were passed, to wit : ' That an effort be made to establish an orphan asylum in this vicinity for those indigent boys whose education, maintenance, and employment are neglected by their parents and friends.' ' That a committee be appointed to solicit subscriptions to this charity, and also a committee to apply to the legislature of the State for an act of incorporation, with authority to hold property, to receive and bind out indigent boys, and to adopt such regulations and by-laws as may be necessary for the government of the institution.'

" At the next meeting a board of nineteen women was chosen to act as directors, and their efforts are described as worthy of the highest praise. Laboring under changes and vicissitudes of one sort and another, the institution has come steadily forward until it has a fine and commodious structure in which to do its work, and a nursery in connection with it cares for a limited number of infants.

" From a report of 1879 it is estimated that more than one thousand children have at different times received the protection of the asylum, and that is fourteen years ago. Many of these have been taken as boarders, on the principle that it is best for parents to support their children, when possible, even if they cannot have them under their immediate care. The average of children provided for in the asylum is one hundred.

" To answer the question if the work has paid, the managers sent out to all those families to whom they had indentured children, making certain definite inquiries regarding the habits and character of the children committed to their care. From the replies to those circulars, and from other sources of information, it appears that, of the children over whose beginnings in life the Orphan Asylum exercised the only care, fully ninety per cent. have maintained habits of integrity, as declared by their honest and useful lives. Eight of the boys, it is to be recorded with pride, have laid down their lives on the battle-field in noble defence of their country. What the character of

these children would have been if left to their own devices, exposed
to the influences from which they were taken,— influences, in many
cases, of the most appalling vice and degradation,— can only be con-
jectured."

Among the self-sacrificing workers that have given their time
for years to the interests of this asylum, and still continue in it,
are Mrs. E. G. Howe, Mrs. Jonathan S. Curtis, and Mrs. Charles
Howard.

NEW HAVEN ORPHAN ASYLUM.

Four years after the Hartford Orphan Asylum was established
New Haven moved on the same line; and, to use their own words.
"they started their Orphan Asylum in a pleasant and human sort of
way." Dr. Jonathan Knight and Dr. Croswell, pastor of Trinity
Church, find suddenly left upon their hands four little orphan children, the youngest only a few weeks old. The two good men, physicians, one to the body, the other to the soul, have met at the bed-
side of the dying mother. The father had died of cholera a few
months before. They cannot bear to send the children to the almshouse. So, knowing the ladies were ready to commence the work,
they call a meeting of gentlemen to encourage them in it. Many a
talk there must have been before this over "those poor little Dan-
iels children."

Many a motherly heart must have compassionated them and
planned for them, and now the husbands and fathers step in to
pledge their support to the plans. At the meeting the following
resolution was passed: "That this meeting cordially approve of the
design proposed by several ladies of this city, to establish an asylum
for the protection and education of destitute orphans within the city,
and will most cheerfully unite with them in any measure calculated
to effect this desirable object." In 1834, at the end of the first year,
it was thought advisable to purchase a house; and a convenient and
commodious location was selected, and the work of bringing in the
children was fairly begun. From this date the asylum went on, ex-
periencing, like all other charities, its depressions and its triumphs,
until the results of its having been long ago established in the hearts
of the people are shown in the bequests and loving benefactions of all
kinds that have been showered upon it. During the war the capacity
of the asylum was taxed to its utmost; and, as it was also a season of

financial depression, the managers experienced much solicitude as to its future support. One of the managers writes, "Little did I imagine at the time what an important part our financially poor asylum was to enact in accomplishing the fulfilment of the promise to the men who bravely went to the front,— that during their absence their families should be kindly cared for, not only for the Second, but also for every regiment in the State, by securing from the legislature aid for indigent families." Another important item is the fact that through the efforts made in behalf of soldiers' children the asylum was first adopted by the community at large as an institution to be valued, cherished, and liberally supported.

" It may seem strange that such efforts were necessary, since to Connecticut belongs the honor of maintaining the indigent children of soldiers during the war more generously than any other State. But many fathers enlisted in regiments of other States, leaving their children with no right to the Connecticut bounty; yet these little ones needed food and shelter, and it fell to the asylum to supply their need."

The plan of this asylum is to find family homes for these children, where they will be brought up in good New England ways; and hundreds of the children have been so placed. The managers feel that they can say with truth that they turn out as well as the same number of children taken from our rural towns, who are not the children of poverty and vice, as so many of these are.

Catholic Orphan Asylums.

The Catholic Orphan Asylums yearly receive many children of their own faith, for whom they provide all necessary support and instruction.

Reform School for Boys.

Next in line for the protection and care of boys came the Reform School, founded in 1853, and located in Meriden.

A main building with a wing was erected, but in 1873 another wing was added to accommodate the rapidly increasing family. Up to the year 1878, writes Mr. Howe, the present competent superintendent, "the school was conducted on the congregate, or prison, system, with cells, barred windows, and all necessary and common appliances of a boys' prison." Mr. Howe began his work at the school at the earnest solicitation of the Reform School Board, as he declares, "with great reluctance and many misgivings." To convert a school established and conducted for twenty-five years upon the rule of absolute authority, to one upon the humane and open plan, where prison appliances should not exist; to inaugurate, instead of prison life, conditions of freedom and natural home rule, calling out the best qualities in each boy by raising the plane of discipline to one of self-respect and self-reliance, where willing obedience should be rendered to all reasonable and wholesome requirements,— was a great undertaking, and might lead to misunderstanding and failure. Mr. Howe with his convictions could undertake it in no other than a reluctant way and spirit; and besides his own fear, lest he might meet with disaster, came the expressed feeling of many that the experiment was a dangerous one. Notwithstanding all that was to be risked in such a complete change in the methods and spirit of the school, Mr. Howe decided to accept the task, and risk his reputation and that of the school in making the departure, where each boy should be permitted the task of conquering himself.

To use Mr. Howe's own words, "Heaven has smiled upon the work, and no State to-day can boast of a better reformatory institution than that of Connecticut."

The boys are cared for now in nice, homelike cottages, with as much of family life about them as may be ; and restraints, says the superintendent, "are only such as would be voted for by any class of intelligent and well-meaning boys." It goes without saying that Mr. Howe's success has made glad the State of Connecticut. Six thousand boys have been sent out from the school, a large percentage of whom, he asserts, "bear interesting testimony to the efficiency of reformatory treatment."

A reform school for boys presents an almost unlimited field for missionary effort, and the earnest work of Superintendent Howe and his devoted wife will tell in Connecticut for generations to come.

School for Imbeciles.

A private school for the instruction of imbecile children was begun by Dr. Henry M. Knight at Lakeville, Conn., in 1858, and was continued by him up to 1861, when it was incorporated as the "Connecticut School for Imbeciles." The school began with one pupil, whom Dr. Knight took into his family.

During the early time Dr. Knight labored with a most Christian and missionary spirit, receiving, says the report of the work, "but very slight pecuniary reward for all the time, care, and energy which he devoted to the effort to create an institution from which these most unfortunate and hitherto much neglected members of the human family in our State might derive some amelioration from their unfortunate condition." The report continues to show his persistent self-sacrificing efforts, and to bear witness to the astonishing results which were accomplished by him in the improvement, bodily and mentally, of the pupils placed under his charge.

An institution of sufficient capacity and with sufficient endowment to embrace all the unfortunates of that class within the State, it was declared, was demanded by all the humane and charitable considerations which have so liberally provided for the insane and for the deaf and dumb; and the claim was made that it appealed as forcibly for aid as did either of these institutions established for the improvement of the conditions of those classes. From these early and heroic efforts a school of large numbers has grown, the family at present numbering one hundred and forty children. Since the death of Dr. Knight the work has been most successfully conducted by his widow and her son, Dr. George H. Knight, with a corps of earnest and conscientious assistants.

INDUSTRIAL SCHOOL FOR GIRLS.

In 1870 the Industrial School for Girls was established, and by the middle of the year, twenty-four girls had been committed to its care. An act was passed by the General Assembly appropriating ten thousand dollars ($10,000) whenever fifty thousand dollars ($50,000) should be secured from other sources. The money was secured, and the work has gone on. The school was established in Middletown, and contains six homes, on ample, well-kept grounds, and has a well-cultivated and stocked farm. Its proper subjects are "viciously inclined girls between the ages of eight and sixteen years."

Its design is not that of a prison to which criminals are consigned for punishment, but that of a temporary place of custody and instruction. The system of discipline and education is specially adapted to the conditions and wants of the girls. As at present arranged, it can accommodate two hundred and twenty inmates. The girls attend school, church, and Sunday-school upon the grounds, and are taught housework, needlework, cooking, and the trade of box-making.

It is every way a desirable home for the classes of girls for which it is intended, but some innocent little girls go there and remain there that should find homes easily outside the institution. The county temporary homes more recently provided we hope in time will shelter all children not viciously inclined who need protection.

County Temporary Homes.

The County Temporary Homes were the next provision made for children ; and, although having been established nine years, and past the experimental stage, still the State at large is not so fully acquainted with them as we could wish. Notwithstanding the good work of the correctional schools, still there was no provision for waifs and strays, or children abandoned by their natural protectors. Accordingly, an experiment was tried without law or legislation. A house in Hartford was hired, and a matron engaged to receive and care for helpless little wanderers at any hour of the day or night, for whom we should find homes as soon as possible.

The Home was humble and inexpensive, but in a few years it had received hundreds of children, thus demonstrating the benediction that such Homes would become to the children of the State. Visiting the almshouses of our State and finding unfortunate children living in the most desolate poverty and neglect, we were determined not only to relieve their distresses, but to change their entire conditions, to brighten their lives, and to be able to secure to them the proper opportunities to become good men and women by the good example, affectionate teachings, and tender personal care that they might receive in well-selected family homes.

Realizing the grand results that had already accrued from our local charity in our comparatively small city, we were deeply impressed with what it might do as a State provision for children needing its opportunities. Urged on, moreover, by our increasing knowledge of the sufferings of these children, and made strong by the sympathy and co-operation of those interested in this question, it was determined that we take a more public step. I had asked the board of a local charity to provide a home for dependent and neglected children, and was not refused; but, instead, we were cheered and blessed by the work it had already accomplished, and now we would go further and ask greater things. We would ask the General Assembly that represented our State to give temporary homes or shelters for the protection of its most helpless class, its dependent children, until other provision could be made; that is, until, as a rule, family homes could be found into which they could go and live. Is not a home the God-given right of every child, we reasoned? Denied that right, how slow its advancement in the proper formation of character! None of us can realize what homes and home ties have done for us,—perhaps because they come, like other indispensable blessings of life, so freely and naturally that we forget to be specially grateful for them; but, when we feel for our own children that love which we accepted as our right, we recognize its power and value.

How we welcome our children to the best there is in our hearts and homes! How we invest our whole natures in them, and hang our hopes unlimitedly and unconsciously upon them! How we rejoice in their growth and development! and how blissful the days that bring them joy and blessing! How we spend ourselves like water in their illnesses! and how no beauty dawns in any day that witnesses their sorrow and distress! How, living, they are our world! and how, dying, they become our inspiration, and among the chief beatitudes of the heaven we hope for! How the precious memories and hopes that abide with us are secret springs to action, and a daily consecration of time and powers for those children whose pitiful faces and wretched lives make mighty appeal to the tendernesses within us!

Moved by the love we all bear for our children yet on earth, and by that same love which, passing with those precious ones into the eternal country, became a part of their immortality, so that we can never again be altogether mortal; warmed through all our nature with the tenderness of this world and with radiations from the world to come,— how can we fail to work unceasingly and to our utmost to give neglected children the homes and friends they need!

We carried a petition to the legislature, asking that a law might be enacted to prevent the further placing or retaining of children in almshouses, and, in fact, to care for any dependent, neglected, or abused child needing such legislation in the State. The bill was not passed, but instead a commission was appointed to investigate as to the necessity of such a law, and report to the next General Assembly such facts and statistics as it might obtain, and to suggest, by bill or otherwise, such legislation, if any, as it might deem necessary or desirable to ameliorate the condition of such children.

Notwithstanding all the discussion which the commission of inquiry excited, it went quietly forward, and performed its work. It went into the almshouses of the State, and discovered nearly five hundred children in them. It went into cities, factory villages, boroughs, large farming districts, and isolated towns. It inquired of clergymen, physicians, and school-teachers in the different towns as to the number of neglected and abused children of whom they had knowledge.

At the end of the year we had gained an accumulation of knowledge-creating statistics that hardly seemed credible even to those seeking the information. The commission returned to the next General Assembly the fact that there were between four and five thousand children of the three classes mentioned — namely, dependent, neglected, or abused children — in the State of Connecticut that needed the State's special care and guardianship, and recommended additional legislation, making it lawful not only to rescue them from almshouses and vicious homes, but also to care for them in the best and most discreet manner, when once they were in the hands of those who would befriend them. We recommended also in connection with our report to the General Assembly that a temporary home be established in each county of the State in which these children might at any time be placed, with a view to finding them good homes as soon as possible in desirable private families.

The bill passed both House and Senate almost unanimously; and upon Jan. 1, 1884, each county had opened its home, and was ready to begin its work.

At about the middle of December, 1883, there were hundreds of children in the almshouses; but when, just before the first of January, the selectmen were notified that at New Year's the Temporary Home of their county would be opened for the reception of said children, some people, interested by ties of blood in these children, suddenly developed an unheard of capacity to support them, showing that their neglect had been from sheer indolence and a willingness that their children should become paupers. And in that and other ways the almshouses were swiftly depopulated. Nearly two hundred and fifty children, however, were placed in the Homes during the first year; and about fifty per cent. of that number were provided with permanent homes in private families, and consequently went off the pauper lists, and are no longer an expense to the towns which have previously supported them. Appreciating our work, the correctional schools informed us of the relief the Homes would be to their crowded ranks, stating that there were large numbers of children, both in the Reform and Industrial Schools, who never should have gone there.

At the end of the first year's work in the Temporary Homes the friends of the enterprise hoped to be able to lay before the legislature some amendments, calculated to facilitate the growth of the work; but, already in advance of it, various petitions were laid before the Humane Committee, praying that a State institution might succeed the Temporary Homes. Foremost among the supporters of this plan of a State institution were the very people who, two years before, had declared that no additional legislation was necessary.

The friends of the State institution admitted that the children would not probably be placed in families so soon from a State institution, but did not know as it mattered much if they did not have any family life for a few years. They urged that in a State institution they could be taught trades; and they believed it better to class these pauper children by themselves, giving them a school in their own building and a chapel for their service, than to tolerate them in the society of other children. On the other hand, the friends of the children considered the fact of a modest dwelling-house in each county of the State, for many reasons, a much more desirable provision than an enormous institution, in which children inevitably congregate, until by very numbers they become demoralized. Even in the county homes the children make a beginning in both home and practical life. The size and appointments of these homes are not greatly disproportionate to the houses into which they will naturally go to live.

It seemed also, to those practically engaged in finding homes for these children, that the plan of their learning trades in the State institution was most impractical, as the elder children, being sought in largest numbers, would naturally be swept out of the institution; while those remaining would range in age from two to seven years, and would seem rather infantine material upon which to depend for apprentices in the different departments of mechanical labor.

The effort to secure a State home had no effect except to establish the Temporary Homes more firmly in the affections of the people who believe in them, and to interest and convert many more to the work who had heretofore known little about it. Intelligent workers felt it truly the beginning of the time when all the forces of true sympathy, right knowledge, virtue, and wise administration had begun to move in converging lines and with united purpose to the relief and rescue of the distressed children and to the succor of imperilled posterity. In finding permanent homes for such children, we claim that no system of "placing out" will ever be successful that does not take into account the deepest needs of the child, and the determination conscientiously to adapt the child to its place. We do not attempt to make a success of it by depending upon letters of recommendation concerning the parties who wish to secure a child. They are, generally, as unsubstantiable (unless the case has been officially investigated and approved) as the overdrawn recommendations of servants, which many ladies have learned to accept with due allowance.

We are not anxious to secure homes of wealth or of excessive neatness or of any special or extraordinary appointments. The work of placing a child in a home is a task that requires natural adaptability to the work. It is a delicate transaction, and one which no bungler can ever wisely carry out. In this work an ounce of affection is worth a ton of intellect. And when, through such efforts, a child reaches a good home, and its pathetic wanderings cease for a while in the quiet haven of rest and benediction which a good home always brings to a child, there is a satisfaction, than which nothing is sweeter, that the worker has tried to follow the example of the Teacher who took a little child, and set it in the midst of the people, to illustrate the laws of the kingdom of God.

All workers are to remember also that, unless they do so save the children from their distresses, they will grow coarse and hard with the brutalities they will learn to practise ; and their hands will reach out into every immoral phase of life, and soil themselves hopelessly by the thousand impurities of the world.

Let every State see to it that the neglected, dependent, and abused children are not hindered from sharing the blessings so freely bestowed upon us as a people. Let not slothfulness, indifference, cowardice, nor ignorance prevent them from working both individually and in unison, until every child has all the rights and privileges which they insure to their own.

HUMANE SOCIETY.

The Connecticut Humane Society was incorporated in 1881 as a society for the prevention of cruelty to human beings and animals, and through it much good work has already been done for the children. They are rescued, and frequently placed in the County Homes and provided with good places.

KINDERGARTEN.

In 1880 we established at Hartford the first charity kindergarten of Connecticut. Public sentiment was sufficiently created in three years' time to aid us in placing back of our single-handed endeavor a board of directors responsible for the effort necessary to enlarge and continue the school. Its refining and Christianizing influence upon the children and their parents was thoroughly demonstrated.

We rejoice to-day that it is no longer confined to the records of unofficial or missionary agencies of prevention; for by bringing the matter before the General Assembly we succeeded in permitting children to enter school at three years of age, and permission also was given to establish kindergartens in the public schools of the State.

In pursuance of this law the several districts of Hartford and those of other cities have already begun the work; and thus the hope of securing this immeasurable benefit to the children through the public schools, and outside the boundary of charity, is beginning to be realized.

SAVING THE BABIES.

There is still another class of children for whom we are now trying to make special legal provision. It is the very young children who are dependent upon the public purse or private charity, and for whom no ordinary asylum or temporary home can properly provide.

The mothers go to the almshouse frequently for a stay of from six months to two years. This provision is much better than none, as it prevents, to a great extent, the temptation for unmarried mothers to abandon their offspring.

For the good of both mothers and children, as well as from public considerations, it is best that they should be kept together whenever it is practicable. To encourage a mother to keep her child with her, and care for it, is to guard her in the strongest manner possible against a repetition of her error; but six months or more in an almshouse so destroys self-respect and fosters the habit of self-dependence that the future support of herself and child is often considered by the mother too much to be undertaken.

Women should be required, therefore, when well and strong, to undertake their own and infants' maintenance after two months of rest, both for the wholesome effect upon them of honest labor, and because the industrious and moral citizen should not be taxed for the support of the idle and licentious.

So far as possible, we find homes for the mothers, where they can take their infants with them. They go into country families, where a kindly regard is felt for them, and where, almost invariably, the children are watched over with especial interest. Occasionally, it is found best not to leave infants in the personal care of their mothers. Women of low moral natures, devoid of conscience and affection, should be helped to go into service, where a part of their wages can be retained to pay for the care of their children by judicious persons, until such time as family homes, free of charge, can be found for them.

It is thought by some impossible to do this; but our experience proves the contrary, as in scores of cases which we have thus managed only two or three women have deliberately refused to support their children or have deserted their place of service. Infants can be provided for only to a small extent in orphan asylums; and experience has shown that in a State foundling asylum, from want of proper care, a large proportion of children do not outlive their infancy. Small homes in each county might be established, under a strict system of visitation and inspection; or, better still, one or two children (never more than three) could be boarded in private families in the country, under the same supervision and inspection which would be given to the county homes.

At present a lamentable number of cases are in the almshouses of the State, and others will continue to be sent there until some law is passed which will secure to this class of children the care they require.

Proposed Home for Incurables.

In the work of caring for her dependent children, Connecticut still lacks an important provision ; and that is a home for her incurables. The law that mercifully secures to the healthy, dependent children a place of shelter and security until they are received into private families, does not contemplate the care of this helpless class of children. It distinctly and wisely says, "Children who are suffering from incurable diseases are *not* included in the provisions of the act." But now that the intelligent and healthy children are protected by the county homes, and the feeble-minded are carefully provided for at Lakeville, the fact is all the more conspicuous that the suffering children, with no earthly future to anticipate, are still left to the mercy of circumstances.

We believe that there are more than one hundred children in Connecticut who, as incurables, need at the present time the comforts of a " Home " adapted to their special necessities.

Hospitals will admit sick and disabled children from the Temporary Homes, and from homes where they cannot receive proper care, and also will treat curable and acute diseases ; but even hospitals cannot receive, and for years care for, incurables, and they do not profess to do it. Therefore, there is among us a class of children more helpless than any other — unless it be the imbecile — for whom no proper provision has been made.

With these facts well known and continually repeating themselves in pathetic instances, the attempt to awaken public interest and urge means for relief should no longer be postponed.

Other New England States, as also New York and Pennsylvania, long since established homes for this class of children, and are able to testify to their importance in the classified and systematic care of every condition of childhood, and even of adult life.

In the past twelve years a member of the Board of Charities has secured admission for several supposed incurables, adults and children, the former to the Home for Incurables at Fordham, N.Y., and the latter to the Home for the Ruptured and Crippled, located on Forty-second Street, New York City, and has supported them while there by allowances from the towns to which they belonged and by private contributions from societies and individuals.

But the objections to using the institutions of other States in the care of our dependent incurables can be readily seen. It is frequently an inconvenience to the asylum so receiving patients, and long intervals are liable to elapse between the application and the time when they can be received. It costs more to support a patient in an asylum in another State than it should in a similar place in one's own State. The expense of travel renders it difficult, and often impossible. for the friends of patients to visit them ; and, when death occurs. it is expensive to bury them there, and almost equally so to bring them home for burial.

In view of all these disadvantages to the patients and to those who support them, it seems imperative that Connecticut should have an institution of this kind within her own borders.

The fact that institutional life for children should be avoided. so far as possible, does not need to be considered here. For a class of incurable and crippled children an institution seems so great a necessity that no objection can be reasonably urged against it.

Such a charity need not be a State institution. But, until such an asylum should become self-supporting by private bequests, the same allowance made by the State for healthy children in county homes might be provided by law, to be used by a board of trustees in the care of children committed by law to a home for incurables.

The choice for many a dependent child must be either such a home or life-long residence in a town poorhouse, tied in a chair or lying neglected in bed.

The Board of Charities has found, in visiting almshouses, a number of suffering children whose cases appeal strongly to public sympathy.

At this time a resolution is before the present legislature to incorporate the Connecticut Children's Aid Society, with permission to care for incurable children ; and a sum of $5,000 is already raised for a home for the latter.

The workers in Connecticut long ago learned that there is no patent machine for the elevation of humanity, no royal road to learning. The products of centuries cannot be at once reconstructed. The measure of success will depend upon the patience. energy. and good judgment which workers individually possess. With organization and wise leadership and the persistent, conscientious labor of many individuals, there may be brought about in a few generations a surpassing reconstruction of the lower grades of society.

CHILDREN'S HOMES IN OHIO.

BY S. J. HATHAWAY, MARIETTA, OHIO,

TRUSTEE WASHINGTON COUNTY CHILDREN'S HOME.

The origin of Children's Homes in Ohio was a horror of the poor-house. Prior to 1857 no provision had been made in this State, either by public or private charity, to save the homeless children, except in the larger cities. The destitute children of the country districts were consigned to the tender mercies of the poorhouses, and allowed to grow up under the baneful influences of imbecility and pauperism.

In the year 1857 Miss Catherine Fay (afterwards familiarly known as "Aunt Katie Fay"), feeling the hopeless and forlorn condition of these children, thus placed in county infirmaries through no fault of their own, resolved to do something for their relief. Here is her own statement in regard to the matter, prepared at the writer's request for the Report of Trustees of Washington County Children's Home, for 1890 : —

FOUNDING OF THE HOME.

In the fall of 1853, while laboring as a missionary among the Choctaw Indians, a physician called on me, and asked me to visit a poor family, where the mother, a New England woman of culture and refinement, had died, leaving five small children. These little ones she had committed to his care ; and he was trying to find homes for them, their drunken father having deserted them. He wished me to adopt a very lovely little girl, two years old. I longed to do it ; but I was a poor teacher, hundreds of miles from home, and it seemed impracticable. She was taken by a man and his wife, who soon after began to sell whiskey to the Indians. One day there was a drunken fight, and the dear child was thrown down the steps of the house and killed. This affected me very deeply ; and the determination was born in my heart to have a home of my own, where I could care for such orphaned and homeless children.

After this time every energy was directed to this object : every dollar was laid up with miserly care for this purpose. I taught two years in Kentucky, and with the money thus earned bought fifteen acres of land, about ten miles from Marietta, Ohio.   There was a small house of two rooms on the land.   About this time I received two legacies from an uncle and an aunt, and began at once to build a larger house.   My plan was to take poor children, and support them myself.

I went to our County Infirmary, and found twenty-six children, associated constantly with older people, many of them of the vilest character.   This was more than I could bear.   I wanted to take them all; but, as I could not hope to support so many by my own exertions, I went to the directors of the Infirmary, and persuaded them to let me take the children at $1 per week.

The first few years were very hard ones.

After the war broke out many soldiers' children were added to the number in my care.   At one time I had thirty-five of these, and felt that they deserved something better of their country than had yet been provided.   I became exceedingly desirous that we might be entirely separated in name and in fact from the "poorhouse," and have a distinct fund appropriated for our use.   In 1864 I conferred with the commissioners about the expediency of applying to the legislature to bring about this change.   A bill was presented to the legislature that year, but was laid aside.   In 1865 it was again presented, and rejected; but in 1866 it became a law.   So the plan, which I had first thought of only as a relief to our own Children's Home, became, in God's good providence, which guided and helped me all the way, the means of planting children's homes all over our State.

TEACHING TRADES IMPRACTICABLE.

Her first plan was to retain the children in the Home long enough to educate them and teach them trades, but this was found impracticable for the following reasons: the expense was an important item, as it required skilled workmen to teach trades properly; and then it was found that all children were not suited to trades, and their time could be more profitably employed in school.

HOME FARMS.

At first it was supposed that every Home should have a farm attached to it, the supposition being that a great deal of farm-work could be done by the inmates.   Consequently, we find many of the Children's Homes of the State are located on farms, at some distance from the county seats; but experience has shown that very little work can be expected from the children. The first Home established by Miss Fay was ten miles distant from Marietta, and when the county authorities took charge, and established a Home under the general law in 1866, the new Home was located about two and a half miles from the city; and for many years thereafter all the Children's Homes of the State followed the example of this first Home. These early ideas as to location and management of Children's Homes were changed and enlarged as time advanced, the doctrine of evolution applying to these as well as other institutions.

LOCATION OF HOMES.

It has been found better to locate a Children's Home near a city or village, so that the children can attend the public schools and mingle with other children of the community, thus reducing as much as possible the liability of their growing up as a class; and, in order to still further remove this danger, many, if not all, the Homes avoid dressing the children alike.

PLACING OUT.

It has also been found that a farm is not necessary, as all the labor, or nearly all, must be hired; and it is about as economical to buy as to try to raise produce to supply the Home, and much better for the children to place them out in good families, where they can have the beneficent influences of Christian households thrown around them, and where they can grow up like other children, taking up such trades and callings as they prefer and such as their different abilities fit them for. In this way the danger of their becoming institutionized by long residence in the Home has been avoided, and the idea of self-dependence inculcated as soon as possible.

No trouble was experienced in finding good homes for the children in private families. People who wanted children to raise soon found that they could obtain them by applying and giving proper references. For a number of years the Children's Homes of the State followed this plan, and placed the children out in the same county or immediate neighborhood of the Home, making no effort to get them away from their early surroundings; but this method was found to be objectionable on account of close proximity to former acquaintances and vicious relatives, who enticed them away after they had become well fixed in good families; and, their early history, being familiar to all, clouded their prospects in life. Consequently, many Children's Homes of the State refuse to place children in the same county in which the Home is located, but seek homes for them in distant localities, where well-to-do-people are found who are willing to take them and bring them up as their own. Many foster-parents adopt them formally, and make them heirs to property. The children are thus given a start in life far distant from the degrading influences of bad relatives and where no trace of their early history can be found. Even their foster-parents are not permitted to know of their previous history, and the whereabouts of the children is carefully concealed from everybody except the officers of the Homes. Those Homes which have adopted the improved plan of placing out children, have a visiting agent or a private institution which has one employed to place out the children, who calls on each child at least once a year, and ascertains and reports as to its condition and prospects; and, if for any cause there should be a misfit, the child is transferred to another family, and so on to another, if necessary, until a home is found where both child and foster-parents are suited to each other. When this is accomplished, the future of the child is assured, as far as it is possible to assure it. Each child is followed in this manner until it becomes of age and is absorbed in the community.

Many of the Children's Homes of the State, however, have not taken this high ground in managing their institutions, preferring the old way of allowing people of the neighborhood to come and take the children, which is undoubtedly much the easier plan of placing out children, but is open to the serious objections above stated.

GROWTH OF THE SYSTEM.

There are seventy institutions in Ohio devoted to saving homeless children. Of these, forty-six are Children's Homes, located in as many different counties, and twenty-four are private institutions, located in the large cities. Besides these there are five State institutions, charitable and reformatory, which, with the exception of the Soldiers' and Sailors' Orphans' Home at Xenia, are not properly classed with Children's Homes.

FIG. 4. SOUTHDOWN HALL WEST

THE CHILDREN'S HOME OF CINCINNATI, OHIO.

BELMONT COUNTY CHILDREN'S HOME, NEAR BARNESVILLE, OHIO.

THE CLEVELAND PROTESTANT
ORPHAN ASYLUM.
1460 ST CLAIR ST

JEWISH ORPHAN ASYLUM.

FAIRMOUNT CHILDREN'S HOME.

"W'hosoever receiveth a little child in My name, receiveth Me."

M. M. SOUTHWORTH. Sunt.

THE MEIGS COUNTY CHILDREN'S HOME AT POMEROY, OHIO.

FRANKLIN COUNTY CHILDREN'S HOME, COLUMBUS, OHIO

FRANKLIN COUNTY CHILDREN'S HOME, COLUMBUS, OHIO.

KNOOP CHILDREN'S HOME, Troy, Ohio.

CHILDREN'S HOME, TRUMBULL COUNTY, OHIO.
LOCATED AT WARREN.

CHILDREN'S HOME, TRUMBULL COUNTY, OHIO.
LOCATED AT WARREN.

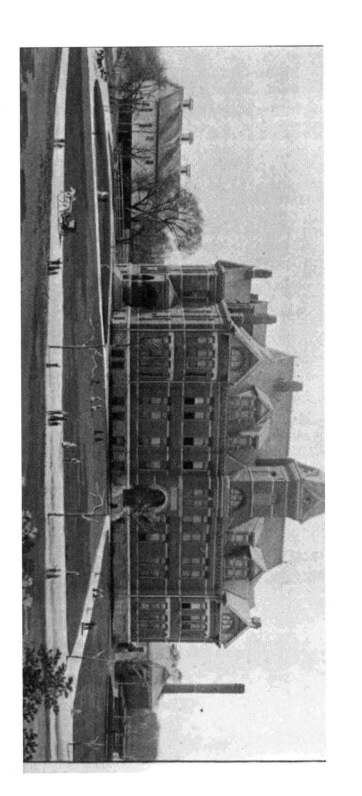

The rapid growth of the Children's Home system in Ohio was largely due to the efforts of the late Secretary of the Board of State Charities, Rev. A. G. Byers, who, having a high appreciation of the work being done by the Children's Homes, did all he could to induce county authorities to establish new Homes. He was a man of rare abilities for the place he held so many years, a man of progressive and advanced ideas in all departments of charitable work. Wherever he went through the State, visiting State and county institutions, he advocated the establishment of Children's Homes.

No Children in Poorhouses.

Another factor intervened which stimulated counties to organize Homes, which otherwise would not have done so. The General Assembly enacted a law prohibiting the keeping of children in county infirmaries, so that counties having no Children's Home must provide for their homeless children in some other way.

Since the date of the law in 1866 there have been established Homes as follows : —

1866 to 1870,	3
1870 to 1880,	6
1880 to 1890,	33
1890 to 1893,	4
Total,	46

All these institutions are supported by taxation, which tax is cheerfully paid by the people. These Homes are managed by boards of trustees, appointed by the county commissioners, and serve without compensation ; and we have the first Home yet to hear from where politics has in any way interfered with its efficient management.

In conclusion, there can be no better way of closing this paper than by quoting from the writer's address, delivered before the National Conference of Charities and Correction at Baltimore, May 19, 1890, as follows : —

The Ohio System.

The object of our plan is to secure the greatest good to the greatest number. Any county in the State may, by a vote of the people, organize a Children's Home.

This plan should rather be called the American plan than the Ohio plan, on account of its democratic breadth and scope. Where in the whole world is there such philanthropy as this, carried on in a business-like way, reaching every political subdivision, and thus affording immediate relief to the suffering and dependent children in every neighborhood of every county of the State?

Responsibility of the State.

The Ohio system is supported wholly by taxation, and it is a tax which the people pay willingly. I have the first grumbler yet to hear who was dissatisfied with the tax. Indeed, why should the State assume the support of one class of dependants, like the aged and infirm, and turn over the dependent children to private charity? There are many beneficent institutions in our large cities, devoted to saving homeless children; and there are a large number of noble men and women doing a grand work through these institutions, which could be done in no other way. Let us thank God for this, but these do not reach the country generally. The thousands of small cities, villages, and rural communities all over the land need Children's Homes, to take charge of their dependent children. The city institutions only reach a limited circle at best. Who, then, shall care for the dependent children of the State? Why, who but the people themselves in their collective capacity, thus distributing the burden over the whole community?

If the State undertakes this work at all, it must make it possible and easy for a dependent child from any locality, no matter how remote, to be placed in a Children's Home; and this, too, without any great amount of red tape or delay; yet how few States acknowledge this responsibility! Most of them do not distinguish between paupers and dependent children: both are consigned to the poorhouse.

Eighteen States, however, according to the last Conference (1889) report on this subject, have provided by law for saving dependent children. These are California, Connecticut, Indiana, Iowa, Kansas, Maine, Maryland, Massachusetts, Michigan, Minnesota, Missouri, Nebraska, New York, Ohio, Oregon, Pennsylvania, Texas, Wisconsin, and the District of Columbia.

This shows the extent to which the idea has advanced that the State should provide for saving these dependants. Twenty-four States have no such laws,— at least, none are reported; and it is presumed that, if they had them, the report would show it. Truly, here is a wide field for the benevolent and public-spirited people of those States to do a great work. The objective point in every State is the legislature, but it must be sustained by public sentiment. Can any one doubt that the people would sustain the legislature of any

CHILD SETTING IN THE WORKHOUSE OR ...

nce founded		Placed in Homes since founded.			Returned to Parents, Friends, or Guardians since founded.	Deceased since founded.	Number in Institution Feb. 15, 1893.			Current Expenses for Year ending Feb. 15, 1893.	Do you employ a visiting agent to place out your children?	Give, as near as possible, the average length of time children remain.
irls.	Total.	By Indenture	By Adoption.	Total.			Boys	Girls	Total			Menth.
81	151	55	–	55	43	7	27	19	46	$5,717.23	No.	45
155	355	138	3	141	131	13	41	29	70	7,400.08	"	3
234	576	272	5	277	154	20	31	10	41	7,232.00	"	7
98	216	95	1	96	66	12	29	21	50	5,006.95	"	–
291	756	145	1	146	289	65	48	20	68	7,753.97	"	10
117	265	162	7	169	69	4	19	7	26	4,150.00	"	12
63	156	21	16	37	37	1	39	24	63	8,000.00	"	15
46	125	28	3	31	–	–	15	12	27	–	"	24
83	230	15	136	152	47	11	24	6	30	2,256.73	"	9
81	225	56	–	56	67	6	56	22	78	7,012.68	"	–
96	213	79	2	81	78	4	31	19	50	5,595.85	"	18
437	1,125	707	–	707	380	38	97	28	125	17,200.17	"	12
173	383	107	3	290	134	6	27	16	43	3,491.31	"	24
145	321	146	1	147	63	3	31	19	50	6,302.00	"	–
31	72	18	3	21	8	–	19	13	32	3,700.00	"	12
–	–	–	–	–	–	3	15	11	26	1,137.79	"	6
38	84	21	–	24	30	–	20	9	29	2,700.00	"	11
201	577	64	17	81	65	16	26	10	36	4,877.44	"	–
124	316	145	3	148	83	6	48	25	73	12,502.48	Yes	18

State in passing such laws? The people's hearts are always right, when the fate of a homeless child is at stake.

It is safe to say that the dependent children now growing up to lives of idleness and crime in those States will in the end cost the public more than would a liberal Children's Home system, extending to every part of those great commonwealths.

> " Through the deep caves of thought,
> I hear a voice that sings:
> Build thee more stately mansions, O my soul,
> As the swift seasons roll!
> Leave the low vaulted past;
> Let each new temple, nobler than the last,
> Shut thee from heaven with a dome more vast,
> Till thou at length art free,
> Leaving thine outgrown shell by life's unresting sea."

NOTE.— A carefully prepared circular was sent out to each of the child-saving institutions of the State, asking for facts which it might be desirable to preserve. The responses to this circular are so fragmentary that it has been found impossible to use them in the preparation of this paper. We are indebted to Mr. Joseph P. Byers, Clerk of the Board of State Charities, for the following carefully prepared statistical table, containing most of the facts which it is desirable to preserve relating to Children's Homes.

CHILD–SAVING WORK IN PENNSYLVANIA.

BY HOMER FOLKS.

OUTLINE.

I. INTRODUCTORY.
II. WHAT THE STATE DOES FOR CHILDREN.
III. WHAT THE COUNTIES DO FOR CHILDREN.
IV. SOCIETIES FOR PLACING OUT.
V. INSTITUTIONS FOR CHILDREN (NON-SECTARIAN).
VI. INSTITUTIONS FOR CHILDREN (UNDER SECTARIAN CONTROL).
VII. THE CONFERENCE ON THE CARE OF CHILDREN.

I. INTRODUCTORY.

The object of this paper is to answer the questions, how large a factor among the organized activities for social betterment is child-caring work, what part of the work is done by the State and what by private beneficence, what are the merits and demerits of the prevailing methods? It does not aim, therefore, to be interesting or convincing, but simply to give an impartial answer, as complete as may be, to the questions above stated. It hopes to prove instructive to the student of practical sociology, when studied in connection with the other papers of the volume.

The oldest of the child-caring agencies of Pennsylvania is the Philadelphia Orphan Society, founded in 1814. Since that date these organizations have multiplied at the rate of one per year, with an extra four in each decade, the present number being 109. The total number of children in Pennsylvania whose support was paid from charitable funds, either public or private, on Dec. 1, 1892, was 11,490. In addition to these there were 2,520 children under the supervision of these organizations who had been placed out in families, without payment, by agreement, indenture, or adoption, so

that the total number of children in the charge of the charitable
agencies of the State was 14,010, or nearly 1 of every 120 of the
total child population of Pennsylvania. Of the 11,490 supported at
charitable expense, 2,906 belonged to special classes, namely: the
blind, 214; the deaf-mutes, 689; the feeble-minded, 855; and the
delinquent, 1,148. Of children *simply dependent* there were 8,584.

These may be divided as follows:--

Boarding in private families,	329
In institutions owned by counties,	87
* In private institutions (non-sectarian),	4,202
In private institutions (sectarian),	3,966

The fourth class is thus divided: in Roman Catholic institutions,
3,042; in Protestant institutions, 932; in Jewish institutions, 92.

The returns as to expenditures are not complete; but replies from
80 of the 109 institutions, including all the larger ones, indicate a
total expenditure for 1892 of $1,834,250. Deducting $429,143, the
amount expended by institutions for the special classes above
named, the expenditure for *dependent* children was $1,505,107. Of
this amount the State contributes $51,850, the counties $44,050, and
private beneficence $1,309,207, of which $463,722 is the expenditure of Girard College.

Of the total expense for caring for dependent children about 7 per
cent. is therefore borne by public authorities, 35 per cent. by Girard
College, and 52 per cent. from other private sources.

II. WHAT THE STATE DOES FOR CHILDREN.

The State of Pennsylvania takes no direct part in the care of dependent children. It has no officials engaged in this work, no central authority to which such children are committed, and, if we except
the schools for soldiers' orphans, which have never been regarded
as charities, has never owned or controlled any institution of this
nature.

The State legislature does, however, grant appropriations from
time to time to a number of the private non-sectarian institutions for
homeless or abandoned children. These appropriations are made at
the biennial sessions of the legislature, and are payable quarterly.

* Including 1,559 in Girard College.

Applications for State aid must be submitted to the State Board of Charities before November 1 preceding the session, together with a statement of endowment, receipts, expenditures, and inmates. After the appropriation is made, the State exercises no supervision over its expenditure, and has no voice in the admission or discharge of the children. The State Board of Charities, however, visits the institutions, and bases its subsequent recommendations for State aid on such visits, and the financial statement before noted.

A list of such appropriations made by the legislature for 1891–92 is as follows: —

1. Northern Home for Friendless Children, Philadelphia,	$10,000
2. Home for the Friendless, Erie,	5,000
3. Pittsburg and Allegheny Home for Friendless Children,	10,000
4. Southern Home for Destitute Children, Philadelphia,	5,000
5. Children's Aid Society of Pennsylvania,	12,000
6. Children's Aid Society of Western Pennsylvania,	12,000
7. Pennsylvania Society to Protect Children from Cruelty,	6,000
8. Home for Friendless Children, Lancaster,	5,000
9. Home for Colored Children, Allegheny,	4,700
10. Children's Industrial Home, Harrisburg,	5,000
11. Home for Friendless Children, Reading,	2,000
12. Memorial Home, Brookville,	15,000
13. Pittsburg Newsboys' Home,	10,000
14. Western Home for Poor Children, Philadelphia,	2,000
Total for 1891–92,	$103,700

There is noticeable a tendency to increase the amount given by the State to private charities for children. The following table exhibits the number of institutions aided, and the amount appropriated for the past eighteen years, and the recommendations for 1893–94.

Years.	Institutions aided.	Amount.
1875–76	1	$10,000
1877–78	2	8,000
1879–80	2	11,200
1881–82	1	10,000
1883–84	5	37,000
1885–86	6	47,000
1887–88	7	40,100
1889–90	13	84,200
1891–92	14	103,700
1893–94 (recommended)	17	157,700

In caring for special classes of children, the blind, the deaf-mutes, the feeble-minded, and the delinquent, the State has pursued a similar policy of aiding already existing private institutions. With the single exception of the Pennsylvania Reform School at Morganza, no agency touching the child problem is under the direct control of the State. To these institutions for the training of special classes State aid is given regularly, and in most cases is the major part of their income. A list of these agencies with appropriations for 1892 is as follows: —

Pennsylvania Institution for the Instruction of the Blind, Philadelphia, .	$30,000
Western Pennsylvania Institution for the Blind, Pittsburg,	12,000
Institution for Deaf and Dumb, Philadelphia,	96,000
Western Pennsylvania Institution for Deaf and Dumb,	30,000
Pennsylvania Oral School for Deaf-mutes, Scranton,	30,700
Home for Training in Speech of Deaf Children,	7,500
Training School for Feeble-minded Children, Elwyn,	103,250
House of Refuge, Philadelphia,	80,000
Pennsylvania Reform School (under State control),	39,693
Total for 1892,	$429,143

III. WHAT THE COUNTIES DO FOR CHILDREN.

The political unit whose duty it has been to make provision for the care of dependent children and to meet the expense of their support is the county. The Directors of the Poor, usually three in each county, have charge of the distribution of outdoor relief, the care of the almshouse and of dependent children.

Previous to 1883 all dependent children were sent to the almshouse. A few of the brighter ones to whom there was no parental claim were "bound out" by the directors to such families as might apply; but the majority remained year after year in the almshouse. I need not enter into the details of this awful system of pauper manufacture. I need not explain how the almshouse surroundings blighted, shrivelled, and debased the life of the child. In 1883 the State Board of Charities, with the Directors of the Poor, the Charity Organization Society, and the Children's Aid Society, secured the passage of a law forbidding the retention of any child sound in mind and body in the almshouse for a longer period than sixty days.

The counties were left entirely free to make such other provision for the children as they saw fit. As a result, nearly every possible method of child-caring is represented in the courses chosen by these sixty-seven counties. The Directors of the Poor keep few records, and publish no report of their work in this line; and hence all former efforts to ascertain the total number of children cared for have been very largely "guess-work." The writer endeavored to gain some accurate knowledge of this field by sending a circular letter to the directors of each county, asking for information on five points, viz.: —

1. The immediate disposition of dependent children.

2. Who has charge of providing permanent homes?

3. The amount of money expended for children in 1892.

4. The number of children supported by the county on Jan. 1, 1893.

5. The number of children who had been placed in free homes and were under the supervision of public officials on that date.

As this was probably the first time the directors had been asked these questions, it hardly needs to be said that the answers were not complete. Of the forty-nine counties in which the county system prevails, replies were received from forty-five. In connection with other sources of information, they point to the following conclusions

1. In eighteen counties the township system of poor-relief prevails. There is no almshouse; and the expense and duties of administration rest upon two overseers in each town, and not upon county officials. These are the sparsely settled counties, and very few children become dependent. Reports from the superintendents of schools of ten of the eighteen counties indicate that the general tendency is to give outdoor relief freely, to avoid breaking up the family. Other cases (one or two each year) are provided for by the overseers by adoption or identure, or very rarely by boarding out.

2. In eight counties, where few children become public charges, no provision is made except that of adoption or indenture and a generous use of that dangerous expedient, outdoor relief. In these counties a local committee of the Children's Aid Society renders valuable assistance in finding homes.

3. In two counties, Greene and Washington, the Directors of the Poor have established under their control "county homes" for children. This method, which is practically that of the children's alms-

house, is not favored as regards its influence upon the children, and is the most expensive system in the State, the expenditure for 1892 being equivalent to a per capita tax on each inhabitant of $0.08 in Greene County and $0.084 in Washington County. Cambria County reports, "Some are bound out, and some are taken care of by their own parents, with a compensation from the county." Its per capita expenditure in 1892 was $0.043.

4. In eleven counties the directors place the children in private institutions, to which is also intrusted the providing of permanent homes. The directors pay usually $1.50 per week while the child remains in the institution, although in Scranton and in York County the private institutions *make no charge* for children received from the directors. The expenditure in a number of these counties was the equivalent of a per capita tax as follows: Lackawanna, $0.021; Huntingdon, $0.034; Dauphin, $0.011.

5. In two counties, Adams and Perry, the directors themselves board out the children until free homes are found. Perry County reports: "Children are placed in private families, and their maintenance paid at the rate of 75 cents per week from the poor-fund, until the children are eight years of age. They are then usually bound to the same families until they are eighteen years of age." Nine children were being paid for January 1, and twenty-two were indentured. Under a similar plan Adams County reports six boarding and fourteen indentured. The per capita expenditure in Perry County was $0.012, and in Adams County $0.017.

6. In twenty-five counties the Directors of the Poor have accepted as their agent the Children's Aid Society. In five of these counties the children are sent temporarily to institutions owned or controlled by the local branch of the Children's Aid Society. The per capita expenditure of these counties for 1892 was as follows: Berks, $0.008; Lancaster, $0.009; Westmoreland, $0.012; Franklin, $0.029; Northampton, $0.041.

In the other twenty-five counties the family plan of the Children's Aid Society is strictly adhered to; that is, the children are boarded temporarily in private families, under the supervision of the Society, until permanent homes — that is, homes without payment can be properly provided. A fuller description of this co-operation between the Children's Aid Society and the Directors of the Poor, which is a striking example of effective co-operation between an official body and a private organization, and is almost entitled to be called the Pennsylvania system, will be given under the head of Societies for Placing Out.

This arrangement seems to be more economical than any other. The per capita expenditure of several of the counties using this plan is as follows: Philadelphia, $0.008; Bedford, $0.011; Blair. $0.008; Bucks, $0.017; Tioga, $0.004; Montgomery, $0.004; Chester, $0.022.

The returns from forty-five of the forty-nine counties indicate that on January 1st, 666 children were being supported at an expense during the past year of $44,050. Including the $51,850 granted by the State to private child-caring institutions, the total expenditure of public money in Pennsylvania for the care of dependent children in 1892 was $95,900.

The "Children's Law" of 1883 has been one of the most humane ever placed on the statute books; but we wish to call attention to one feature which, in our opinion, admits of improvement. The sixty days' stay allowed the child at the almshouse influences the Director to make every possible effort to find a free home himself for the child before the close of the period, and thus save all farther expense to the county. This tendency is re-enforced by the natural unwillingness of officials to turn over to others any of their prerogatives. We do not believe, however, that the Directors of the Poor, men of personal worth but of many business and political cares, are best fitted for the task of placing out children. Of this work they make no report to any power in the heavens above or in the earth beneath; and they keep very few records. " To Mr. Jones, who lives just over the hill," is an actual specimen and a fair sample of the total record of children who have left the almshouse in this manner. The last question in the list, " How many children placed out in families are now under supervision?" was evidently, in many cases, something of a puzzler. Among the replies are the following: "thirteen last year (up to that time the books were badly kept)," " About ten, as near as can be told," " From fifteen to twenty," " About seventy-five (estimated)," "About ten." Certainly, such supervision leaves much opportunity for grave dangers. In one county of Pennsylvania, in which the Directors had steadily refused any volunteer assistance in the supervision of the children, a boy bound out by the directors was so overworked, beaten, and starved that death was the direct result.

The Directors were good men personally; but they were busy men; and by no means experts in child-caring. This system of irresponsible placing out by men unaccustomed to such work is radically wrong. A work involving such responsibilities, and in which so much is to be learned by experience, should be placed by statute in the hands of some central authority, or at least be guarded by a system of careful inspection by some higher power.

IV. Societies for Placing Out.

We mention first among these, on account of its relations to the public authorities, the Children's Aid Society of Pennsylvania. Organized in 1882, it addressed itself to the task of providing for homeless children by means of placing out. Its first and greatest work has been its co-operation with the Directors of the Poor of the various counties. Since 1883 it has been the agent of the city of Philadelphia for all Protestant children who become public charges; and, as this co-operation explains the workings of the society in many other counties, we venture to describe it somewhat in detail. Its method is the family plan, pure and simple, the society owning no institution whatever. The afternoon of the day on which the child is brought to its office, it is, after a bath and proper precautions, taken to a private family in the city, who know about the society, and have agreed to receive children without previous notice for a reasonable remuneration. Here it remains for a few days or weeks, and then is transferred to a home in the country, usually at a distance of from forty to two hundred and fifty miles. Here, under favorable conditions, it awaits developments. If the parents die or disappear or forfeit all claim to the child, it may then be placed in a "permanent home"; that is, with a family who receive it "as their own child" and without payment, and with whom it is expected to remain until it reaches the age when children usually leave their homes. Very frequently it is thus kept permanently by the same family with whom it has been boarded, the only change being that the payment ceases, and the child is not to be removed except for unjust treatment. This is briefly the history of a child dependent upon the city of Philadelphia. He may have two or three temporary or boarding homes before he is finally settled permanently. Payment is usually at the rate of two dollars per week in the country and three dollars in the city.

The work of the society has, therefore, been an actual, practical, legitimate social experiment to solve the question, How far can the family plan meet the problem forced upon us by homeless childhood? An experience of ten years indicates that the family plan is in itself able to meet the whole of the problem. It not only furnishes favorable conditions for the healthy physical development of the child and the learning of the thousand lessons of industry, self-control, thrift, and affection which make up the early years of ordinary childhood, but it tends to diminish the number to be cared for. It does not appeal to the imagination of weak parents, stimulating the unloading of children upon the public, which is unquestionably the effect of an imposing institution.

For all children sent by the city authorities the society receives an allowance of two dollars per week while the child is boarded. The amount paid the country family by the society is usually two dollars per week, the society furnishing at its own expense clothing, schoolbooks, medical attendance, etc. There is no possible incentive for the society to retain children at an expense to the city longer than is necessary. The city has also a salaried officer whose duties are to pass upon all applications to place children upon the expense list of the city, to look after parents or relatives who should resume the charge of their children, to inspect the work of the society in selecting homes, and to exercise supervision over children placed in permanent homes. The number of dependent children supported by Philadelphia was on Jan. 1, 1893, 144. The total expenditure for 1892 was $8,630, or the equivalent of a per capita tax of $0.008. In New York City the expense for the same purpose was nearly equal to a per capita tax of $1.00.

The various county committees formed by the main society seek to do for the Directors of the Poor of the various counties what the Central Society does for Philadelphia. The Central Society maintains constant communication with its county committees, and by reason of its greater experience often takes charge of difficult cases from the counties. When the children are particularly troublesome, or relatives interfere, or the family name is unfavorably known, the main office often removes the children to a distant part of the State. The work of the main office is conducted under the supervision of the managers by a corps of eight salaried officials, two of whom are men. One assistant gives her whole time to the problem of homeless mothers with young children, providing for them service places to which they can take their children. Four workers are travelling almost constantly, investigating families who have applied for children, visiting children who have been placed out, or taking children to or from their homes. Having relied so largely upon the family plan, the society has given much attention to the elaboration of the details of its administration, and has thrown around it every possible safeguard. Its investigation of a family is systematic and exhaustive, and is carefully recorded. The applicant fills out a blank containing twenty-six questions relating to the various phases of the family life; viz., church relations, distance from school, size of farm, occupation, number of members of family with their ages, etc. A study of this return usually reveals the real motive of the application, and gives the data for an opinion as to the *material* fitness of the family. Their moral fitness is ascertained by sending a list of questions to six of the neighbors, stating that their replies are confidential, and that the appeal to them is not known to the applicant. A personal visit completes the investigation. After the child is placed out, his welfare is ascertained and protected by from one to five personal and unannounced visits each year, by a monthly report from the teacher of the public school, and a quarterly report from the pastor. The society uses neither indenture nor written agreement, the terms being perfectly flexible, and subject to change from year to year to suit the circumstances of each individual case.

Boarding out, carefully guarded, proved to be for the unfortunate and in many cases wayward and degenerate children of the almshouse such a really reforming, developing, regenerating agency that the society has recently extended the work to the care of the younger children from police stations and the criminal courts, and apparently with equal success.

The history of the Union Temporary Home is instructive in this connection. Organized in 1855 for the work indicated by its name, it maintained for thirty years an institution in Philadelphia. Its managers then became convinced that their method was not securing the objects originally intended, sold their institution, invested the proceeds, and have since used their income in the payment of the board of children in private families, working in co-operation with the Children's Aid Society and through its office. From their report for 1892 we quote: "We have closely watched the development of hundreds of cases under this plan, and at the close of our sixth year are prepared to assert more strongly than before that it is the best method of caring for these unfortunate children."

The Home Missionary Society, organized in 1835, has for many years combined the work of placing out homeless children with its other ministrations to the poor. The number under supervision at the close of the last fiscal year was 378. This society places out by indenture, and only in free or permanent homes. The average age of the children placed out is stated in its last report at eleven years. The Society for Educating Orphans in Jewish families uses only the family plan, and payment is at the uniform rate of $3 per week. The number of children in its charge Dec. 1, 1892, was thirty-two. The Jewish Home and Orphan Asylum combines the boarding-out system with its institutional work. At the date of its last report nearly one-fourth of the children in its charge were boarded in families.

Unlike New York and Massachusetts, the placing-out agencies of Pennsylvania have not sent children to the "Far West." A disproportionately large number have, however, been sent to Delaware and New Jersey. The former State especially, notwithstanding its small area and population, furnished a far greater demand for children under indenture than did Pennsylvania. Many of the placing-out societies found that they were actually sending more children to Delaware than to any other State. One institution stated in 1887 that of the white boys indentured, fifty were in Delaware, thirty-five in New Jersey, and thirty-three in Pennsylvania. This remarkable capacity for the absorption of homeless boys about fourteen years of age into the community was found to indicate unwholesome conditions for placing out. Many boys ran away, the school term was short, and the term for work long. Entirely apart from the moral character of the people, this matter of rearing boys from the age of twelve to the age of eighteen was altogether too much of a *business*. Most of the institutions now send very few children to Delaware; and the number sent to New Jersey is, for similar reasons, decreasing.

V. Institutions for Children (Non-sectarian).

The desire to shelter, warm, clothe, and feed friendless children has usually expressed itself through an institution where such children may be sheltered, warmed, clothed, and fed in generous numbers, the whole process being under the direct inspection of its supporters. There are forty-seven such institutions, non-sectarian in control, in the State, eighteen of which are in Philadelphia.

The greatest of these child-caring institutions, and one which lies very near to the heart of Philadelphians, is the Girard College for Orphans. The fact that it is called a college need not cause us to forget that it is a child-*caring* institution, the wealthiest and one of the largest in the land. The average age of the 137 boys admitted in 1891 was eight years and two months, and the average age of those discharged sixteen years and eleven months. The average duration of college or institutional life is, therefore, little short of nine years. Girard College is worthy of a volume. It is mentioned here to indicate the fact, often overlooked, that it is a large factor in the child-caring work of the city, and that its influence should be taken into account by any student of the subject. Admission is limited by the terms of the will to " poor white male orphans between the ages of six and ten years." The term "orphan " is held to include any fatherless child whose mother has not remarried. The "waiting list" numbered 503 on Jan. 24, 1893; and about two years now intervene between application and admission. About 70 per cent. of the 1,559 pupils in the college Jan. 1, 1893, were admitted from Philadelphia, and 30 per cent. from other parts of the State. The value of the endowment, and buildings of Girard College is reckoned at $15,500,000, and is steadily increasing. The magnificence of this endowment will be better understood when we remember that the endowment of all the other child-caring institutions of Philadelphia is but $2,000,000,— a magnificent sum in itself, but insignificant compared with the Girard estate. The total value of the real estate owned by the 217 private institutions for children and adults of the Empire State of New York, is but $20,000,000. The endowment of Harvard is stated at $11,500,000, and of Yale at $10,000,000.

What Girard College is for boys, the Foulke and Long Institute,

organized in 1887, is for girls, except that it does not admit pupils
under eleven years of age, and is a much smaller institution. Regular courses of study, three years in length, are offered in housekeep-
ing, dressmaking, and business. Of the forty-five other non-sectarian institutions for children, we note that, in general, they are small
institutions. Thirty of the forty-five have less than fifty inmates
each, five have between 50 and 100, nine between 100 and 200,
and only one more than 200. Their aim is less purely educational
than the two institutions we have noted, and, in general, it may be
said that they are only temporary stopping-places, from which the
child is returned to family life, either with his parents or by adoption
or indenture.

As to conditions of admission the institutions vary greatly. Many
do not observe, or at least do not announce, any inflexible rules.
Others make specifications as to age, sex, legitimacy, mortality of
parents, residence, etc. There is also a great variation in the terms
offered to parents; i.e., complete surrender or obligation for partial
or entire support. Other conditions being fulfilled, there yet remains the condition that there shall be a vacancy. To secure admission for a child to a " Home " is not the easy matter it might appear. Worthy parents often find it very difficult, while unworthy
ones often find it possible. Some central agency which could sift
the worthy from the unworthy, and impartially refer each worthy
case to the proper agency, assuring itself that it was received, is
greatly needed.

The institutions also vary greatly as to the length of time children may remain. The Orphan Society, the oldest institution of the
city, indentures girls at fourteen and boys at twelve. Most institutions place out as circumstances warrant and opportunities offer.
Statistics as to the duration of institutional life of children discharged
are not published in the annual reports. Each institution has its
own method of investigating applications for children and of supervision of placed-out children.

It is greatly to be desired and strictly in keeping with their responsibility to the public that all institutions should state in their reports full particulars as to parental relations and age of children received, the length of stay and disposition of those discharged,
and definite information as to the supervision of those placed out by
indenture or agreement.

VI. Institutions for Children (under Sectarian Control).

All religious denominations seem to agree in at least one point, that it is their duty to make some provision for homeless children. It is doubtless true that religious motives have inspired the great amelioration in the lot of children cared for by the public, and have brought into existence many institutions and societies which are non-sectarian; but we have a more direct recognition of the duty of the Church in this matter in the existence in the State of forty-four child-caring organizations under direct denominational control, and sheltering at the latest report 3,877 children, about 45 per cent. of the dependent children of the State. The Roman Catholic Church, whose care for orphans dates back in Philadelphia to 1829 and in Pittsburg to 1840, has under its charge 28 of these institutions, with a population of 3,042. With regard to the Roman Catholic institutions we venture three observations : -

1. They present about the only instance of extended, effective co-operation among child-caring agencies. While in too many cases the non-sectarian and Protestant organizations are separated by jealousies and distrust, the seventeen institutions in the archdiocese of Philadelphia present an organized rational system.

2. The predominance of the religious orders in all Catholic institutions emphasizes and deepens every item of religious belief or training which may have found a place in the child's life.

3. While the Church disclaims a preference for institutional life, and distinctly asserts that the family plan is its ideal, it is unquestionably true that in its practical workings their system allows large place for institutional life. The average number of inmates in their institutions in Pennsylvania is 103; while the average in the Protestant institutions is 63, and in the non-sectarian 80. This is undoubtedly to some extent due to the greater difficulty of placing children in Catholic country families.

The 14 Protestant institutions of the State, representing 9 different denominations, are now caring for 932 children; and the 2 Jewish institutions, for 92 children.

It should be said of all these institutions that the term "sectarian" applies only to their management. In the admission of children, so far as the writer can learn, there is no formal discrimination on denominational grounds.

We are not here concerned with the question as to whether the motive which led to the establishment of these institutions was simply love for the children themselves, or whether there was mingled with it a desire to, at the same time, by careful training, increase the number of the "faithful" of that particular faith. Nor do we ask whether that motive is now a factor in their administration. If the churches *should* desire to increase numbers through sheltering, clothing, and caring for homeless children, we think no one would object. It is worthy of note, however, that Pennsylvania has provided that the expense of such forms of "church extension" shall be borne by the churches, by inserting in its Constitution, Art. 3, Sect. 18, "No appropriation shall be made to any denominational or sectarian institution, corporation, or association."

VII. THE CONFERENCE ON THE CARE OF CHILDREN.

We have, then, in Pennsylvania 109 child-caring agencies, to whose care are now intrusted 14,010 of its future citizens. Each of these agencies has its own history, its own line of work, its own fund of experience, and has learned its own lessons. One of the most evident needs, therefore, is that these organizations shall meet on some common ground, confer with each other as to the proper division of the field, learn to have mutual confidence, and to profit each by the experience of the others. Such a movement as this was the Conference on the Care of Children held in Philadelphia on Jan. 25 and 26, 1893. To this conference all the child-caring agencies of the city and vicinity were invited, and were joined by representatives from many other States. All matters of business and routine were arranged in advance; and four sessions, of three solid hours each, were devoted to papers and discussions on the various phases of child-caring work. After the reading of each paper, its writer was subjected to a "running fire" of questions, which proved to be probably the most instructive and certainly the most entertaining feature of the conference. At the first session, devoted to dependent children, three papers were read, presenting its three phases: viz., boarding out, placing out from a central institution, and "the legitimate use of an institution." The second session considered exhaustively the investigation of homes and the supervision of placed out children. Four short papers were presented from four different societies, stating their methods and experience. The system of the Roman Catholic Church was presented by a representative of one of its institutions, and was discussed by the lecturer of the Philadelphia Ethical Society. Various means of improving the condition of children in their own homes closed the session. The third session was devoted to delinquent children: three papers again, on the cottage system, the farm school, and the family system. The last session was given up to the care of foundlings and the work of the Society to Protect Children from Cruelty, with a closing address from Professor Francis Wayland,— a plea for centralization and for a greater exercise of the authority of the State in protecting and caring for exposed and neglected children. A committee was appointed to consider the subject of permanent organization.

THE HISTORY OF CHILD-SAVING WORK IN THE STATE OF NEW YORK.

BY WILLIAM PRYOR LETCHWORTH, LL.D.,

EX-PRESIDENT OF THE ELEVENTH NATIONAL CONFERENCE OF CHARITIES AND CORRECTION, EX-CHAIR-
MAN OF THE COMMITTEE ON SAVING WORK FOR CHILDREN OF THE SIXTH, EIGHTH, TENTH,
AND TWELFTH CONFERENCES OF CHARITIES AND CORRECTION, AND CHAIRMAN OF THE
COMMITTEE ON DEPENDENT AND DELINQUENT CHILDREN OF THE
NEW YORK STATE BOARD OF CHARITIES.

One hundred and sixteen years have passed since the founding of New York State by the adoption, in 1777, of a constitution for a State government. The State was then sparsely populated. Even thirteen years later it numbered only 340,120 persons, less than half the population of Virginia at that time; but so rapid has been its advancement since that its population in 1892 was 6,513,343, and the assessed valuation of the real and personal property within the State was $4,114,099,324. Meanwhile, its burdens have proportionately increased. Its beneficiaries in the care of charitable institutions, and its prisoners in jails, penitentiaries, and State prisons, at the close of the fiscal year of 1892, numbered 85,363; and the expenditures for charitable purposes, and in connection with the above-named institutions during the year, were $19,426,020.

The experience of so populous and wealthy a State, active in its multifarious industries, inexhaustible in its resources, possessing varied attractions for all kinds of people from all parts of the world, and being, at the same time, the gateway for an immense heterogeneous immigration, is invaluable to those having to deal with some of the difficult problems of the nineteenth century. In considering the successive stages of development attained by humane effort in New York State, we will confine our attention to that branch of the subject known as Child-saving Work.

Prior to the adoption of a State Constitution there did not exist in the territory now included in the boundaries of the State any institutions of the character of special homes for children. During the Dutch occupancy of the New Netherlands the wants of this frugal and thrifty people were few, and their affairs were managed with strict regard to economy. The assessment of one-twentieth of a penny on all houses, and one-tenth of a penny on all lands under cultivation, formed the fund for the support of the poor. There was elected by the people an officer called a Schout, who, with four Burgomasters, was charged, among other duties, with that of extending relief where needed. They were Fathers of the Burghery, guardians of the poor, of widows and orphans, and were the principal church wardens. Although this system included destitute orphan children, it would appear that, at this early date, there was a lack of suitable provision for them; for complaint was made on one occasion by the local authorities to their " High Mightinesses " in Holland that no orphan asylums or hospitals were provided for the colony.

Under the English colonial government, by an act of the General Assembly of the colony of New York, passed in 1754, overseers of the poor were authorized to apprentice poor children ; but we hear of no special provision being made for those who were not eligible to apprenticeship on account of their helplessness or tender years. The English colony left a legacy to the State of a system of relief developed in the mother country, which was inseparably connected with Church and State ; to wit, the parish or vestry system. The money to support this system was mostly raised by taxation, and the ruling idea of the time was to furnish the smallest sum that would provide the necessaries for actual existence. Under this system it was evidently the aim to make the lot of the dependent as hard as possible. Gradually, the parish or vestry plan gave place to a more secular form ; and relief, being no longer monopolized by the Church as its almoner, was distributed by the officers of the people. The church divisions of the State gave way to civil divisions : and the care of the poor, no less than the education of youth, became one of the functions of civil government.

The prolonged struggle for American independence left the people in a needy condition. There was a scarcity of money, a distrust of credit, and at the same time a pressing demand for means to develop the resources of the country. There was much suffering, and many children of the soldiers who had fought in the cause of freedom were destitute and homeless. In this great emergency private benevolence came to the rescue. A mother's quick perception comprehended the situation, her active sympathies were turned to the orphaned and destitute ; and it is to the honor of her sex that a woman first inaugurated for homeless children a grand system of philanthropy in a State that was destined to become a mighty commonwealth.

DEPENDENT CHILDREN.

The earliest accounts we have of a purely benevolent system for the care of dependent children are in connection with the work of the New York Society for the Relief of Poor Widows with Small Children, which was founded by Isabella Graham in 1797. It had for its object the care of such worthy and respectable widows with small children as could not provide the means of obtaining even the necessaries of life. The managers had no building where they received and cared for beneficiaries, but visited the widows and fatherless, supporting and encouraging them until the days of their helplessness were past, and the dependent mothers became self-supporting. The city was divided into thirty-eight districts, and a manager appointed for each. It was a condition that the applicant must be a widow of good character, having young children, and that she was willing to exert herself for her own support, and was not receiving aid from the almshouse. The work of the society was conducted on a principle similar to that of the present Charity Organization Societies, the members acting the part of friendly visitors, seeking out the destitute, giving intelligent counsel, and extending relief to them in their homes.

It was in connection with the operations of this society that its founder came to realize the necessity for a Children's Home. In 1806 she collected twelve full orphaned, homeless children in a small cottage in the village of Greenwich, since absorbed in the city of New York, and with the aid of her daughter, Mrs. Bethune, Mrs. Sarah Hoffman, and Mrs. Elizabeth Hamilton, began a work which is still conducted under the name of "The Orphan Asylum Society in the City of New York," an act for the incorporation of which was obtained from the legislature in January, 1807. The first meeting of the trustees of this corporation, notable as being the first in the State to provide a special home for destitute orphans, was held at the City Hotel in New York, April 2, 1807, on which occasion twenty orphan children then under care were presented to the friends who were supporting the enterprise. The society filled a public want, but through the first years of its existence it had to struggle with debt and depend on the liberality of its friends.

Passing for the present the work organized by members of the Roman Catholic faith, the next work undertaken for children under Protestant auspices was in the village, now the city, of Utica, in 1830. Like that in New York, it originated with a small band of benevolent women, who were organized as a society to relieve the distressed. Three little children, in a condition of peculiar distress, coming to the notice of the society, one of its members, Mrs. Sophia D. Bagg, was unwilling to leave them to the cold charity provided by taxation, and undertook, with the aid of her associates, to maintain them. The need of establishing some kind of asylum care for children of this class, where they could have the advantages of a home and Christian instruction, was so urgent that a meeting was called by the society, and steps were taken to form an orphan asylum society, which was incorporated the same year under the title of the " Utica Orphan Asylum." The building now in use is conveniently planned, and is situated in the midst of beautiful grounds on the outskirts of the city.

About this time an important work was begun in Albany under such peculiar circumstances that it seems proper to particularize them here. A young lady was reading to an invalid convalescing from a serious illness the memoirs of the celebrated missionary to India, Ann H. Judson. The listener, Mrs. Orissa Healy, and the reader, Miss Eliza Wilcox, together formed a resolution to enter upon missionary work; and, after the recovery of Mrs. Healy, Miss Wilcox offered her services to the American Baptist Mission to Burmah. But, as the way did not open for serving in this quarter, it was decided by both the ladies that there was missionary work at their own doors. The result of the resolution formed in the sick-chamber was that Miss Wilcox gave up her position as teacher in a school; and the two ladies, after visiting the asylums for children in New York City, engaged quite limited and unpretentious quarters for the purpose of carrying out their intentions. The first child received was an unpromising girl, and the next a homeless boy of doubtful antecedents. For a week they constituted, with the two ladies, the entire household; but it was not long before seventy children were under their care, and a warm interest was manifested in the enterprise by the citizens of Albany. In 1831 the work was incorporated under the title of "The Society for the Relief of Orphan and Destitute Children in the City of Albany." The work of the society under the succeeding administration of the late Rev. Timothy Fuller, and as continued by his son, has been highly prosperous.

The ravages of the cholera in 1832 left a large number of destitute orphan children in the city of Brooklyn. In this emergency an association of women was formed to provide permanent shelter, care, and religious instruction for the homeless ones. This led to the incorporation in 1835 of the Orphan Asylum Society of Brooklyn, which has been continued to the present time under the direction of a board of lady managers, having an advisory board of gentlemen. It still fills a large field of usefulness.

These institutions were followed by the establishment of the Troy Orphan Asylum in 1833, the Society for the Relief of Half-orphan and Destitute Children in the City of New York in 1835, the Buffalo Orphan Asylum in 1836, the Rochester Orphan Asylum in 1837, the Onondaga Orphan Asylum in 1841, the Leake and Watts Orphan House in New York City and the Hudson Orphan Relief Association in 1843, the Society for the Relief of Destitute Children of Seamen at West New Brighton, Staten Island, in 1846, the Orphan Home and Asylum of the Protestant Episcopal Church in the City of New York in 1851, the Cayuga Asylum for Destitute Children at Auburn and the Oswego Orphan Asylum in 1852, the Five Points House of Industry in New York City in 1854, the Poughkeepsie Orphan House and Home for the Friendless in 1857, the Jefferson County Orphan Asylum at Watertown in 1859, the Union Home and School* for the Benefit of the Children of the Volunteers at New York in 1861, the Ontario County Orphan Asylum at Canandaigua and the Newburg Home for the Friendless in 1862, the Davenport Institution for Female Orphan Children at Bath in 1863, the Sheltering Arms, on the family system, in New York in 1864, and the Southern Tier Orphan Home at Elmira in the same year.

Under the auspices of the German Lutheran Church there was established in 1864 the Evangelical Lutheran St. John's Orphan Home of Buffalo, which comprises two departments,— one for boys on a large farm at Sulphur Springs, near the city, and one for girls in the city. In 1866 the Wartburg Farm School was established for

* The Union Home and School has been discontinued.

German children at Mt. Vernon, Westchester County, also under the auspices of the Lutheran Church.

In 1869 a work for neglected and destitute children was begun at Cooperstown, Otsego County, by Miss Susan Fenimore Cooper, under the title of the "Orphan House of the Holy Saviour." In the same year the Susquehanna Valley Home was established at Binghamton. In 1870 Gerrit Smith gave a site and building for the Madison County Orphan Asylum, which was located at Peterboro. On the basis of a work conducted by the Ladies' Relief Society at Lockport, Niagara County, the Lockport Home for the Friendless was incorporated in 1871. The Home for the Friendless at Plattsburg was incorporated in 1874. Subsequently there were incorporated various institutions for the care of orphan and destitute children in different parts of the State.

In connection with the charitable labors of the Protestant Episcopal Church, a work on behalf of unfortunate and destitute children is conducted by the church charity foundations and church homes in Brooklyn, Utica, Rochester, and Buffalo. An important work under the auspices of the same church, based on the family system, was established at St. Johnland, Long Island, by the late Rev. Dr. Muhlenberg. The House of the Good Shepherd in Rockland County, and the Orphan Home of St. Peter's Church at Albany, are also conducted under the auspices of the Protestant Episcopal Church. The sisterhoods of this church are likewise variously engaged in New York in an extensive work for children, in connection with the relieving of general distress.

In 1817 an important work was inaugurated on the part of the members of the Roman Catholic communion, by the establishment of the Roman Catholic Orphan Asylum in the city of New York, which was incorporated by an act of the legislature in April, 1817, under the name of the "Roman Catholic Benevolent Society in the City of New York." It was reorganized in 1852 under the name of "The Roman Catholic Orphan Asylum in the City of New York," thus consolidating under one management several societies having the care of children that were then maintained in the city under Roman Catholic auspices. The powers of the corporation are exercised by a board of managers, of which the Archbishop, or Ordinary, of the diocese is the president.

The objects of the society are to provide for the destitute and unprotected orphan and half-orphan children of both sexes, and to educate them in the Roman Catholic faith. It is difficult to arrive at a correct estimate of the number of children that have received the benefits of this organization and that have been restored to usefulness and to society by its devoted efforts. In its early history it had to struggle with many difficulties in consequence of limited means.

In 1826 an extensive work was organized in Brooklyn for the benefit of children of Roman Catholic parents. It was incorporated, in 1834, under the name of "The Roman Catholic Orphan Asylum Society in the City of Brooklyn, in the County of Kings." It includes the Roman Catholic Male Orphan Asylum and St. Joseph's Female Orphan Asylum, both conducted by Sisters of the Order of St. Joseph, and St. Paul's Industrial School for older girls, conducted by the Sisters of Charity. The number of children under the care of the society Oct. 1, 1892, was 1,663. During the years of its existence it has proved to be a powerful regenerative agency.

A work under Roman Catholic auspices was begun in Utica, in 1834, under the direction of a band of Sisters of Charity, who were delegated from the Mother House of the order at Emmittsburgh, Md. The asylum was opened in a plain dwelling-house, and had connected with it, as now, a large day school. The early days of the institution were dark and discouraging; but under the courageous Sisters, headed by Sister Perpetua, it struggled on, sometimes without a dollar in the treasury, and finally reached a condition of prosperity.

Benevolent work of this character, conducted under Roman Catholic auspices, was extended by the establishment of St. Patrick's Orphan Asylum in the city of Rochester in 1842, St. Vincent's Orphan Asylum Society in the city of Albany in 1845, St. Vincent's Female Orphan Asylum in Buffalo in 1848, the House of Mercy in New York the same year, St. Joseph's Male Orphan Asylum at Limestone Hill near Buffalo in 1849, the Troy Male Catholic Orphan Asylum and St. Vincent's Female Orphan Asylum at Troy in 1850, St. Vincent's Orphan Asylum at Syracuse in 1852, the

Institution of Mercy in New York and St. Vincent's Male Orphan Asylum at Albany in 1854, the Convent of the Sisters of Mercy in Brooklyn in 1855, St. Mary's Orphan Asylum at Dunkirk in 1857, the Orphan Asylum of the Holy Trinity in Brooklyn in 1861, St. Mary's Boys' Orphan Asylum at Rochester in 1864, and St. Stephen's Home for children in New York in 1868. Others of like character have since been established throughout the State.

The work done by the charitable of this faith is, in some respects, unique. With hardly a single exception,—indeed, I know not a single one in the State,—the burden of the work is assumed by some religious order in the church. Most of these orders are composed of women who are specially trained for their work, to which they devote their lives without compensation. The orders most prominently represented are the Sisters of Charity, the Sisters of St. Joseph, the Sisters of Mercy, and the Sisters of the Good Shepherd. The Christian Brothers are also in charge of orphan asylum work, mainly in the education of boys.

The Hebrews have not been backward in providing for the wants of children of their faith deprived of support from parents, and thus becoming public dependants. The oldest of the institutions established for this object had its origin in a simple incident. In the spring of 1820 an Israelite, who had been brought in a critical condition to the City Hospital, expressed a wish to see some of his co-religionists before his death. He had been a soldier in the war of American Independence, and was without money or friends. The fact becoming known to a few of his religious belief, they visited him, and collected some money for his support. Shortly afterwards he died, and about $300 was left in the hands of those who had assisted him for their disposal. They decided that this small sum should be used as a nucleus to found a benevolent society, to whose members assistance could be given in time of need. This led to the establishment, in 1822, of the Hebrew Benevolent Society. After various attempts made later to combine the Hebrew Benevolent Society with the other benevolent interests of the Hebrews in New York City, this was finally accomplished by the incorporation, in 1860, of the Hebrew Benevolent and Orphan Asylum Society.

In 1878 the Ladies' Deborah Nursery and Child's Protectory in

New York was incorporated.   Children are received here who are committed by legal authority, and are instructed in trades and household duties until able to support themselves.   In the same year was organized in Brooklyn the Hebrew Orphan Asylum.   The Hebrew Sheltering Guardian Society of New York, which has two separate establishments,— one for boys and one for girls,— was incorporated in 1879.   There has also been established at Rochester the Jewish Orphan Asylum Association of Western New York, which was incorporated in 1881.

The children in these institutions are thoroughly instructed in the elementary branches of an education, and are taught useful trades. Except in rare instances, they find their way to independent support in after years.

A benevolent desire on the part of Swedish people residing in different parts of the State to provide a special home for bereaved children of their own nationality led to the establishment of the Gustavus Adolphus Orphans' Home at Jamestown, which was incorporated in 1883.   Its affairs are controlled by a board of seven directors elected by the New York Conference of the Scandinavian Lutheran Augustana Synod.   The capacity of the institution is for about one hundred children of both sexes.   The main building is a substantial structure located on eighty-four acres of land.   Gardening, farming. and the care of stock employ the male children out-of-doors, and the girls are thoroughly instructed in domestic arts within doors.   The asylum is of the nature of a permanent home, the children not usually being placed out until they have reached maturity.

In 1836 a few benevolent persons deeply interested in homeless colored orphan children, and impressed with the conviction that some special provision should be made for them, formed a society, and undertook to establish an asylum for their care.   About $2,000 was obtained by small subscriptions, and an attempt was made to rent a house; but so strong was the prejudice against the colored race that, after several months of unsuccessful effort, it was decided to purchase a building, which was accordingly done.   The house was furnished by the friends of the project, and at times the food of the inmates was mainly supplied from the tables of the members of the society. Limited resources did not permit the hiring of school-teachers, and in the beginning of the work forty pupils were regularly taught by members of the association. The asylum accommodations being insufficient, some of the children received were boarded in families in the country. In 1842 the city gave to the society, called the "Association for the Benefit of Colored Orphans in the City of New York," twenty lots of ground, upon which a plain, substantial building was erected, capable of accommodating one hundred and fifty children.

During the New York riots in 1863 the asylum was assailed by a furious mob, and was pillaged and burned to the ground. The children, however, were quietly removed without injury, and temporarily provided for by the city on Blackwell's Island. Subsequently buildings in the country were rented for their accommodation. In the following year $20,000 was given to the association by Chauncey Rose. With this and other gifts, and the sum of $73,000 allowed by the city for the destruction of the buildings and $170,000 derived from the sale of the old site, other property in the upper part of the city, overlooking the Hudson, was purchased at a cost of $45,000; and the present spacious and convenient edifice was built.

The present number of inmates in the institution is two hundred and eighty-six. Destitute colored children whose parents are living are now received, as well as orphans and half-orphans. The children are usually indentured. Parties taking them pay the association annually a stated sum. This is deposited in the bank to the credit of the treasurer of the association. The child holds the book, and when it is of age the money is paid over to it.

The exigencies of the War of the Rebellion led to the establishment of another institution for colored children in Brooklyn, which was incorporated in 1868 under the title of the Brooklyn Howard Colored Orphan Asylum. The work was organized in 1866 under the name of the Home for the Children of Freedmen, and was designed to relieve colored people coming North who could not obtain situations. As the children of such were not admitted into the New York asylums, it was necessary to make other provision for them. Some of them were taken into private families. S. A. Tilman had twenty such children in his house over six months. Until the present asylum could be opened and the children admitted there, they were maintained by the benevolent and by donations from the Freedmen's Bureau during its existence. There are at the present time one hundred and thirty children in the institution.

———

A peculiar work, having its origin in private benevolence, is that for Indian children, which is carried on by the State on the Cattaraugus Reservation, under the corporation known as the Thomas Asylum for Orphan and Destitute Indian Children. The name perpetuates the memory of one who was imbued with that spirit of love and justice which guided William Penn in his early intercourse and dealings with the Indians.

The nucleus of the asylum was an industrial school for Indian girls, established by the Society of Friends. It was a free school, and so continued for fifteen years, till about 1845. At this time there was a change in the Indian government on the Reservation, the pagan element losing control, and the party called the New Government, which gave up wigwam life, with its hunting and fishing, for the more civilized pursuits of agriculture, assuming the direction of affairs.

Through the advice of Philip E. Thomas, of Baltimore, a philanthropic member of the Society of Friends, who had always taken a great interest in everything pertaining to the welfare of the Indians, the school, which had been closed, was reopened as an asylum, under the patronage of the New Government. The Rev. Asher Wright and his wife, who for over fifty years devoted their lives as missionaries to the Indians, were the active workers in the new departure.

The asylum struggled on with its limited means till 1855, when it was considered advisable to procure a charter of incorporation from the State. This was secured; and a board of trustees, composed of five Indians and five whites, representing different religious denominations, assumed the responsibility of management. This act of incorporation secured for the asylum much-needed annual contributions from the State, which, together with means derived from private sources, were sufficient to enable it to carry on its work.

In 1875, however, an amendment to the State Constitution, which prevented the giving of State aid to private charitable institutions, cut off from this asylum quite a source of support, and rendered a reorganization necessary to its continuance. Through the efforts of the friends of the Indians, an arrangement was made by which the institution was turned over to the State, and the work is still continued under its direction.

The asylum is now controlled by a board of trustees composed of both Indian and white trustees, as formerly; but they are appointed by the governor and confirmed by the Senate. The scope of the work has been enlarged, and children of both sexes are received from all the reservations of the State.

The average number of children annually cared for is about one hundred, and they remain in the institution until they are sixteen years of age. They receive a good education in the common English branches, and are taught various industries suited to their years, including farming and gardening. The girls receive training in domestic work, in sewing, cooking, and laundrying. Music is also taught, in which some have made remarkable progress. Many of the children have scrofulous tendencies. They usually come from wretched homes, where they have suffered from want and exposure, and are received in feeble health. The asylum care soon effects a marked improvement in them. The institution aims, by intellectual and industrial training and by the inculcation of moral and religious principles, to enable the children in their changed condition to become self-supporting.

The first institution in the State for the care of foundlings was established in Buffalo. Before the enterprise was undertaken, lying-in women, infants, and foundlings were obliged to be taken to the Buffalo Hospital of the Sisters of Charity. The institution was incorporated in 1852, under the name of Saint Mary's Asylum for Widows, Foundlings, and Infants; but its work was not actively entered upon till later. In 1854, owing to the crowded condition of the Hospital, it was determined at once to make other provision for lying-in patients; and cottages were erected on land given by Louis Le Couteulx for this object. The lying-in patients were transferred there, and placed in charge of the Sisters of Charity. In the enlargement of the work the cottages have been displaced by a capacious brick edifice.

The great need of public provision in the city of New York for infants of the class termed foundlings, and for the relief of women in destitute circumstances and about to become mothers, aroused the sympathies of a noble woman, Mrs. Cornelius Du Bois, whose generous feelings were deeply stirred by a painful incident that demonstrated to her the need of some special organization for the protection of such mothers and infants; and she did not rest until she had established, in 1854, the Nursery and Child's Hospital in New York City.

The impelling motive in the founding of this charity was the thought — and it was most repugnant to this Christian lady — that the children of the poor had to be sacrificed for the benefit of the children of the wealthy, which was done when mothers were forced to accept employment as wet-nurses, and thus deprive their own offspring of the aliment necessary to their existence.

To the Nursery was subsequently added a country branch, modelled upon the cottage plan. This was located on Staten Island. The cottages are planned on modern sanitary principles, and patients can be easily isolated in case of the appearance of contagious or infectious diseases. To this institution Mrs. Du Bois gave her assiduous personal attention during her lifetime.

Both the city nursery and the country branch have maternity wards attached. The mothers of children born out of wedlock are kindly treated, and helped to honorable courses of life. The children are cared for by the institution until proper provision can be made for them in families or otherwise. A number are boarded in private homes, under the supervision of the officers of the nursery. At the age of four years the children are transferred to the country branch, if not suitably placed in families before. Sick children are also sent there for the benefits of country air.

It is claimed that infant mortality materially diminished in New York City after the nursery went into operation. The benefits of this institution have been extended to 33,018 inmates.

In 1865 work in this direction was enlarged by the establishment of the New York Infant Asylum. The prevalence of infanticide, suicide, and moral abandonment among homeless and despairing young women impressed the projectors of the asylum, and led them to organize an institution which has since grown to large proportions. As the managers assert, it is now so organized that, by its methods of mercy and care, a helping hand is extended to the homeless mother and infant, and to the friendless and cruelly forsaken young woman on the eve of her greatest want, when woe and terror make such acts of mercy the plainest duty of Christian charity.

The institution consists of a city establishment on Tenth Avenue and a country branch at Mount Vernon, Westchester County. It is governed by a board of lady managers representing many Protestant denominations, and by a like constituted board of gentlemen acting as trustees. In a quiet way it has enlisted the co-operation and support of many prominent people of the city.

In 1869 the Roman Catholic Sisters of Charity entered this large field of Christian usefulness in New York City, beginning their work on a small scale at a private house in Twelfth Street, under the leadership of Sister Irene. When describing to the writer the struggle they had to make in order to establish the work, Sister Irene said: "We commenced with two cups and saucers. The first morning we had to beg our breakfasts. We slept on straw on the floor the first year, rolling the mattresses up during the day."

From this beginning has grown the large and imposing institution known as the New York Foundling Hospital, which covers the block bounded by Third and Lexington Avenues and Sixty-eighth and Sixty-ninth Streets, and includes a country branch at Spuyten Duyvil. The city institution comprises a main structure, a children's hospital, a maternity hospital, and other necessary buildings. The country branch is designed for delicate and convalescent children, and has accommodations for two hundred and fifty inmates.

In connection with the work is maintained an outdoor department, where children are placed out to nurse with respectable married women who have lost their own infants. These are required to produce a physician's certificate of fitness; and they are constantly under the supervision of a special officer who visits and inspects the homes, and also under the vigilance of the Society of Saint Vincent de Paul, whose members are scattered throughout the different parishes. At stated periods the nurses are required to present themselves, with the babies under their care, at the hospital for medical inspection. Upwards of a thousand infants are daily cared for in this way.

The object of the Sisters from the first has been to prevent infanticide and preserve lives which otherwise would have been sacrificed to hide the mother's shame. It was soon found that the co-operation of the mothers was essential to successful work; and, this being secured, a reflex reformatory influence was exerted upon the latter. Only children born in New York City are received.

The ultimate disposition of such of the children as are not returned to the mothers has been a subject of solicitude on the part of the Sisters. Various plans have been adopted, and within recent years the experiment of finding homes for them in the West has been tried with signal success. About 6,000 of the children have been thus provided for.

Prior to June 30, 1891, the title of the corporation was "The Foundling Asylum of the Sisters of Charity in the City of New York"; but at that time it was changed to its present form.

From the organization of this charity in 1869 down to October, 1892, a period of twenty-three years, there were received into the institution 23,210 infants and upwards of 4,500 needy and homeless mothers. As further showing the magnitude of the work, it may be said that its expenditures during the past year were about $300,000.

Work of this kind, conducted under both Roman Catholic and Protestant auspices, has been extended to other cities of the State.

A foundling hospital having a capacity for two hundred and twenty infants is maintained on Randall's Island by the Commissioners of Charities and Correction of New York City. Prior to 1866 foundlings and other infants becoming a charge upon the city were sent to the almshouse on Blackwell's Island and placed in charge of nurses; but the mortality under this system was fearful, being nearly ninety per cent. In 1866 a matron, who was aided by a corps of nurses, was employed to take exclusive charge of the infants in a special department; and more watchful supervision was extended over them. The mortality still continued, however, to be great. In 1868 the present foundling hospital was built, and placed under the control of a resident physician, who is aided by a visiting and consulting medical staff. There is also a matron and a staff of paid nurses. Since then the mortality has gradually and greatly decreased. During the fiscal year ending June 30, 1892, it was 19.76 per cent. This was based on an average of both foundlings and infants having mothers. At the date of April 10, 1893, there were one hundred and eighty infants and sixty-one mothers. Each mother is required to nurse her own child and another infant.

As a part of the work for the care of infants should be mentioned that comprised under the title of Day Nurseries. These are institutions having generally for their object the rescuing of children where families have been broken up by intemperance, or on account of various other causes. The children are kept during the day, thus enabling the mother to go out and earn her own support, and contribute also to the maintenance of her children. Prominent among the institutions of this character is the Brooklyn Nursery. One of the latest of this class is the Crêche, established by Miss Maria M. Love, and conducted by her under the auspices of the Charity Organization Society of Buffalo.

A work for the relief of suffering children was begun as early as 1842, and, like many other beneficent undertakings, owes its origin to a member of the medical profession. Dr. Thomas Knight, of New York, in his clinics among the medical schools of the city, saw the need of an institution for the care of the large class of crippled children, whom he had been accustomed to treat gratuitously and as best he could, without adequate surgical appliances and means of affording proper diet and nursing. Persistent in his efforts, which were long continued amid many discouragements, a beginning was at length made by his taking a limited number of such children into his own house. He was finally successful in establishing in New York City that magnificent charity known far and wide as the Hospital for the Relief of the Ruptured and Crippled.

The work for sick and suffering children has been extended by the creation of other establishments for their relief.—notably, St. Mary's Hospital of New York and the Child's Hospital of Albany, both doing excellent work under the charge of sisterhoods of the Protestant Episcopal Church.

In addition to the work of these institutions, which is carried on continuously through the year in permanently organized hospitals, there are summer hospitals and sanitariums by the seashore and

elsewhere.   The large establishment of the " Health Home " of the
Children's Aid Society on Coney Island is a fine example of this
kind of hospital.   In this connection may also be mentioned the
summer hospital at Charlotte, on the shore of Lake Ontario, near
Rochester.   This institution is under the supervision of Dr. Edward
Moore, who is especially interested in it, and who has found it to be
the means of saving the lives of many infants.   A series of cottages
simply constructed are ranged along the margin of the lake, where
the greatest benefit can be derived from the cool breezes.   Children
accompanied by their mothers or nurses are taken here from the
city.   The hospital has been in operation for several summers, and
is still in a flourishing condition.

There are various organizations of a complex character in the
State, whose work includes that of child-saving.   Among the earliest
of these should be mentioned the American Female Guardian Society and Home for the Friendless, organized in 1834.   Up to 1849 it
bore the name of the American Female Moral Reform and Guardian
Society : then its name was changed to that of the American Female
Guardian Society, and in 1887 the name was again changed to its
present title.

The objects of the society, as stated significantly by the large-
hearted women who projected it, are to " prevent crime, diminish the
victims of the spoiler, and save the perishing."   It began its work
in small quarters under the old Tract House in Nassau Street, New
York City, and has steadily grown till it now occupies a spacious
home on Thirteenth Street, and maintains twelve large industrial
schools in various parts of the city.   In the schools the aspirations
of the children are stimulated to higher aims by instruction and discipline, and the refining influences of association with the lady
teachers.   The children are prepared for entrance into the public
schools, and the girls are taught sewing and other branches of
domestic work.   The society also maintains a nursery for children
given over to it, and a home for girls working in stores and shops in
the city, who, unable to defray the expense of living at a boarding-
house, have their needs met at a very low rate.   It covers a broad
sphere of usefulness in the great city of New York, and is well sustained through the personal efforts of large numbers of ladies of high

character. The expenditures in carrying on the work during the year ending Oct. 1, 1892, were $113,185.95.

Children are committed to the society by the courts, and are bound out in families. In case of debased parents, to whom such children are likely to belong, an effectual separation is secured, greatly to the advantage of the child.

A somewhat similar field is occupied by the Children's Aid Society, founded in 1853, and made familiar to the public by the writings of Mr. Brace in his book on "The Dangerous Classes." That most eminent laborer in the cause of child-saving holds an imperishable place in the annals of saving and reform work.

During the forty years preceding 1892, in which this society conducted its work for neglected and destitute children in New York City, it found homes and employment for 75,000 homeless boys and girls: in its twenty-one industrial schools situated in different parts of the city 275,000 poor children have been trained, encouraged, and aided; in its boys' and girls' lodging-houses for homeless and vagrant children 370,000 boys and girls have received kindly advice, shelter, and instruction. A particular presentation of the work of this society will be made to this Conference by C. Loring Brace, who succeeded his father in the great work to which he devoted his life. The good accomplished by the society through its industrial schools, night schools, lodging-houses, free reading-rooms in New York City, its summer charities, and the placing of children in homes in the West can only be appreciated by one who makes a study of the work in all its vast ramifications.

While some of the Western States have legalized the placing of children in families within their borders by Eastern societies, thus showing their approval of the practice, complaints have been made from time to time in the meetings of the National Conference of Charities and Correction against the immigration of such children, some of whom, it was asserted, ran away from their guardians, and became vagrants and criminals. Conceding this to be so, if we consider the question dispassionately, looking to the interests of the whole country and not to those of any particular State, we must conclude that the work of the society has been of incalculable benefit. Had the children whom the society has placed in the West been left to roam the streets of New York, the great mass of them would have become vagrants and criminals; and, as such are itinerant, they would have infested the Western States as well as the Eastern, and increased the number of the dangerous classes in every State of the Union. By placing these in Western homes, the great majority of them have been made good citizens, to the immeasurable advantage of the country at large.

Work of a cognate character was taken up in Brooklyn by the Children's Aid Society ten years after the pioneer organization had been established. The programme proposed by the movers was sufficiently comprehensive; to wit, "the protection, care, and shelter of friendless and vagrant youth, furnishing them with food and raiment and lodging, aiding and administering to their wants, providing them with occupation, instructing them in moral and religious truths and in the rudiments of education, and, with such means as the society can properly employ, endeavoring to make them virtuous and useful citizens."

It began its operations by opening a lodging-house for street boys. Industrial schools followed, and the work rapidly grew to large proportions. In addition to its other work the society now maintains a day nursery and a seaside home. Thousands of children have been taken from the streets and placed in good homes, thousands of girls have been taught, among other things, to use the sewing-machine, and want and destitution have been relieved.

Work of a similar kind for reclaiming friendless and vagrant youth has been extended to other cities of the State.

———

It is creditable to the State of New York that it should have been among the first States of the Union to move in measures for the relief of deaf-mutes. The New York Institution for the Instruction of the Deaf and Dumb is one of the oldest of its kind. At the time of its founding there was but one school for deaf-mutes in America, that at Hartford, Conn., and not more than twenty-five in Europe. The first steps were taken for the organization of the New York institution in 1816. It was incorporated in 1818, and in May of the same year was opened for pupils. For the first two years an experiment was made with a system recommended by Dr. Watson of England, including articulation, but with results so unsatisfactory that it was abandoned for the methods of Sicard, which were followed with some success until the succession of Dr. Harvey P. Peet as principal, who introduced methods largely his own, by which the teaching was governed during his term of thirty-six years. He was succeeded by his son, Isaac Lewis Peet.

From 1818 to 1857 the New York institution was the only one in the State devoted to the instruction of deaf-mutes. In 1857 the Roman Catholic order of the Sisters of St. Joseph opened an institution for the same class in Buffalo, called Le Couteulx St. Mary's Institution for the Improved Instruction of Deaf-mutes. Since then the work has been extended by the establishment of the Institution for the Improved Instruction of Deaf-mutes, in New York City; the Central New York Institution for Deaf-mutes, at Rome; the Western New York Institution for Deaf-mutes, at Rochester; St. Joseph's Institution for the Improved Instruction of Deaf-mutes, at Fordham, under the charge of the Sisters of St. Joseph; the Northern New York Institution for Deaf Mutes, at Malone; and the Albany Home School for the Oral Instruction of the Deaf. The last-named is a small institution recently established for young children, to whom instruction is imparted by the articulation method in connection with the kindergarten. The Fordham institution has a branch at Throgs Neck and another in Brooklyn. These institutions are all private corporations. In the case of the one at Malone the money for the land and buildings was appropriated by the State; and State appropriations have also been made for construction in others, including a liberal appropriation to that at Rome. The methods of instruction *
employed differ in different institutions. Of late years the articulation method is becoming more general. Several of these institutions have recently introduced kindergarten instruction.

As to the manner of admission, indigent deaf-mutes between the ages of twelve and twenty-five years may be sent to the institutions by the Superintendent of Public Instruction, the State paying $250 per annum for each. The counties, through superintendents or overseers of the poor, may send indigent children between the ages of five and twelve years, for which the counties pay $300 per annum. After the age of twelve years these become State charges.

As a means of preparing the inmates of these institutions for self-support in after life, a great variety of trades and occupations are

* A comprehensive exposition of the New York State system for the education of deaf-mutes will be found in the report of Commissioner Stewart, which is embodied in the report of the State Board of Charities for the year 1892.

taught, which include the following: carpentering, cabinet-making, scroll-sawing, wood-turning, wood-carving, metal work, engraving, cane-seating, shoemaking, tailoring, printing, farming, gardening, foundry work, drawing, water-color and oil painting, modelling in clay, type-writing, photography, sewing, knitting, embroidery, dressmaking, shirt-making, cooking, baking, and laundrying. In some of the institutions the pupils are employed in a greater variety of ways than in others. The industries common to most of the schools are shoemaking, printing, tailoring, carpentering, cabinet-making, sewing, and cooking.

Statistics show that, in proportion to the growth of the population, the increase in the number of deaf-mutes is small, and that during the past decade it has hardly been appreciable.

The attention shown by the benevolent and by the State to the deaf and dumb has secured ample provision for them; and the names of Peet and Gallaudet will ever be held in reverent esteem for their life-long devotion to the interests of this class.

———

While it is gratifying to know that New York was one of the first States in the Union to move in measures for the relief of deaf-mutes, it is also greatly to its honor that its citizens should have been the first in the country to establish an institution for the amelioration of the condition of children deprived of the sense of vision, and that this enlightened action should have had its origin in a spirit of pure benevolence.

The New York Institution for the Blind was incorporated by an act of the legislature in 1831. It is a private corporation, directed by a board of managers, who assume the responsibility of management from special interest in the work, and is under the charge of Mr. B. W. Wait, who has devoted his life to the undertaking.

The fact that blindness has the tendency to develop many peculiarities seems to have been well understood by the projectors of the charity; and efforts are made to teach the pupils that they are not different from other children, save in the loss of sight. Out of the older methods of teaching,— the Braille and the McClelland,— combined with the Morse point principle in telegraphy, the superintendent has ingeniously developed what is known as the New York Point System, by which the blind can not only read the thoughts of others, but write their own, take notes in class, write music, and avail themselves of many aids that, in a considerable degree, ameliorate their loss of sight. Naturalness of life is kept up throughout the establishment, and teachers and pupils are brought as much as possible into pleasant social relations.

The instruction imparted is of a high character, and includes the foundation work of the kindergarten. In the musical course particular attention is given to intellectual development by the study of harmony, music history, etc. By the use of the point system of printing the study of literature and music is extended beyond what it was formerly possible to teach.

Various industries are taught, such as cane-seating, mattress-work, piano-tuning, sewing and knitting by hand and by machine, crochet-work, bead-work, and regular instruction in cooking.

An interesting feature is the savings-bank system, by which pupils are enabled to save the earnings from their work to form a little fund to begin life with on leaving the asylum.

This provision for the blind was supplemented in 1865 by the establishment of a State institution at Batavia, which is managed by a board of commissioners appointed by the governor and confirmed by the Senate. It was fortunate in its opening to secure the services of a distinguished specialist, Dr. A. D. Lord, who had formerly been superintendent of the Ohio Institution for the Blind. He labored faithfully and devotedly until his death, after which the work was conducted for some time by his estimable widow. For the past ten years the institution has been under the superintendency of Arthur G. Clement.

The pupils are here instructed both in the line-letter and point-print systems. The aim is to give a good education, covering the ordinary range of studies. A kindergarten is maintained for the younger children. Music, as in the New York institution, forms an important part of the training; and piano-tuning is taught. Among the industries are cane-seating, mattress-making, broom-making, shoemaking, sewing, knitting, crocheting, and bead-work. There is need in both institutions of increased facilities for object-teaching.

It is a noteworthy fact that the increase in the number of the blind is small in proportion to that of the other defective classes, except the deaf and dumb. These two institutions meet the requirements of the State. The early attention given to cases of redness or inflammation of the eyes, the improved methods of the oculist, and the aid rendered by physicians in dispensaries in accordance with the philanthropic instincts of the profession, have contributed largely to the diminution of blindness in the State. A wise beginning in legislation has been made, requiring midwives to report the first appearance of redness of the eyes in the case of the newly born; but the law needs to be, and doubtless will be, amended, to render its working more effectual.

To the New York institution the State pays annually for pupils from its own domain two hundred and fifty dollars per capita toward its support. This does not, however, meet the whole expenditure: and the benevolent purpose active in its management is consequently kept alive. In the State institution the entire support falls upon the State, and there is no opportunity for the exercise of the virtue of self-sacrifice. The results of both systems seem to show that a benevolent purpose entering into the management tends to imbue every act with its own spirit; while the atmosphere enveloping an institution wholly supported by the State is likely to foster an interest in patronage, and detract from the high aims which such an institution should inspire.

Formerly, before any special provision was made for feeble-minded children, both those in the poorhouses and such as roamed the streets were sadly neglected. Their helplessness, on account of their mental infirmity, subjected them to the ridicule and abuse of the coarser natures about them; and they soon became brutalized and even dangerous. At the time when the attention of philanthropists was particularly directed to the feeble-minded there were in the poorhouses of the State large numbers of them, and their presence there and their imperfect protection resulted in increasing their numbers and perpetuating pauperism.

Although Dr. Edward Seguin, of Paris, as early as 1838, had demonstrated the practicability of imparting to idiotic children the benefits of an education, it was not until thirteen years after that the State of New York took measures to provide for the care and instruction of this class of dependants. The New York Asylum for Idiots was then organized: and Dr. H. B. Wilbur, who had opened the first school in the United States for weak-minded children, at Barre,

Mass., in 1848, was placed in charge. The school was begun near Albany, but in 1855 it was removed to Syracuse, where it was permanently established. Dr. Wilbur conducted the institution with great success until the day of his death. It was designed to furnish an education to those who were capable of being benefited by instruction, and did not contemplate more than the education of children. For adult males it now has a department situated on a farm five miles distant.

For girls and women of the feeble-minded and idiotic class the State has established at Newark an institution for custodial care during that period of their lives when they are liable to be the victims of the unprincipled, and give birth to offspring of their own kind. Here they are made useful to the extent of their abilities in sewing and domestic work.

A bill was passed by the legislature at its last session, making provision for unteachable children of both sexes, and for custodial care of adult male and female idiots at Rome, Oneida County, in what was formerly a department of the poorhouse. This action is greatly regretted by those specially desirous of maintaining, as at Newark, a complete separation of feeble-minded girls and women from adults of the opposite sex, and it must be regarded as a retrograde step.

Prior to 1824 the only public receptacles for pauper children were the town and city almshouses. In these ill-conditioned places they were brought into intimate association with the debased; and their welfare, both as to health and morals, was jeopardized.

In 1824 a law was passed enabling counties to erect county poorhouses for the shelter of their paupers, in which all county charges might be cared for under a county system. The county houses were placed under the control of the county officers of the poor, who were elected by the people. There may now be three such officers, or but one, as the Board of Supervisors of the county may decide. The county plan was rapidly adopted, as it lessened the expenses of towns. All the sixty counties of the State have built poorhouses, except Schuyler and Hamilton. In the latter county paupers are still boarded in families (as is done in some parts of Massachusetts) or aided by outdoor relief. There are now but four of the old-fashioned town almshouses maintained in the State.

At first, vagrants, tramps, and petty offenders might be committed by magistrates to county houses, they being designed for correctional as well as charitable purposes. After the establishment of district workhouses or penitentiaries, however, offenders against the statute were seldom committed to the county poorhouses. These institutions immediately became convenient receptacles for pauper children, and were usually overflowing with them. The town overseer of the poor, in dealing with a family of dependants coming under his care, found that the easiest way to dispose of them was to provide a conveyance and take the family, consisting, perhaps, of both parents and half a dozen children, with what household effects they might have, to the poorhouse. Unloading them at the door, he drew a long breath of relief, with the satisfied feeling that he had done his whole duty. The means of caring for the children here were in every respect unsuited to their needs, and their condition was deplorable. They were subjected to associations that were corrupting to both body and mind. They acquired habits of idleness sure to lead to pauperism and crime; while their moral and religious education was almost entirely neglected.

In some poorhouses attempts were made to educate the children by hiring a teacher and fitting up a room for a school; but their minds had become so poisoned by the poorhouse atmosphere that the most conscientious efforts of experienced teachers were unable to apply an antidote and arouse healthful mental activity. To counteract the effects of poorhouse influences upon the children seemed as impossible as the curing of disease in a pestilential atmosphere. Many of the children had been in the poorhouse for periods ranging from five to ten years: others had been born there. Some had come from families that had broken down through misfortune or crime; and in others the pauper taint was inherited, it having been carried through one, two, and sometimes three generations. In the case of the latter the poorhouse had created a controlling element in their natures, which unfitted them for admission to virtuous homes. The girls grew up to maturity, and often became the mothers of illegitimate offspring, thus adding continually to the pauper class and increasing the public burden.

Philanthropic people, desiring to rescue dependent children from suffering and crime, had established from time to time, on the basis of private benevolence, orphan asylums in different parts of the

State, and endeavored to gather into them all homeless and destitute children. But Boards of Supervisors were slow to lend them
aid, because the children could be supported more cheaply in the
county houses than elsewhere; and large numbers were retained in
the latter places. Some of the counties, however, availed themselves
of the advantages offered by the orphan asylums; and in a few others
the county officers, partly by indenturing and partly by using asylums, kept their poorhouses tolerably free from children.

Notwithstanding the efforts that had been put forth by the benevolent to save children, at the time of the organization of the
State Board of Charities in 1867, the public system of caring for unfortunate children in the poorhouses and almshouses* of the State of
New York was a gigantic evil. In his first report to the Board,
which was for the year 1868, Secretary Hoyt directed attention to
this grave abuse. There were then in these establishments, according to official figures, 2,257 children, including those of New York
and Kings Counties.

In 1873, Governor Dix, in his annual message to the legislature,
recommended that "an inquiry be made into the condition of the
pauper children in the several counties, with a view to making some
provision by which they might be saved from contamination by association with old and incorrigible offenders." The same year I was
appointed by Governor Dix one of the commissioners of the State
Board of Charities, and my sympathies were particularly aroused for
the neglected children to whom the governor had alluded in his
message. I decided to give the subject of their care my special
attention; and to this work devoted three successive years of my
life.

Efforts to correct this evil were made in different directions:—

1. By urging superintendents of the poor to deny children
admission to the poorhouses, and to provide for them temporary
family care till homes could be secured in which they might be
placed permanently.

2. By recommending, in hearings before county Boards of Supervisors, that they take action directing children to be removed from
the poorhouse and placed in families, orphan asylums, or other
proper institutions.

3. By appeals to benevolent persons connected with charitable or-

* Where the words " poorhouse " or " almshouse " occur, they are used synonymously.

ganizations throughout the State, asking their aid and co-operation in attempts to rescue these children.

In these efforts I was uniformly supported by the State Board of Charities and its worthy Secretary.

In 1874, by request of the State Board of Charities, in connection with an inquiry made by the Board into the causes of pauperism and crime,— an inquiry which extended to the mental and physical condition and antecedents of 12,614 pauper inmates of the poorhouses and almshouses of the State,— I made an examination into the condition of the children of all these institutions, upon which I reported in January* and December † of the following year. A chart accompanied the report, showing, among other things, the relative proportion of the sexes, of legitimate and illegitimate children, of native and foreign born parents, of temperate and intemperate parents, the porportion of children having mothers in the poorhouse, and of children that were born in the poorhouse.

At the time of making this report the efforts put forth by public officials, including the action of many superintendents of the poor, combined with the efforts of philanthropic workers, had secured the voluntary relinquishment, in a majority of the counties, of the system of rearing children in the poorhouses. Feeling that the time had arrived for legislative interference, I recommended in my report the enactment of a law which should forbid the retention of children in any of the poorhouses of the State. This recommendation was adopted by the State Board of Charities, and resulted in the enactment of what is known as the Children's Law (Chapter 173), which passed the legislature April 24, 1875. This law required that all healthy and intelligent children over three years of age should be removed from the poorhouses and placed in families, orphan asylums, or other appropriate institutions. It was afterwards amended so as to include all children over two years of age.

There was much opposition to the enforcement of the new measure, but the claims of humanity were finally acknowledged. It was wisely enacted that the law should not go into operation until the following year. In the meantime I conducted a large correspondence with county officials, and was present at numerous hearings before

* See Eighth Annual Report of the State Board of Charities, pp. 161-245, transmitted to the legislature Jan. 15, 1875, Senate Document No. 15.

† See Ninth Annual Report of the State Board of Charities, pp. 93-417, transmitted to the legislature Jan. 14, 1876, Senate Document No. 19.

them for the purpose of removing opposition to the coming change. During the same year I visited nearly all the orphan asylums* in the State, and other institutions having the care of children, then numbering upwards of one hundred and thirty, for the purpose of examining into their condition, of conferring with officials respecting the contemplated change, and urging upon them the adoption of an active placing-out system, in order to provide room for the new-comers. Some of the asylums were reluctant to receive any but selected children from the poorhouses, such as had not been within them long enough to be seriously contaminated. Within two or three years every county in the State having a poorhouse conformed to the law without compulsory action.

This important legislation received the approval of all interested in child-saving work. It has been sustained by the press, and is now popular with every class of officials. The county visitors of the State Charities Aid Association, as well as the visitors appointed by the State Board of Charities, have been watchful in seeing that the law has been observed. The reform has been complete and effectual, and there are now virtually no healthy, intelligent children over two years of age subject to the soul-destroying influences of the county poorhouses or city almshouses of the State.

— —

A few months before the Children's Law went into operation, Oct. 1, 1875, the number of dependent children in the orphan asylums and institutions of like character, exclusive of day nurseries, day industrial schools, children's lodging-houses, and juvenile reformatories, was 12,199. It was naturally expected that after the law took effect the number of children in the asylums would be much larger. It is true that the public burden through keeping children in asylums rather than in the poorhouses is increased, in spite of the large voluntary contributions by the benevolent toward their support; but, if we consider for a moment the advantages to society and the State accruing from this plan, whereby moral and religious instruction is given to a class of children who, but for this, would eventually largely swell the pauper and criminal classes, the increased cost sinks into insignificance. Instead of the Children's Law

* A report then made of these institutions may be found in the Ninth Annual Report of the State Board of Charities, pp 221-730, Senate Document No. 19.

operating, however, to increase greatly the number of children in the asylums, it has had but a slight appreciable effect in this direction, as the number * of the children in the asylums in 1875 was in the proportion of 1 to 391 of the population, and six years later it was as 1 to 358 of the population.

For cause or causes that will be variously accounted for by different authorities on the subject, there was a large increase in dependent children in institutions of the class under consideration in the eleven years interval between Oct. 1, 1881, and Oct. 1, 1892. The number remaining at the latter date was 24,074, being 1 to 270 of the population. The total expenditure in connection with orphan asylums and institutions of like character for dependent children, exclusive of the Thomas Asylum for Orphan and Destitute Indian Children, and not including juvenile reformatories nor institutions for the defective classes, during the fiscal year ending Sept. 30, 1892, amounted to $4,359,932.01. Toward the support of the inmates in the orphan asylums and institutions of like character there were received : —

From county Boards of Supervisors,	$527,996.68
From cities,	1,491,346.26
From individuals for the board of inmates,	159,636.94
From legacies, donations, and voluntary contributions,	819,127.06

There is not a little uneasiness, if not dissatisfaction, in the public mind over the large expenditure for children under institutional care in this State; and the extraordinary expansion of the asylums may well cause anxiety in the minds of the benevolent, through fear that this now rapidly growing system may be crushed by its own weight. Even among the strongest advocates of the present system are found those who are convinced that many of our asylums have grown to unwieldy proportions; that the numbers congregated within them forbid that individual treatment and social intercourse with superiors which is desirable to the elevation of the inmates; and that the monotonous routine and restriction incident to the discipline and handling of large bodies, and the long detention under this system, tend to the process aptly termed "institutionizing." In consequence of these tendencies, it is averred that the asylum system is losing its hold upon popular favor. It would therefore

* The statistics relating to dependent children are from official returns made to the State Board of Charities.

seem well for asylum managers to consider to what extent these criticisms are true, and, if found to be just, endeavor to correct them. I have strong faith in the beneficence of these institutions; but I would have the length of time spent within them reduced, the children sooner restored to family life, and the public burden in this way lessened. It would seem prudent for the managers of these institutions at once to put in operation an active placing-out system, as was done in 1875, when the Children's Law was about to become operative.

It should be borne in mind that this accumulation of children is not altogether composed of those eligible to situations in families. Some, through hereditary causes, some, on account of ill usage or neglect, have impaired constitutions, and are affected in one way or another with some weakness that renders it extremely difficult to find families willing to receive them. There are others physically sound, but mentally affected, and for this reason are not desirable in families. Another class who need constant supervision and watchful care are girls of weak judgment who are approaching maturity, and are a source of anxiety to those responsible for them. There are, besides, numbers of children in the asylums belonging to parents who are struggling to preserve their independence, and keep the family from becoming public charges. These are usually boarded at a slight charge, and the asylum has no judicial control over them. Among them are found many that are half-orphans.

The placing out of children from the asylums is not an easy task, and it requires constant stimulus. Inaction is more natural than action; and, when children are once received into these institutions, it is easier to allow them to remain there indefinitely than to set about seeking homes for them. So time slips away; and the child grows up in the institution, when it would have been better developed and better fitted to struggle with the world, had it been early restored to family life. Besides, the details of asylum management are so numerous that the placing out of children is sometimes deferred for lack of time to devote to this branch of the work.

The large accumulation of children in asylums in Buffalo, Erie County, some years ago, became the subject of public controversy. The Board of Supervisors complained that the cost of their support was unreasonably large, in consequence of their prolonged stay in the asylums. The matter was finally disposed of by the Board of

Supervisors appointing two agents who were charged with the duty of co-operating with the asylum officers in placing out children. The desired object was speedily attained; and the arrangement, which is still continued, has proved satisfactory to all concerned.

This incident suggests the question whether the State might not establish, in connection with one of its departments, an agency to assist asylums in finding homes and placing out children. The same agency might be of service in dealing with juvenile delinquents upon a plan similar to that adopted in several other States of the Union.

It is claimed by some that there is reason for the assertion that the power held by the numerous magistrates in some counties, to commit dependent children to asylums, has tended to increase unnecessarily the number of children in asylums, and that many are thus committed whose parents are able to support them. At one time the magistrates of Brooklyn exercised this power. It was taken from them in 1880, and only the officers of the charity department were permitted to commit children at the expense of Kings County to the asylums. The result was a large diminution of children in these institutions.

It is customary for superintendents of the poor, in placing children in families, to indenture them. Owing to the frequent changes of officials, the duty of looking after them till maturity is theoretical rather than practical. Formerly the custom of indenturing * was more prevalent in placing out children than at present. It is now growing into disuse, it having been found that, where there was dissatisfaction existing on the part of the foster-parent or the child, it was better to change than to insist upon a relation which was irksome to both. The greater proportion of children leaving the asylums are returned to parents.

In 1873 a law, the principle of which was taken from the French statutes, was passed for the adoption of children, which is growing more and more into favor, and has been attended with very satisfactory results. The principles of this act define adoption to be the legal act whereby an adult person takes a minor into the relation of child, and thereby acquires the rights and incurs the responsibilities of a parent in respect to such a minor. A married man cannot

* This power of apprenticing or indenturing was conferred upon overseers of the parish in 1750. When the parish system was superseded by the town system, the town overseers of the poor were given the same power; and a like power was conferred upon county superintendents of the poor in the establishment of the county system.

adopt a child without the consent of his wife, nor a married woman without the consent of her husband. The consent of the parents (except in cases of abandonment) and of the child, if over the age of twelve, is necessary before adoption. The county judge before whom the parties must appear makes examination, and, if satisfied that the moral and temporal interests of the child will be promoted, makes an order of adoption; and thereafter the parents are absolved from further responsibility in respect to the child. It is thenceforth regarded and treated as the child of the person adopting it, possessing all the rights and subject to all the duties of that relation, except certain rights of inheritance, and conveyances by deeds, wills, devices, and trusts.

There is no uniform rate of compensation paid by counties or municipalities to asylums for the maintenance of children committed as a public charge. By some counties the price allowed for support is but $1.00 per capita a week, while in New York City the sum is $110 a year. For such asylums as maintain schools an allowance is made for education in proportion to the number of pupils instructed.

The prevalence of ophthalmia in some of the larger institutions for dependent and delinquent children, and the tendency to overcrowding in them, led to the enactment by the legislature, in 1886, of a law, entitled "An Act for the better preservation of the health of children in institutions," Chapter 633. The act provides that every institution for the classes named shall have connected with it a physician in good professional standing, whose duty it shall be, upon the admittance of any child into the institution, to examine it, and certify in writing as to whether it is apparently suffering with diphtheria, scarlet fever, measles, whooping cough, or any other contagious or infectious disease, especially of the eyes or skin. It shall also be the duty of such physician, "at least once a month, to thoroughly examine and inspect the entire institution, and to report in writing, in such form as shall be approved by the State Board of Health, to the board of managers or directors of such institution, and also to the Board of Health within the district or place where the institution is situated, its condition, especially as to the plumbing, sinks, water-closets, urinals, privies, and dormitories, and also as to the physical condition of the children and the existence of any contagious or infectious diseases, especially of the eyes or skin, and as to their food, clothing, and cleanliness; and also whether the officers of such institution have provided proper and sufficient nurses, orderlies, and other attendants of proper capacity to attend to said children, to secure to them due and proper care and attention as to their personal cleanliness and health." An important requirement of the law is that every dormitory shall be well ventilated, that the beds shall be separated by a passage-way of not less than two feet, and shall have a circulation of air beneath them; and, further, that in the dormitories of every such institution six hundred cubic feet of air space shall be allowed for each bed or occupant.

An additional protection to the inmates of these institutions is afforded in the supervision exercised over them by the State Board of Charities. It is made the duty of the commissioners of the Board not only to inspect the State institutions, but also the private corporations for these classes; and the Board is required to report upon them annually to the legislature, making at the same time such recommendations as it may deem proper.

JUVENILE DELINQUENTS.

Previous to the year 1824, when the Society for the Reformation of Juvenile Delinquents was established, juvenile delinquency was treated as a crime to be punished; and the laws on the statute book of the State of New York regarded it as such. The importance of the legislation creating this society can hardly be overestimated. The names of the philanthropic gentlemen connected with its establishment include those of Griscom, Colden, Gerard, Stephen Allen, Maxwell, and other well-known public men of the time. They recognized the necessity of securing control of the classes needing reformation, and fully believed in the beneficial effect upon them of cleanliness, decent clothing, sufficient food, good schooling, industrial training, and moral and religious instruction. The founding of the society was considered at that time as a great advance; and Governor Clinton, in his message to the legislature, pronounced it "the best institution ever devised by the thought and established by the beneficence of man."

The work was begun Jan. 1, 1825, in a building in the south

part of Madison Square, which had been the United States arsenal. In 1839 it was transferred to Bellevue at Twenty-third Street and East River, and in 1854 to Randall's Island.

The society is a private corporation, controlled by a board of managers elected by the stockholders, who serve without compensation. It receives both sexes. The buildings, known as the House of Refuge, are of brick, in the Italian style of architecture, and are arranged on the congregate plan, forming a line nearly a thousand feet in length along the Harlem River. The approaches are gravelled and lined with shade-trees, while fountains and other attractive objects adorn the grounds in front. A stone wall twenty feet high separates the girls' from the boys' department.

The class committed to the custody of the society are delinquents between twelve and sixteen years of age,* and it includes the incorrigible. Many of the subjects committed for treatment here come from the worst quarters of New York City, and are most unpromising. The discipline is kind, but firm; and the educational system includes industrial, intellectual, moral, and religious instruction. Under what is termed the Freedom of Worship Act, which passed the legislature of 1892, mass is now regularly celebrated here. For the Protestants religious instruction continues to be imparted by a Protestant divine. An efficient corps of teachers have charge of the school work, which is under the direction of the Educational Bureau of New York City.

In school the older and more vicious boys are separated from the younger and more innocent, and a kindergarten is maintained for the younger boys. The exercises here include paper-folding, paper-cutting, and paper-pasting. The boys receive a good school education, commencing in the grade they are fitted to enter.

Formerly, the labor of the children was let at a stated price per day to contractors, the institution exercising supervisory control. The contractors furnished the material and the instructors, while officers of the house were placed in each shop to maintain discipline. Although this plan secured better financial returns, it was encumbered with many objectionable features. Among these were the following : the receipts did not favor an expected proportional reduction of the public burden ; an outside element, governed by

---

* Formerly children were received from the age of six to sixteen years. In 1881 a law was passed forbidding the commitment of children under twelve years for any offence less than felony to either this institution or the State Industrial School at Rochester.

mercenary motives, was brought into the institution and interfered with the discipline; there was a tendency to overwork the boys, and thus unfit them for school and general educational work; the time essential for recreation was curtailed; and the boys, becoming imbued with the idea that they were simply factors in money-making, were reluctant to work. This system was continued until 1884, when an act of the legislature set it aside, and a different method was substituted, with industries directly controlled by the institution.

The principal industry now carried on is the making of hosiery, at which two hundred and eighty-four inmates are employed. A considerable number are engaged at printing, some at shoemaking, tailoring, carpentering, and gardening. The others employed are occupied in various duties about the premises.

The discipline is based upon a system of grade markings: punishment takes the form of increased time in military drill and deprivation of play, corporal chastisement now being rarely resorted to. It is the aim, by means of the education, discipline, and habits of industry inculcated, to enable the inmates to become useful, self-supporting citizens on their return to the outer world.

The girls' department is under the supervision of a board of lady visitors, subordinate to the general board. It has a separate school, with the ordinary range of studies. The principal industries here are sewing and laundry work.

The number of children admitted to the institution since its first organization is 24,705. The number indentured is steadily diminishing: the greater proportion are discharged to parents or relatives, and the indentured class is composed almost entirely of orphans or children whose parents have abandoned them. The present capacity of the institution is for seven hundred boys and two hundred girls.

Another institution of this class is the State Industrial School at Rochester, formerly the Western House of Refuge, which was established in 1848. It is controlled by a board of managers appointed by the governor and confirmed by the Senate. It is a large establishment on the congregate plan, capable of accommodating about eight hundred inmates.

The institution was designed at the outset to receive not only all classes of juvenile offenders, but also persons under eighteen years of age convicted of felony. It having been intended to include among its inmates the more mature and desperate class, it was planned much after the style of a State prison rather than that of a reform school for boys and girls. Although the interior has been greatly changed by the removal of strong doors and gratings, the huge iron entrance-gate and the high stone walls about the building still remain, presenting externally its former forbidding aspect.

The institution received both males and females from the time of its establishment till 1850, when, upon the recommendation of its board of managers, the legislature prohibited the commitment to the refuge of any but members of the male sex, and limited the age of commitment to sixteen years. Twenty-five years later a retrograde movement was made, by the passage of an act providing for a female department under the same management, and the commitment to the refuge of vagrant girls and those convicted of criminal offences. This department was established immediately adjacent to that of the boys, and consisted of two buildings surrounded by stone walls twenty-two feet high. In 1887 the larger of these two buildings was destroyed by fire; and it was thought by many specially interested in child-saving work that this catastrophe opened the way for a return to the principles departed from in 1875, and for the establishment for girls of a separate institution on the cottage plan. It was demonstrated from the experience of other States that the same number of inmates could be better provided for in this way for less money than was appropriated by the legislature to rebuild on the old site; but local material interests triumphed over philanthropic aims, and a building was erected upon the site of the one burned.

The inmates are instructed in the ordinary common school branches, as also in free-hand drawing. Religious teaching is given by both Protestant and Roman Catholic divines. A graded system has been adopted, and the boys are drilled in military exercises. Discipline is maintained by a change of grade and extra drill. Most of the boys consider the lowering of their standing the severest punishment that is inflicted, as this prolongs their stay in the institution. Corporal punishment is rarely inflicted, and then only in chronic cases and as a last resort. Of late years greater freedom has been allowed. Those on the grade of honor are entitled to special privileges, such as being taken on short parades and as escorts to the city. The managers say: " It is a significant fact that boys who are sent out into the city upon their honor disdain to take advantage of the trust reposed in them. Sometimes the same boys will attempt to scale the walls and escape, selecting the very highest place for their attempt."

The State Industrial School at Rochester was the first to inaugurate one of the greatest reforms in dealing with juvenile delinquents ever effected in this country. This was the introduction of the teaching of trades in connection with the scientific principles underlying them, which followed close upon the passage of the law of 1884 abolishing the system of contracting the labor of children in these institutions. Instruction in the mechanic arts had been introduced into several of the higher educational institutions of the country; but it had never reached a reform school until it was taken up at Rochester, and so modified there as to meet the exigencies of the institution. The success attending it has been unparalleled. At present the trade school includes a carpenter-shop, a pattern-shop, a blacksmith-shop, a foundry, a machine-shop, a shoe-shop, a tailor-shop, a mason-shop, a printing-office, and a bakery. A large amount of excellent work is done by the boys. One of the large buildings in the yard was constructed by the inmates of the institution, who learned the art of building in the trade school. In addition to the beneficial effects of this training on the boys while in the institution, it is of great value in enabling them on leaving to find remunerative employment and hasten their restoration to society.

The present board of managers are desirous of doing away with the prison-like appearance of the buildings, and of remotely separating the work for girls from that for boys, advocating, in general, advanced views on juvenile reformation. It is therefore believed that the gloomy walls and formidable iron gates, tending to inspire fear, if not to cause despair, in the minds of the young, will ere long be removed. The example set by Governor Bagley, on assuming the reins of government in Michigan, in demolishing the stone walls about the State Reform School at Lansing, is worthy of imitation elsewhere.

At the beginning the institution was located upon the outskirts of the city; but it is now surrounded by improved property in a thickly populated district, and its real estate has become very valuable. I have ventured the suggestion that the question is worth considering whether the present plant should not be sold and the money re-invested in property of large dimensions in the country, where greater space can be cheaply obtained, and a new departure taken in the interests of this class. Such action would be in accord with that recently taken by the board of managers of the House of Refuge in Philadelphia, who purchased an attractive site at Glen Mill, apart from the confusion and turmoil of the city, where they developed, in the midst of extended grounds, a beautiful institution on the cottage plan, which is divested of all prison-like characteristics. Notwithstanding the example set by other States in the adoption of the cottage system in caring for this class, whereby a better and more extended classification can be effected, contamination from the association of the hardened with those who are less depraved can be prevented, and a nearer approach to family life can be attained. The reformatories in New York State, with one exception, that of the Burnham Industrial Farm, have had no development in this direction.

Early attention was given to the class of children included under the head of truant, friendless, and neglected. In the city of New York in 1851 the New York Juvenile Asylum was established in the interests of these children. It is controlled by a board of directors, and is under the immediate charge of a superintendent, a physician, and a corps of officers and teachers. It is desirably situated at Washington Heights, and is built on the congregate plan. The children are received from seven to fourteen years of age. It has a reception house in the lower part of the city, from which, after a detention of from fourteen to twenty days, children are transferred to the institution proper.

The schools are graded and conducted in the same manner as the public schools of the city. Instruction is given in the common branches, and industries suitable to immature years and such as can be carried on by hand are taught. There is no kindergarten depart-ment; but three classes, averaging sixty pupils each, are instructed by methods practically kindergarten. The children make most of their clothing, and thus contribute to their support. The aim of the institution is to prepare its inmates for family life, and to restore them to natural conditions as soon as possible.

A Western agency is maintained, through which many children are placed in homes. If the first family secured for the child proves unsuitable, it is withdrawn and tried in one or more families till a suitable one is found. This Western agency supervises the children, and maintains a watchful oversight over them until they arrive at an age when such supervision is unnecessary.

The whole number of children that have received the benefits of this institution since its organization is 29,468. Of this number, 531 were sent to Illinois and indentured to farmers; 1,198, about 300 of whom were colored, were placed in homes near New York; and the remainder were returned to their friends. "The majority of those sent to the West," Superintendent Carpenter says, "have done well, many of them remarkably well. From all the information we have been able to obtain, about 90 per cent. of the children that have been discharged from the asylum have turned out well. Those sent West to Illinois have had better opportunities than those remaining in this part of the country."

In 1853 the legislature, by the passage of the Truant Act, sought to enlarge work of this kind by empowering cities to make provision for truants; but the attempt did not prove a success.

Under this act was founded the House for Idle and Truant Children at Rochester, which I visited in 1875. This visit was quite unsatisfactory. The methods of discipline were found to be censurable; and, except in the educational department, the institution seemed to fail in its object. It was authoritatively stated that the number of cases reformed did not exceed 10 per cent. of the number of cases committed. The managers were appointed by the common council, and for that reason the institution was more or less political. It was afterwards discontinued.

A similar institution established in Brooklyn under the same act, and about the same time, was also found to be purely political and a medium for dispensing city patronage. The managers were appointed in the same manner as those at Rochester by the common council. A visit to this institution left a still more unfavorable impression on my mind than that at Rochester. This plan of reformation was found to be a failure, and was subsequently abandoned.

In 1863 the members of the Roman Catholic communion entered upon the great work of juvenile reform by the establishment of the New York Catholic Protectory. Roman Catholic citizens of New York had long felt the need of an institution where poor and vicious children having Roman Catholic parents might be cared for and educated in accordance with their own faith; and they succeeded in securing, in 1863, an act to incorporate the Society for the Protection of Destitute Roman Catholic Children in the City of New York. The name was changed to its present title in 1871.

Among the founders of this institution must be noted the name of its first president, Dr. L. Silliman Ives, who devoted his life to its establishment and expansion. The most Rev. Archbishop Hughes was also one of the pioneers in this charity. The services of the Christian Brothers were secured to take charge of the boys' school, while the Sisters of Charity held a like position in the girls' department.

The work was begun in two comparatively small buildings in Thirty-sixth and Thirty-seventh Streets; and a three years' struggle was maintained through pecuniary and other embarrassments, when, in 1867, the present farm in Westchester County was purchased and fitted for occupation. The Protectory comprises numerous buildings arranged on the congregate plan, and situated in the midst of extensive grounds.

Excellent schools are maintained. Map-drawing, typewriting, plain and ornamental drawing, and plaster-moulding are taught in addition to the ordinary branches. The industrial feature of the Protectory is specially marked, and includes printing, type-setting, a bindery, a folding department, and an unusually extensive shoemaking branch. A military corps is maintained among the boys, and the exercises are considered very beneficial. The boys have stated hours for labor, for study, and for recreation. After performing certain tasks they can go and play. Kindergarten methods have been introduced into the female department; and the industrial training here, as elsewhere, is thorough. The following industries are pursued: kid, silk, and merino glove-making, shirt-making, the making of ladies' waists, dressmaking, embroidery, lace-making, and plain sewing. Practical lessons in domestic economy are given.   Recently, a cooking branch has been added; and cooking is taught on scientific principles.   Type-writing and stenography have been introduced here as well as in the male branch.   The discipline is mild: that of a corporal character is said to be seldom necessary.   Although about ninety-five per cent. of the boys are committed by magistrates, few of them are really incorrigible, so that the Protectory has to do with a more hopeful class than the House of Refuge on Randall's Island.

The inmates are kept until they reach maturity or are fit to be discharged.   Most of them are returned to parents or guardians.   Some are indentured.

Since 1863 the blessings of the Protectory have been bestowed upon over seventeen thousand boys and nine thousand girls.   The vast growth of this charity is shown by the number of its inmates which, Sept. 30, 1892, was 2,374, and by the fact that, beginning with nothing thirty years ago, it has steadily increased its work till the expenditure for the maintenance of children during the year ending the date last named, amounted to $283,381.20.   Toward the maintenance of the children the city of New York makes an annual per capita allowance of $110.

"The Society for the Protection of Destitute Roman Catholic Children in the City of Buffalo," which was incorporated in 1864, receives the same class of children as are committed to the Catholic Protectory at Westchester.   The delinquent boys are placed in St. John's Protectory, at West Seneca, near Buffalo, and the delinquent girls are intrusted to the care of the Sisters at the House of the Good Shepherd in the city.

St. John's Protectory was opened under the supervision of Father Hines, who, with the aid of the boys, erected the first brick building on the grounds, out of brick made by their own hands.   The good Bishop Timon was specially interested in, and largely aided, the enterprise.   Various industries are pursued here, and an excellent school is maintained.   The Protectory is now in charge of Father Baker, who is aided by the Sisters of the Order of St. Joseph. The institution receives no aid from the State, and only the small sum of one dollar a week per capita from the county of Erie for the support and training of the inmates. The remainder of its income is derived from the voluntary contributions of the benevolent. The institution is doing a good work.

_____

With the object of reforming a class of idle and refractory boys that infested the streets of New York, the municipal authorities in 1869 purchased a ship called the "Mercury," and fitted it up as a marine training school. The boys were instructed in seamanship in the harbor of New York, and occasionally some of them were allowed to make voyages on merchant ships. It was found, however, that the less vicious boys were still further demoralized by intimate association with the incorrigible ones; and, after a trial of about six years, the experiment was abandoned.

_____

A divinely inspired thought in the breast of a philanthropic resident of New Jersey, Frederick J. Burnham, led him, in 1885, to devote a valuable estate of about six hundred acres, situated near Canaan, in Columbia County, to the saving of unfortunate children, by the establishment thereon of an industrial school. By Chapter 332, Laws of 1886, such a school was incorporated and placed under the management of twelve trustees. In recognition of this valuable gift the corporation was named the Burnham Industrial Farm.

The estate is well secluded from city distractions, and with its forests, groves, and beautiful lake, affords ample opportunities for a variety of sports and healthful recreation, including swimming, boating, and fishing.

The undertaking is wholly philanthropic. The institution receives no aid whatever from the State. The property and concerns of the corporation are managed by a board of twelve directors, four of whom are elected each year. They serve without compensation.

The corporation undertakes the support, education, and training of such boys as may legally come into its custody and care. "Any justice of the peace, police justice, or other committing magistrate or officer is authorized to commit to this corporation, with its consent, any boys between the ages of seven and sixteen years, deserting their homes without good or sufficient cause, or keeping company

with dissolute or vicious persons against the lawful commands of
their fathers, mothers, guardians, or other persons standing in the
place of a parent; or any such boys found wandering in the streets
or lanes of any city or village, or in the highways of any town without guardianship, and practising dissolute or vicious habits."

The plan of reformation and the system adopted at the Burnham
Industrial Farm are best set forth in the following language of the
earnest and philanthropic director of the institution, W. M. F.
Round: —

You ask me to tell you something about the characteristics of
the institution here. They are mainly those of the Rauhe Haus,
following out Wichern's maxim, that the strongest walls are no walls
and that the strongest force is the spiritual or moral force. I have
always believed that this force, administered with discretion, would
hold any class of men or boys. But moral force is not to be bought
and paid for like sugar or cloth; it is not a power like steam that
can be gauged and its cost and power figured. It is something so
subtle, and yet so sure, that no one has ever seen it, and still there
is no one but that has felt it. I found that there could be no administration of this principle with paid employees, and that the success
of the experiment here, as the success of Wichern's experiment, de-
pended upon the character of those who made them. The result
of this has been the organization of the order of St. Christopher, a
non-sectarian order of consecrated Christian men who are in training
for lives of institutional usefulness. The little band of men is called
a brotherhood simply as meaning rather more than the word society.
A pledge of intention to enter upon institutional life is signed by
each, and a promise to stay three years and six months in training,
with an opportunity of a release from this promise at the end of six
months should it be found that it is mutually advantageous to have
such release effected. Thus far the only institution that the Order
of St. Christopher has undertaken is the Burnham Industrial Farm.
This institution was taken under great disadvantages, is not wholly
adapted to the work of the brotherhood, but thus far has been quite
as successful as could be expected, considering that there was no
endowment except the farm itself and that it is entirely dependent
upon rather uncertain voluntary subscriptions.

The underlying principle of the Burnham Industrial Farm is this:
That there is something in every boy, however bad, that answers to
firm, kind, just treatment, and something that can be developed into
usefulness by a system of industry, training, and recreation that occupies the entire time of the boy and keeps his thoughts from the
old influences that have made for unrighteousness in his character.
The ideal surroundings of ordinary society would effect the same

results ; but the ideal surroundings of ordinary society do not exist, except under conditions that are made for them. It is the aim of the Burnham Industrial Farm to create these conditions, and to intensify them in such a degree that they will continually bear upon the boy. He is made to feel that uprightness is profitable to his soul and conducive also to his worldly welfare. He is made to labor and to feel the thrill of delight from steady, honest labor honestly performed. He is made to understand the rewards of labor by a small payment given to him from the moment he becomes an inmate of the Farm. He is made to understand that all progress in the simple life of the Farm here depends upon uprightness and industry, until he has acquired the mind and body habit of uprightness and industry. When he has acquired these so that the impulse to do the right thing follows the motive to do any act, then he is fitted to become a member of outside society, and his discharge is effected. Thus far, every boy that has been honorably discharged (or rather honorably paroled; for we, under the law, can give no boy his discharge until he reaches twenty-one years of age) has justified the judgment of the Brothers, and the boys are all doing well.

The methods adopted at the Burnham Farm are these: steady training in some industry by which the boy can earn his living when he goes from the Farm; a fair common-school education; a course in civics, music, and military drill; and the strictest simplicity of life and careful teaching as to the care and development of the body. Although I cannot consider the system entirely out of its experimental stage in this country, I feel amply justified in continuing the experiment, and hope to enlarge its scope both as to the organization of the brotherhood and an increase in the work of the Burnham Industrial Farm.

This unselfish enterprise must receive a cordial welcome by every one interested in child-saving work, and the career of the institution will be watched with deep interest.

The number of inmates in the juvenile reformatories of the State on the 30th of September, 1892, was as follows:—

Society for the Reformation of Juvenile Delinquents (House of Refuge, Randall's Island)	500
State Industrial School, Rochester	761
New York Juvenile Asylum	1,085
Catholic Protectory, Westchester	2,374
Society for the Protection of Destitute Roman Catholic Children at the City of Buffalo	173
Burnham Industrial Farm	83
	4,976

KINDERGARTEN WORK.

The extent to which kindergarten work has been taken up is one of the most hopeful signs of the times. Mrs. Sarah B. Cooper, on the Pacific coast, has set a grand example for philanthropic enterprise, which has been followed on a smaller scale in different parts of the State of New York by the establishment of free kindergarten schools, the great good resulting from which it is impossible to estimate. Kindergarten work is conducted, too, in nearly all the institutions of the State where there are dependent young children. Kitchen-garden work, by means of free schools, as well as under orphan asylum instruction, has of late years been rapidly and widely extended. The very efficient work of Miss Emily Huntington, of New York City, should be mentioned in this connection.

COMPULSORY EDUCATION.

The history of child-saving work would not be complete without some mention of preventive endeavors, as shown in the movements to secure regular attendance of children at school. The law for effecting this object in this State, which was enacted in 1874, has proved of little practical value, except, perhaps, in New York City, for lack of the machinery for its adequate enforcement. Many efforts have been made to secure a compulsory education law capable of enforcement, but for one reason or another it has never found a place upon the statute-book.

There is great need for legislation of this kind, so framed as to make it obligatory upon every locality to provide sufficient school accommodations. The failure to provide such has had much to do with making the law ineffectual. There can be no doubt but that the strict enforcement of a properly constructed compulsory education law would greatly reduce the number of children who roam the streets in our large cities and become depredators upon society through idleness and the temptations it offers. In England, Prussia, and France the education of the young is considered of the greatest importance, and stringent compulsory educational laws are not only in existence, but are also enforced. If, under monarchical governments, these are thought to be necessary, how much more are they

needed in a government the very foundation of which rests upon the
intelligence of the people.

Societies for the Prevention of Cruelty to Children.

An important part of the child-saving work of the State is that
conducted by societies for the prevention of cruelty to children.
These organizations exist in different cities of the Commonwealth.
The first of the kind ever established was the New York Society,
which was incorporated in 1875. Its first president was John D.
Wright. He was succeeded by Elbridge T. Gerry, who is still at
the head of this indispensable organization.

The objects of the society are, to seek out and rescue those unfortunate little ones whose lives are rendered miserable by the constant abuse and cruelties practised upon them by the human brutes
who happen to possess their custody or control. Ample laws for
the protection of this class had been passed by the State previous
to 1875, but there was no organization to see that they were enforced. This the society attempts to do. Its beneficent powers
cover a wide range of usefulness. They extend to the preventing
of abuses such as kidnapping, abduction, abandonment, improper
guardianship, begging, the use of unnatural violence, the endanger-
ing of the health or morals, etc. From the founding of the society
to the first of January of the present year, 69,737 complaints were
received and investigated, which involved the care and custody of
over 209,000 children; 24,581 cases were prosecuted, 23,947 convictions secured, and 36,359 children rescued and relieved. The
present superintendent, Mr. E. Fellows Jenkins, who has been connected with the society since its organization, says: "At the present
time fewer cases of actual physical cruelty are found, but neglect
and moral cruelty still exist, as well as many other wrongs to children which this society is called upon to endeavor to remedy. Almost every phase of child-work now, particularly that connected with
the courts, is placed in the hands of the society for examination,
which is able, through the very active co-operation of its sister organizations, both in this country and abroad, to present to the
courts and magistrates a very full report, upon which they may act
understandingly in making dispositions of the children brought before them."

Under Sect. 3 of Chapter 30, Laws of 1886, any society incorporated for the prevention of cruelty to children "may prefer a complaint before any court, tribunal, or magistrate having jurisdiction, for the violation of any law relating to or affecting children, and may aid in presenting the law and facts before such court, tribunal, or magistrate in any proceeding taken. Any such society may be appointed guardian of the person of any minor child during its minority by a court of record of this State or by a judge or justice thereof, and may receive and retain any child at its own expense upon commitment by a court or magistrate."

Through the work of the societies of this kind in New York State great numbers of children are rescued and placed in institutions suited to their moral and physical condition.

FRESH-AIR CHARITIES.

In the broad field of charity there is no work that has enlisted the sympathy of so many people in all ranks of society as that which has enabled thousands of poor children, packed away in hot attics and fetid basements, to enjoy the blessings of God's freest gift,— fresh air. The city missionary worker, the country farmer in his busiest season, the so-called soulless corporation director, the humble artisan, and the princely capitalist, all cheerfully co-operate in carrying on this blessed work.

The plan of taking children from crowded and ill-ventilated city tenement houses to the country for a brief period was first put in practical operation in New York State by Rev. Willard Parsons. He believed that these children, whose bodies were enfeebled by impure air and a lack of wholesome food, could be physically benefited by a short stay in the country. Accordingly, in 1877, he gathered up nine very poor and needy children in New York City and took them to the small village of Sherman, in Pennsylvania, as guests of some of his parishioners who had promised to receive them. After the lapse of two weeks they were returned to the city and other children were brought out, until sixty in all had enjoyed this privilege. The average per capita expenditure in their behalf was but $3.12.

Mr. Parsons was now so fully convinced of the wisdom of his plan that he determined, if possible, to extend the work. The following year the interest of others was aroused, and the New York *Evening Post* engaged to raise the necessary funds to carry on the work through the summer months. This it continued to do for four successive summers, during which time 9,220 poor children were sent out from New York City to various points in the country. The work of raising funds was then transferred to the New York *Tribune*, which created a department familiarly known as the " *Tribune* Fresh-air Fund," and the work was enlarged. During the summer of 1882, the children sent out numbered 5,500, and last summer 15,267 poor children had a two weeks' outing in the country, besides upwards of 25,000 who were given day excursions. Since the beginning of the work in 1877, the large aggregate of 199,317 children have had this two weeks' stay in the country, and 81,650 have been sent out for one day. The money expended in behalf of those who had a two weeks' vacation amounted to $278,609.39, all of which was raised without any outlay for salaried collectors. The per capita expenditure has varied in different years, ranging from $3.36 to $1.83. In transporting the children the railroads have generally given low special rates.

In providing families to receive the children an agent goes from town to town and calls upon the clergymen, sees the local editors and a few leading citizens, and explains the object of his mission. This is usually all that is necessary to arouse the co-operation of localities and secure the admission of the children into the country homes. The real labor of the work comes in selecting and preparing the little ones for the journey. Children must be selected who have no contagious disease and from houses where no such disease exists. In making discriminations the local Board of Health is brought into service, it being a requirement of law that all cases of contagious disease must be reported to the Board of Health. A large force of earnest workers lend a hand in selecting the children. They represent the Church Missions, Bible Missions, Hospitals, Dispensaries, Industrial Schools, Day Nurseries, and other organizations. Then the children are in such a condition of uncleanliness that they have to be scrubbed and cleaned, and frequently new clothing has to be purchased for them. No family would be willing to receive them in their ordinary condition, and it is important to the continued success of the work that there should be nothing about the children to excite the aversion of the people that so kindly throw

open their homes to them.   The labor involved in this part of the
preparation is aptly illustrated in the language of a kind lady
voluntarily engaged in mission work, who undertook to prepare one
hundred and twenty-five children for their journey, and who reported
upon them as follows: "All of the No. 2's have now been thoroughly oiled, larkspurred, washed in hot suds, and finally had an
application of 'exterminator.'   All this I have done in the church
to be as sure as possible that they are safe to send away.   Ninety
have been thus treated, and I hope Mr. Parsons will send for them
before they become again contaminated."

The work of benefiting poor children by removing them from the
hot city to places where they can breathe the pure air of the country has been extensively carried on by other methods in New York
and other cities of the State.   The Children's Aid Societies of New
York and Brooklyn have their seaside homes, and summer homes
for poor children may be found elsewhere in the State by its inland
lakes and among the hills.   New York *Life* has secured a deserted hamlet of about twenty cottages pleasantly situated and
converted it for the summer months into a village with a happy
population of about three hundred of these city children.

Sixteen years have passed since the "Fresh-air" movement was
inaugurated.   Its results have more than met the expectations of
its projectors.   Besides the physical improvement of the children, a
purifying and ennobling element has been added to their environment by letting into their lives a glimpse of something better, of
which they had never before dreamed.   The youthful mind, with its
quick intuitions, at once perceives the desirability of the orderly, industrious life of the country people : ambition and hope are awakened,
and the future of a child is very likely to be determined by such
brief views of a better way of living.

In connection with the work, it is gratifying to reflect that there
are so many people in the country, many of them in humble circumstances, who are willing to open their doors to these peculiar guests
and to accept the responsibility and bear the burden and expense
of their care, with no other motive than that of doing good to others
less favored with the bounties of Heaven than themselves.

Conclusion.

In closing this review I cannot but feel deep regret that the circumstances attending its preparation should have been such as to make it impracticable for me to do little more than briefly allude to the origin and the character of the leading branches of child-saving work carried on in the State of New York. I would have liked to describe more fully the principles and methods governing and guiding the different kinds of work, and to include a reference to all the varied benevolent efforts put forth to save unfortunate children.

The work in this State has not been free from mistakes ; but these should be judged from contemporaneous advancement, and not from the standpoint of to-day. Besides, it should be remembered that it is more difficult to make progress in the older States than in the new ones, because of established precedents. The question uppermost when any change is proposed is that of utilizing what already exists. In adopting new ideas old foundations must be removed, cherished associations set aside, and prejudices overcome. In new States there is an unobstructed field in which to project reforms, and such embarrassments do not exist.

In whatever light we may view this work in New York, it cannot be said that a narrow spirit has been shown in conducting it. On the contrary, the State and local authorities have been liberal in contributing to its support, the personal sacrifices that have been made in its behalf by numberless devoted men and women, actuated by the highest motives that can inspire human action, are immeasurable, and the results attained have been of incalculable value to the State and to humanity.

STATE PUBLIC SCHOOLS FOR DEPENDENT AND NEGLECTED CHILDREN.

BY G. A. MERRILL,

SUPERINTENDENT OF THE MINNESOTA SCHOOL.

The plan of work for the prevention of child dependence which we are to present is that by which the State takes charge of its dependent, neglected, and ill-treated children, and provides for them homes in private families, through a central institution acting as an agency for their reception and distribution. It is not simply a theory proposed, but a plan of work, successful in operation, with results to show.

This plan originated in Michigan, and has been adopted in Minnesota, Wisconsin, and Rhode Island. In many of its features it differs from all other institutions, and has secured for the State which inaugurated it an enviable reputation. No other State has attained such results in the care of dependent children as have been reached through the State public school of Michigan. As that institution is the one after which the others are more or less perfectly modelled, to give the plans adopted in its organization is to give, in effect, the plans adopted in the other States named.

THE MICHIGAN SCHOOL.

Before the establishment of the State Public School at Coldwater, Michigan, as other States do now, in the absence of any other provision for them, allowed her dependent children to be placed in the county poorhouses with adult paupers, and reared in all of the vices and disorderly courses that prevail among the inmates of such houses.

Municipal and private associations had contributed in some degree to their relief. Orphan asylums founded by religious orders of the church and by associated effort outside of the church had

done a beneficent work with a limited number. Still, there were
hundreds of children unreached by these agencies. With minds
keen and bright, innocent of any wrong act themselves to account
for their condition, doomed to a degraded life at public expense,
they appealed strongly for assistance.

The first official action looking to their relief was suggested by
Governor H. P. Baldwin, who, after visiting several of the State institutions, county jails, and poorhouses, recommended in his inaugural
message to the legislature of 1869 the appointment of a board of
commissioners to examine into the condition and management of
these institutions. Pursuant to this recommendation, the legislature authorized, by joint resolution, the appointment of such a commission to examine and consider the whole subject relative to the
organization and management of the institutions referred to, and to
report on or before the meeting of the next legislature. The governor appointed the commission during that session. The researches
of the gentlemen composing this commission extended not only to
the State and county institutions in Michigan, but into similar
institutions in other States.

They embodied the information gained by their investigations in
an able and comprehensive report, setting forth facts and arguments
that were strongly convincing in favor of a revision of the laws
relating to the State and county institutions. While this report
covered many questions relating to social reforms, the problem of
the children occupied a conspicuous part. The number of children
under sixteen years of age in the poorhouses was shown to be about
600. Touching incidents, illustrating the fact that poorhouse life
affords no helpful influences for children, were given ; and, in view
of the failure of private and municipal organizations to reach more
than a few who were in need of help, recommendations that favored
putting the machinery of the State government in operation in their
behalf were offered. Governor Baldwin, in submitting this report to
the legislature of 1871, called attention in his message to the recommendations of the commissioners for the relief of the dependent
children, and asked for legislation in their behalf.

The subject was of such importance as to insist upon a hearing,
and was referred to a joint committee, of which Hon. C. D. Randall,
of Coldwater, then a member of the Senate, was chairman. Mr.
Randall, in writing of the consideration of this subject in the legis-

lature, says: "The commissioners suggested three plans of relief, seeming to prefer them in the order named, as follows: first, establish a State agency by which dependent children could be removed from the county poorhouses and placed directly in families; second, remove them from the county poorhouses to private orphan asylums, the expense of their support therein to be paid by the State. If neither of these plans proved practicable, then: third, establish a State primary school 'after the plan of that in Munson, Mass.' Preference and prominence was given the plan second named, in the following language: 'It would be well for the State to encourage the establishment of private orphan asylums by placing therein as many of these children as the officers of these institutions are willing to receive, and allowing them an amount for their maintenance which would equal the expense of keeping them in the almshouses.' Neither of these plans was fully adopted, the legislature proving the more radical, and establishing an institution, though in some respects like the Massachusetts one, yet being a school, and not a penal establishment. It was new, and, as an educational, preventive scheme, far in advance of any before proposed."

The joint committee, to whom had been referred petitions urging the appropriation of money in aid of private orphan asylums, looked with disfavor upon the plan of aiding private institutions with money from the public treasury. "Besides this," to further use the language of Mr. Randall, "the granting of such aid would tend to involve our State in the same political embarrassments it had others, where aid had been extended to sectarian schools and asylums; that this sectarian aid savored too much of the union of Church and State, and was against the settled policy of our government."

The task of preparing a bill that would eliminate from the project the objectionable features of other systems — namely, the giving of aid from the State treasury to private or sectarian agencies, and the uniting of purely preventive work with that which is reformatory and deals with the subject after the commission of crime — fell to the chairman of the committee. His idea was to embody in the bill "an educational preventive project based on our common school system, having no regard to our penal or reformatory systems." He further says: "Reports of commissioners of various States, especially in Ohio and Massachusetts, furnished useful suggestions, but none the basis for the organic law of the proposed school; for they all treated of institutions of a mixed character, partly penal or reformatory, none having treated of an institution purely preventive, beginning with children before they had become criminal. Michigan already had a Reform School, so there was no good reason for establishing one of a mixed character. Governments, through all the ages, had never treated the dependent children question correctly. The poorhouse and workhouse, the industrial schools, have always, especially in England, received the innocent and criminal alike, and put them under the same treatment, with the same associations. Under this régime dependent children became criminals; and the governments, not as a remedy, but as a necessity, erected large and expensive reformatories and prisons, to reform or punish those whom earlier preventive treatment, in all probability, would have saved to a better fate. It was believed, when the question of the plan of the school was considered, that, while reformatories were necessary and useful, yet with the dependent children prevention was much more just and economical, and had in itself far more the elements of safety. As education was conceded to be the best preventive of pauperism and crime, especially when assisted by moral and religious training, in drafting the plan of the proposed school it was the aim of the author to construct the school directly on the educational basis of our common school system, combining temporary support of the younger dependent children in a home under the supervision of the State during minority. So on that plan was the bill drawn, disconnected entirely from our penal system, so that no taint of crime on sentence or suspension thereof should attach to any inmates; so that none in after-life should ever have cause to blush that he had been a ward of the State in a school where the house had been built and the school maintained by the system of taxation that supports the common schools of the State."

The bill thus drawn was fully considered by the joint committee, which consisted of sixteen members, and reported to the Senate with a written report unanimously favoring its passage. Lest the end to be attained by this institution might be misunderstood, the report of the joint committee called especial attention to the fact that it was to be used as a temporary residence where the children might receive home care, and a term in school pending the selection of homes for them. The following extract from the committee's report sets forth this feature of the plan, and it has been adhered to by the management: "Your committee earnestly and unanimously recommend the passage of the accompanying bill, by which the State will become the guardian of these children, and, taking them as wards into its control, will provide for them suitable homes in good families, and until that can be done will maintain and educate them in a State Public School. . . . That the children, and any one interested in their behalf should only recognize the proposed establishment as a temporary home while the child is on its way to its natural place in the family."

The bill embodied an appropriation of $30,000 with which to carry the act into effect. It received favorable action by the legislature, and was signed by the governor April 17, 1871. The first buildings were erected in 1873, and the school was opened for the reception of children in May, 1874. Thus came into existence what is known as the Michigan system of caring for dependent and neglected children.

The law establishing the institution provided for the appointment of a board of five commissioners for the term of two years, to select a site and erect the first buildings. This board of commissioners was to be.succeeded by a Board of Control of three members, appointed by the governor and confirmed by the Senate, each holding the office six years, the term of one member expiring each two years. In this board were vested the general supervision and government of the institution and its work of placing children in homes. In this board was also vested the power to appoint a superintendent, matron, and such other officers, teachers, and employees as might be necessary, each to hold office during the pleasure of the board. The board was also authorized to fix the salaries of the officers and employees, subject to the approval of the governor. The members of the board were to serve without pay, except they were allowed their expenses and a per diem of three dollars for the time actually occupied in the discharge of their official duties. Senator Randall was appointed a member of the board of commissioners to locate the school, and at the expiration of his term on this board became a member of the Board of Control, which position he held continuously until 1891. As the member of the board resident at the home of the institution, he had much to do in developing the plan he had formulated in the State Senate. Governor Bagley, who succeeded Governor Baldwin and was in office during the organization of the school, took a deep personal interest in its welfare, and lent his aid in putting the plan into operation.

The superintendent, who resides on the premises, is the chief officer of the institution; and to him are delegated large powers in matters relating to the management, and with him is largely the responsibility of success. The name of Mr. Lyman P. Alden, who was superintendent during eight years of its successful career, is inseparably connected with the history of the Michigan school.

In directing the work of construction and organization, it was the purpose of the board to adhere to the policy proposed by the projectors of the enterprise, and outlined in the law for the guidance of the management.

The plan indicated included in its requirements provisions for the proper maintenance, education, and industrial training of such a number of children as might need to be cared for in the institution until they could be fitted for and placed in approved homes.

Special emphasis was placed on the idea of securing to the children the distinctive features of home life, even while in the school. Cottage buildings, with homelike arrangements, afford the best facilities for the realization of such results ; and the cottage system of building was in the beginning adopted. However, some of the features of a congregate system were embodied, for the purpose of securing better economy in administration. In grading and conducting the schools maintained in the institution, better system and a nearer approach to the common schools, into which the children must enter after leaving the institution, can be secured by having the school-rooms in one building apart from the several cottages, which are the homes of the children. Also, a central dining-hall and kitchen, where the food can be cooked and served for the entire family, can be furnished and operated at less expense than several smaller ones could be. The buildings consist of the administration building, nine cottages in each of which a family of children lives, a school-house, hospital, engine-house, laundry, and barns, all distributed according to design, over an elevated and most charming plat of ground, beautifully decorated with trees, shrubs, and flower-beds. The surroundings in themselves are conducive to good results in the uplifting of the little children that find a home here.

In the entire organization the effort has been to give the pupils the highest benefits possible at a reasonable cost to the State. The

old life is shut out, and they enter here a community governed and maintained under high moral and Christian standards. The lives of these infants, heretofore darkened by much trouble and pinched by neglect, are brightened and expanded; and during the few months which they spend here they are given a foretaste of the benefits awaiting them in the homes to which they are going.

Each cottage is occupied by a family of from twenty-five to thirty children, under the care of a lady who bears a very close relation to them, living with them and giving her entire time to their welfare. The individuality of each is preserved. The interiors of the dwellings are tastefully decorated with pictures and plants; and beautiful, well-kept lawns surround each building. Every vantage-ground is used to uplift the children. They are carefully guarded, and kind but firm discipline is maintained. They are not walled in nor kept in. The children spend their evenings in the cottages, the family circle being a special feature,— a time for friendly talks, the reading of pleasant stories, and general mutual improvement. Before retiring, the evening prayer is said, in which all join.

There can be supplied in an institution much that is of great value to a child,— regularity of habits in work, in play, in school, and in diet. While the average time of detention in the institution is not long enough to teach a trade for life occupation, the farm and garden, engineer's department, sewing-room, and other departments of the institution afford facilities for occupation, so that every child old enough has some daily task suited to its years and condition.

The school-house on the premises, not far from the cottage homes, is supplied with the best modern apparatus and books; and, when "school calls," the children leave home and go to school, as in the village. Ladies of high talent for primary work are selected as teachers, and the common English branches are taught. A well-equipped kindergarten is an especially interesting and important feature of the school department.

The children take their meals in a common dining-hall in the administration building, each family having a separate table and eating by itself.

The cottage, or family plan, is found to be entirely satisfactory, and with the congregate cooking and dining plan combines economy with efficiency. The capacity of the school can be increased simply by the addition of cottages.

But all that is done for the children in the institution is only the preparatory process to open before them new advantages and avenues of life.

The greatness of the institution consists not merely in the number and extent of its buildings, nor in the large number of children that it can house in them, but in the number of these children that it can graft into the homes of the people we wish to have them become identified with, and where they will have the advantages of school and church enjoyed in the more enlightened and prosperous communities.

The plan organized in Michigan for the purpose of carrying into effect the provisions of the law for placing the children in homes and for maintaining supervision over them after they are placed, which the projectors of the enterprise wisely contemplated, connects the institution with a system of county agents. This was provided for by an additional act of the legislature in 1873. By the terms of this act the governor was empowered to appoint, in each county, an agent of the State Board of Commissioners for the supervision of penal, pauper, reformatory, and charitable institutions, now known as the State Board of Charities and Corrections. Among the duties of these agents is that of finding homes for the children of the State Public School, and of visiting them after they have been placed.

The Board of Control has power to appoint an agent of the school, known as the State Agent, to have charge of this work. His duties are prescribed by the board, and include the visiting of each child placed out as often and at such times as may be deemed needful. Very full and accurate information is obtained from all children placed out, by means of these agencies. A careful examination of the home and surroundings of each applicant for a child is also made by one of these agents, and no child can be placed in a home until it has been approved after investigation in this way. While it is believed to be best for the children to place them in families in due time, the protecting hand of the government is not to be withdrawn, even after the family has been given their immediate care; and, lest some should be placed where they will be ill-treated, the authority to visit, advise, and recall is reserved.

When a child is placed in a home, an indenture agreement is entered into by the Board of Control, represented by the superintendent or State agent of the school and the parties taking the child. This contract secures to the child kind and proper treatment in health and sickness as a member of the family, a term in school each year, and the payment of a small sum of money at the expiration of the indenture contract. After a term of trial this indenture contract becomes operative. A clause is always inserted providing for the return of the child on request, in case its interests should require such action. The board may consent to the adoption of children. This is desirable in many cases, and is encouraged when the relations between the family and child are shown to be mutually cordial, after they have lived together long enough to become well acquainted with each other.

As a result of the operations of the State Public School in its native State, all children of sound mind, and not physically defective, have been removed from the poorhouses; and, while the population of the State has increased nearly 60 per cent. since the establishment of the school, child dependence has decreased over 50 per cent. All of the dependent children needing State care are being provided for through this single institution, with a capacity to accommodate less than three hundred, at an annual cost of about $33,000 for maintenance. In 1874, when this school was established, there was a dependent child for every 2,223 inhabitants. In 1890 there was a dependent child for every 7,256 inhabitants. Had the number of dependent children increased in proportion as the population increased, as is the case in most States, Michigan would be supporting now over 900 children instead of 300, which is about the average number, including those who are defective and supported by the counties.

This is reversing the usual order, and is a record of which any State might well be proud.

The following tabular statement sets forth interesting facts with regard to the work of the school : —

GENERAL SUMMARY, DEC. 31, 1892.

Received since school opened, ...	3,317
In families on indenture, ...	1,058
In families on trial, ...	70
Total number in families under supervision of the school, ...	1,128
Remaining in the school, ...	208
Total number of present wards, ...	1,336

Returned to counties from which they came, ...   417
Died in families and in the school, ...   114
Adopted by proceedings in the courts, ...   287
Have become of age, ...   174
Have been declared self-supporting, ...   475
Restored to parents, ...   442
Married, ...   72

                                                          3,317   3,317

In 1889, at the request of the Board of Control, a law was enacted
for the better protection of ill-treated children. This law provides
for the removal of children from the custody of parents or guardians
who grossly ill-treat them, and describes the process by which they
may be placed under the care of the State Public School. One section of the law mentioned describes an ill-treated child in the following language : —

An ill-treated child is hereby declared to be : —
First, one whose father, mother, or guardian shall habitually violate or permit such child to violate the provisions of sections one.
two, five, and six of this act.
Second, one whose father, mother, or guardian habitually causes
or permits the health of such child to be injured or his life to be en-
dangered by exposure, want, or injury to his person, or causes or
permits him to engage in any occupation that will be likely to en-
danger his health or life or deprave his morals.
Third, one whose father, mother, or guardian is an habitual drunk-
ard, or a person of notorious or scandalous conduct, or a reputed
thief or a prostitute, or one who habitually permits him to frequent
public places for the purpose of begging or receiving alms, or to
frequent the company of or consort with reputed thieves or prosti-
tutes with or without such father, mother, or guardian, or by any
other act, example, or by vicious training depraves the morals of
such child.

The Minnesota School.

The position of Minnesota on matters of charity and relief for the
suffering has ever been wise. She has stood true in most regards
to the best interests of her citizens. Conditions here are more
favorable than in many older and more populous States, and the
number of dependent children has not become large. Doubtless
local conditions affect the child problem in each State to a greater
or less degree. Large cities, as in New York, Ohio, and Pennsylva-

nia, furnish a large number of youthful vagrants. It is important, therefore, that the citizens of the younger States study well this problem, which in many communities has become one of difficult solution, largely through neglect.

The adoption of this system by Minnesota was in response to a recommendation by Governor Hubbard, in his message to the legislature of 1885. Following the governor's suggestion, the idea was embodied in a bill, and became a law during that session. The law as it stands embodies all the essential features of the Michigan law, varying from it only in some minor features in order to conform to the different conditions of this State.

In the opinion of some who recognized the merits of such a child-saving agency, the time had not come for its application in this State. Later developments, however, have shown that the work was begun none too soon; and the results have proven the wisdom of taking this advanced step. Upon investigation it was found that children were being maintained as paupers in the poorhouses, with no means of instruction; others by the counties, in wretched abodes: and still others, in larger numbers, in the cities, whose only homes were the streets and tenements of ill-repute. The legitimate fruit of neglect in matters of social reform, as in others, is bitter; and in Minnesota, had the practice then in vogue been continued, the unfavorable conditions now present in many densely populated communities would have resulted. The time had fully come for the beginning of this work by the State. A longer delay would have imperilled the lives of many children who have been rescued, and made a larger expenditure necessary to meet the increase in child-dependence which such delay would have caused. Minnesota has achieved fame in the establishment of the splendid school system represented by her common schools, normal schools, and great university; and she has more recently established the State Public School, to extend to those poor children whom the former fail to reach the advantages enjoyed by their more fortunate fellows. Education under normal conditions is the remedy she applies for the prevention of child-dependence. The State Public School is maintained by taxation on property the same as are the public schools, and the underlying principles which led to its establishment are the same as those which prompted the establishment of the free school system.

But the extent of aid given is more than that of education. As has been shown, the State becomes the guardian of the children, and takes them as wards into its control, with the end in view of giving them a fair opportunity of becoming useful citizens,— men and women who will contribute something to the wealth, virtue, and intelligence of the community. And, through the plan arranged for reaching the children in every county, the benevolent purpose of the State is effectively carried out. In each county of this State there is a board of county commissioners, consisting of five members, residing in different sections of the county; and it is the duty of each of these men, whenever there is in his district a dependent, neglected, or ill-treated child, to at once take steps for its removal to the State Public School. The Probate Court is the authority designated to decide upon the eligibility of applicants for admission; and the process of law in this court, which places the child under the guardianship of the State, cancels the parental authority, if the parents are living. This absolute surrender of parental rights has a deterrent effect upon people who would be inclined to throw off the burden of supporting their children if this were not the case. The law also guards against the undue separation of parents and children. The children come to the school as pupils only, the process of admission being divested of every feature resembling a criminal proceeding. The ages at which they may be admitted are between two and fourteen.

The history of the school in Minnesota covers a period of eight years, while the time since it was opened for the reception of children covers only about six years. The selection of a site and the erection of the first three cottages, for which purpose an appropriation of $20,000 had been made by the act of establishment, occupied nearly two years. The buildings were completed in the fall of 1886, and the first children received just before the opening of the new year 1887. The legislature of 1887 generously appropriated $70,000 for buildings and permanent improvements, which enabled the board to provide buildings and appliances of sufficient capacity with which to more efficiently conduct the operations of the institution.

The premises consist of a hundred and sixty acres of land, the gift of the citizens of Owatonna, adjoining and overlooking that city. The land is rolling, well drained, and affords an attractive site. The Chicago and North-western Railroad crosses the farm; and a

COTTAGE.—MINNESOTA SCHOOL.

switch has been laid to accommodate the school, so that all goods in car-lots are delivered on the grounds.

There are eight principal buildings, irregularly located on an elevated plat. The main building occupies a central position; and grouped around this are three cottages, the school-house, engine-house, water tower and laundry, hospital, and a residence for the superintendent or State agent. The main building consists of a central section and two wings, the central section being used for administrative purposes, one wing for a cottage for the younger children, and the other containing an assembly hall on the ground floor and sleeping-rooms for teachers on the second floor. All, except the hospital, school-house, and officers' residence, are constructed of brick; and all present a cheerful and homelike appearance.

Modern conveniences in heating, cooking, and lighting, have been introduced, to secure efficiency and economy in administration.

Besides the buildings described there are barns of sufficient capacity to accommodate the needs of the farm. The situation of the buildings affords good drainage, pure air and water, and a diversified and most charming landscape view. The present capacity is for 120 children, while 150 are now passing through the school yearly. The total cost of the outfit is $138,000.

Among the honorable names connected with the history of this project in the North Star State is that of Senator C. S. Crandall, who has been identified with the institution from its inception, first as a member of the Board of Commissioners appointed to locate and organize the school, and later as the resident member and president of the Board of Control. The other members of the board, as it is now constituted, are Dr. L. P. Dodge, of Farmington, and Hon. O. W. Shaw, of Austin.

In Minnesota there is no county agency system, as in Michigan, the work of visiting the indentured children and investigating the homes of applicants being done by agents of the school, appointed by the Board of Control in the same manner as the superintendent and other officers of the school are appointed. This plan has given entire satisfaction; and the work of the agents who are selected in this way is, as a rule, more carefully done than that of the county agents who receive their appointment through the governor. The framers of the Minnesota law recognized the importance of the visiting agency, both as a means of obtaining proof of the good character

AS SENT TO HOMES.

AS RECEIVED.

of the homes offered for the children and in the supervision that should be constantly maintained over them after they have been placed in homes. This feature was embodied in the act of establishment; but the failure to provide funds for carrying it into effect delayed its application until 1889, when such provision was made. Its effects are now conspicuous to the advantage of both the children and the State. The agents appointed in this way are familiar with the work of the institution. They have opportunities for studying the children. A requisite to success in locating a child wisely in a home is a knowledge of the home proposed joined to a knowledge of the traits of character and habits of the child. The permanent well-being of the child is promoted by as few removals and transfers from one home to another as possible; hence the importance of great discretion in placing a child in its first home. A failure in the first trial often discourages the child, and causes him to go with reluctance to the second place. While this will not always hold true, experience proves that the most successful cases of indenture, and those which result favorably on the first trial, are the ones in which the children are studied with reference to the particular homes into which they are to be placed. The State Public School plan is favorably constituted for the realization of these ends.

A temporary place of detention is a necessity, in order to do the wisest work in placing children. Many are of a neglected class, and need to have the filth of the slums removed and the poorhouse marks erased.

A term in school awakens undeveloped intellects, and gives an opportunity to study the individuality.

No intelligent child in Minnesota need go without a home. None mentally and physically sound, above two years of age, can be found in the poorhouses of the State. These facts attest the efficiency and adequacy of the system that has been put into operation here; and it is believed that having begun in the early history of the State, before the number of dependent children has become large, the expense of caring for them will be reduced to a minimum, and the highest results for the benefit of the children and the reduction of the dependent classes will be reached. The satisfactory condition of Minnesota can perhaps be better seen by comparison with other States. California, with a population a little less than that of Minnesota, is caring for 4,000 children in private or sectarian asylums, at an annual cost to the State of $250,000. Minnesota is supporting an average of 130 children, at an annual cost of $23,000, and is maintaining supervision of 500 that have been placed in homes, at an annual cost of $2,000, making the total annual cost to the State for dependent children $25,000. By comparison Michigan presents an equally satisfactory showing. In New York, where the same policy is pursued as in California, according to official reports over 20,500 children are supported at public expense, at a cost exceeding $2,000,000 annually; and, as no determined effort to place the children in homes is enforced under such a provision of government, the tendency is to multiply institutions as well as inmates, with the consequent increase of the public burden. An economic and hopeful phase of the State Public School plan is that the agencies at work promptly relieve the public burden, and have thus far proven adequate to care for the children that have been thrown upon the public for support.

The following statement shows the number of children received into this school up to Dec. 31, 1892, and how they have been provided for : —

GENERAL SUMMARY, DEC. 31, 1892.

Received since school opened,	697
In homes on indenture,	414
In homes on trial,	43
Present in the institution,	136
Total number of present wards,	593
Died in families and in the school,	15
Attained majority,	3
Restored to parents,	38
Adopted by proceedings in the courts,	12
Returned to counties,	22
Declared self-supporting,	14
	697 697

All that has been accomplished for these children is not told in these brief statistics. This work cannot be brought under review so as to be seen by all in its fulness. It can best be appreciated by those who can see the children as they are brought in from the streets and by-ways, and then again after they have been transplanted into worthy homes.

THE WISCONSIN SCHOOL.

In essential features the State Public School of Wisconsin is identical with those of Michigan and Minnesota, the statute under which it is organized being in the main a copy of the Michigan law. In that State, as in the others, public sentiment demanded the abandonment of the old poorhouse system of caring for dependent children. Modern civilization everywhere revolts at the sickening spectacle of innocent children being kept in close contact with the paupers of ill-repute of both sexes which the average county poorhouse harbors.

The act authorizing the establishment of this institution was passed at the session of the legislature in 1885, and embodied an appropriation of $30,000 with which to erect the first buildings. Its management was vested in the State Board of Supervision of charitable, penal, and reformatory institutions, it being the policy of that State to place all of its institutions of the character named under the management of one board.

Soon after the enactment of this law the Board located the proposed institution at Sparta, accepting an offer of a tract of land, containing about one hundred and sixty-four acres, in consideration of the payment by the Board to the authorities of Sparta of the sum of $3,000, which the law authorized for the purchase of a site. The site is an attractive one, and affords a charming landscape view. The location is easily accessible by different lines of railroad, and offers good advantages for carrying on the work of the institution.

The law required that it be established on the cottage plan. The Board of Supervision visited the Michigan school, which had been perfected after years of actual work, and profited by the eleven years of successful experience of that institution. The facilities, in the way of buildings and equipments, that have been provided in Wisconsin, afford accommodations for about 250 children.

As in the institutions already described, there is an executive building, surrounded by cottages for the accommodation of the children, and other necessary out-buildings. Some of the cottages here are larger than those of the other institutions, and consequently the number of children placed in each is larger.

The first buildings were completed in the fall of 1886. The

governor issued a proclamation, dated Nov. 13, 1886, declaring the school open; and the first children were received a few days later.

This institution seems to have met with general favor in Wisconsin, and received cordial support. It is well organized on the same general plan as those previously described, and is recognized by the people as a useful and necessary agency to lessen the dependent classes.

As in Minnesota, the work of visiting and supervising the children placed in homes, and of investigating the homes of the people who apply for them, is done by agents of the school appointed by the Board of Supervision.

The testimony of Wisconsin is added to that of Michigan and Minnesota that this is a work for the betterment of human society that is effectual.

Following are some statistics taken from the last official report of this school : —

GENERAL SUMMARY, SEPT. 30, 1892.

Received since the school opened,	851
In homes on indenture,	235
In homes on trial,	315
Escapes,	15
Sent or transferred to Industrial School,	14
Committed to Industrial School,	2
Remaining in the institution this date,	210
Returned to counties by order of Board,	25
Died when with families and in the school,	11
Adopted by proceedings in the Probate Court,	12
Married,	2
Returned to homes by order State Board,	1
Vacation,—visiting parents, Veterans' Home Waupaca,	12
Hospital for the insane,	1
Indentures expired,	3
	851 851

THE RHODE ISLAND SCHOOL.

Rhode Island also enrolled herself in the line of preventive work in the year 1885, in the establishment of the State Home and School for Children at Providence, for the education and protection of those of her children who have no safe home of their own to turn to.

The legislature conferred upon the State Board of Education the management and government of this institution, disconnecting it entirely from the punitive system of the State. The following is an extract from the report of the board for the year 1886 : "The State Home and School established last year continues to give flattering promise of filling a most important eleemosynary sphere. Its local tion apart from the penal institutions, notwithstanding the admirable manner in which those institutions are conducted, and upon a beautiful tract of rich farming land, where the boys may become interested in healthful work, is most fortunate, in view of the broad moral purpose with which the Home was founded." The cottage plan of building was adopted.

The management of the school continued under the Board of Education until 1891, when, by an act of the General Assembly, it passed to a Board of Control, consisting of seven members.

Conditions in this State seem to have been somewhat unfavorable to the operation of the placing-out plan, and it has not been carried to the extent that it has in the other States spoken of in this paper. Consequently, large results in this special feature, which has been emphasized in connection with the other schools, are not shown. The extent of the territory and number and character of the inhabitants that contribute to each institution, as well as receive those that are placed out from each, must be considered in making comparisons.

The latest information received from this school is for the year ending Dec. 31, 1891, and is embodied in the following exhibit : —

GENERAL SUMMARY, DEC. 31, 1891.

Received into the Home, ...		240
Placed in homes, ...	107	
Returned to authorities, ...	10	
Died, ...	5	
Ran away, ...	6	
Sent to the State Farm (temporarily), ...	1	
Remaining in the Home, ...	111	
	240	240

Underlying this experiment, which has been successfully tried in four States, there are principles which are founded in true philanthropy and wise policy. The plan has been examined by eminent authority in America and Europe, and commended. In it are united the elements of efficiency, adequacy, and economy. The plain testimony of facts, as shown by the results accomplished, must constitute the ground upon which the people judge of its merits. To the people of these States the plan has commended itself, and the results are thoroughly satisfactory.

STATEMENT FROM THE TRUSTEES OF THE STATE PRIMARY AND REFORM SCHOOLS.

BY MRS. GLENDOWER EVANS.

[EDITED BY ELIZABETH C. PUTMAN.]

STATE PRIMARY SCHOOL, MONSON.

The State Primary School at Monson is an institution for the care of the dependent and neglected children of the State. Here, too, a number of little juvenile offenders, last year sixty-eight boys and four girls, deemed by the court too young or too irresponsible to go to a reform school,* are cared for; also a few adults, chiefly women who have been allowed to accompany their children from the almshouse.

The institution is situated upon a farm of one hundred and thirty-four acres on a hillside overlooking the town of Palmer. The location is admirable; but the great barrack-like building, in which the superintendent and his family, the officers, and all the inmates live, has a most unhomelike aspect, and is regarded by the trustees as a mere makeshift, to be replaced, as they hope, before long by cottages. Meanwhile the arrangements of the building oblige the institution to be conducted upon the congregate plan.

The children sleep in dormitories,—there are ten of them,—and eat in a great dining hall. They play in yards enclosed on two sides by low fences, each with its playhouse attached. Three separate recreation yards are provided,—one for the older boys, one for the younger boys, and one for girls and little children.

About one hundred and ninety-seven feet removed from the main building stands a hospital where the diseased and crippled children,

---

* The superintendent, when asked whether, in his opinion, it would be wise to make a distinct and separate provision for dealing with the two classes now received at Monson,— namely, these little delinquents and the simply dependent children,— answered that of the latter class few literally innocent children come to the school, but that those who have been taken into the custody of the State Board because of neglect on the part of parents, if over ten years of age, are very apt to know all the evil: that 95 per cent. of the offending children who are sent here are the fruit of neglect, and are not a different class from the rest.

ARRIVAL OF SOME CHILDREN.

DEPARTURE, STATE PRIMARY SCHOOL, MONSON.

together with those who may be temporarily ill, are cared for. This is under the charge of a resident physician, whose constant vigilance and attention to small or chronic ailments are invaluable. Fifty-nine feet beyond is an isolating hospital for contagious diseases. This building is seldom used; but, when contagious disease breaks out, as it will do from time to time, this provision for absolute isolation usually prevents the contagion from spreading through the institution. Of late years, to guard against the introduction of such diseases, a suite of rooms in a remote part of the main building has been set apart as a quarantine for new-comers; and here all children under ten years of age are kept for the first two weeks after their admission.

The school-rooms, graded in five divisions from the kindergarten to the grammar, form the most satisfactory feature of the institution. The methods of teaching are, on the whole, up to the time. Object lessons, either by paper-folding, drawing, clay-modelling, or woodwork, are in use in all the grades; and gymnastics are practised several times a week. Some of the children attend school for only one session a day and work the other half,—the older boys upon the farm, the younger boys and the girls about the house and grounds or in the sewing-room. Considering these short hours and the constant flux of the population, it is remarkable that the school work stands as well as it does. When the institution is remodelled upon the cottage system, the trustees are of one mind that general school-rooms for graded schools must be maintained.

While the trustees use every effort to make the State Primary School as good a home as possible for its little inmates, they believe that, by its very nature, an institution must be a poor substitute for a natural home. No officers, however devoted, can care for thirty or more children, whom they supervise during a section of a day, as a man and wife or some motherly woman could for one or two who should become members of their household; and, though the Primary School children are kindly treated, and seem on the whole happy, it is touching to note how they crave such notice and love as is the natural lot of every child in a normal family.

Moreover, in an institution where they live in groups, they must of necessity think and act in narrow lines and under constant rule and tutelage: small room can be given to initiative and independence. They are wholly shut off from the stimulus that comes from taking part in the varied interests of the community and from the responsi-

STATE PRIMARY SCHOOL MONSON, MASS., CLASS IN SLOYD.

bility of independence. They have little chance to learn the value of money or the imperiousness of the old law, that man must work if he would eat. In view of this, it is not surprising that institution-reared children should prove far more apt to become dependent in after life than are children of the same class who have been boarded out; and, as before noted, the agents engaged in placing out State wards find that free homes can be secured for children who have been at board in private families full two years earlier than for those who come direct from the Primary School. Accordingly, the trustees have for years been urging every child out for whom a place could be found. The accompanying diagram will show the progress made in this work during the past year : —

Ratio (in Percentage) of Number placed out to the Average Population.

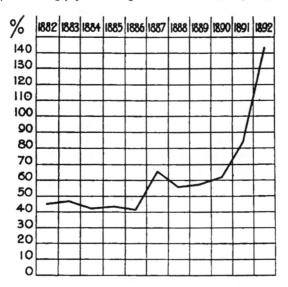

Thus it will be seen that in 1892 one hundred and forty-two per cent. of the average population has been placed out; that is to say, nearly half again as many children as are to be found at the school have gone out to homes during the past year. While the total number of inmates cared for during the year was 744, the average number was only 293, the first time the average had fallen below 300.

The number at present in the school is 178; and placing out is being briskly continued, the superintendent cordially assisting the State Board's agents in the work by having the children ready for placing at short notice.

The total number of new-comers admitted during the year was 415, of whom 92 were "dependent," 72 "neglected" children, and 72 "juvenile offenders," 68 of whom were boys; also 5 not classified. 172 other children were returned from places, of whom 99 had been placed out within the year. The school contained 329 inmates at the opening of the year, and at the close, Oct. 1, 1892, 271, while on March 31, 1893, there are only 178.

But the population of the school cannot go on diminishing indefinitely; for many of the children need the shelter of an institution, as, for instance, new arrivals waiting to be fitted into the right places, others who are so lawless that a short period of taming is necessary to make them acceptable in a private household, others who have been returned from places as unsatisfactory, there usually being fifty or more of these in the school who are too old to be boarded, and who have been returned perhaps several times from places. In addition there is always a very considerable number who are physically or mentally incapable. It seems probable that, when every available child has been placed out, there must still be provision at this institution for about two hundred.

The appropriation was $51,700; salaries, $18,300; for current expenses, $33,000, besides $9,000 for boarding out. This latter sum was in addition to the appropriation for that purpose granted to the State Board of Lunacy and Charity. The weekly cost per capita of children * in the institution was $3.38, and of children at board $1.94.

---

* In 1866 there were over 800 children in the three State almshouses, in 1867 over 700, in 1869 nearly 500, and in 1892 there were only 257.

When in 1882 the experiment of boarding out was inaugurated, it was feared that, as the expense of the school does not diminish in proportion to diminished numbers, money paid for board outside would prove an actual outlay for which there would be no adequate return, as, at the age of ten, when board should cease, the children would come back in great numbers to the State Primary School, helpless to earn their own way for several years.

On the contrary, it has been found that, of 200 boarded children who had reached the age of ten while at board, only 13 have returned to the institution, while 19 have been discharged to their own people, and 168 have found free homes with their foster parents or others.

Schooling is secured for these children as a matter of course. The visitor employed by the State Board to select from the abundant applicants those best suited to care for the children writes: " We visit the [public] schools as well as the homes, thereby interesting the teachers, who, in a majority of cases, take a deep interest in those under our care. Our children average well with others in mental capacity, standing high in their classes at school, and often carrying off the prizes at the end of the term for punctuality, perfect recitations, and excellence of deportment."

THE LYMAN SCHOOL FOR BOYS AT WEST-BOROUGH, MASS.

The institution now known as the Lyman School was formerly known as the State Reform School. It was founded in 1846 and opened in 1848, at the instance and with the aid of the Hon. Theodore Lyman, to be "a manual labor school for the employment, instruction, and reformation of juvenile offenders." Mr. Lyman had in view a school for vicious young persons who had but just entered upon a lawless career. His suggestions were, however, disregarded, and the limit of age for commitment was fixed at sixteen. When the school-ship was established, the limit for admission to the school at Westborough was reduced to fourteen years of age; but the school-ship proved a disappointment, and in 1872 was abolished. The limit

NOTE.

GOVERNMENT.

Trustees.—Seven trustees, two of them women, appointed by the governor with advice and consent of council, for terms of five years, with the title "Trustees of the State Primary and Reform Schools," having charge also of the State Primary School and of the State Industrial School. They are also a corporation to succeed to the trusts of former trustees of the State Reform and State Industrial Schools, the treasurer of trust funds giving $5,000 bonds. By-laws subject to approval of governor and council.

Officers.—Superintendent and physician annually elected by trustees, their salaries subject to approval of governor and council. Superintendent must be resident at the school, has general charge and custody of the boys and the appointment of all his assistant officers, subject to approval of trustees, and is responsible for their conduct.

Each family house contains beds for thirty boys, and is officered by a master and matron, assistant matron and teacher. There are also an assistant superintendent, a principal of schools, a teacher of manual training, a teacher of physical culture, a teacher of printing, an engineer and carpenter, a steward and baker, a truant officer, a watchman, a matron, a nurse, and seamstress.

COMMITMENT.

Boys become pupils of the school only through commitment by the courts. Only boys between the ages of seven and fifteen years may be committed. Term of sentence is during minority. Boys may be released upon trial if their conduct gives promise of future good conduct.

A COTTAGE OF THE LYMAN SCHOOL FOR BOYS, WESTBOROUGH.

for commitment to the Reform School at Westborough was then raised to seventeen. The discipline, perhaps necessarily, became in many ways that of a prison. A few boys were lodged in the three cottages; but the greater number lived in the congregate departments, slept in cells, and took their recreation in high-walled yards, the influence of the more vicious too often prevailing throughout the institution.

The result of this attempt to discipline boys mature in vice under a system planned for younger offenders was felt to be most unsatisfactory, and a radical reorganization was demanded both by the trustees of the institution and by the public. The opening of the Massachusetts Reformatory at Concord in 1884 made this reorganization possible. The limit of age for commitment to the Westborough School was reduced to fifteen years of age, the unwieldy, prison-like building was applied by the State to other uses, a new piece of land was bought, and the Westborough Reform School, rebaptized the Lyman School for Boys, was transferred to its present quarters. The new methods of the institution and the results were fully stated in the last report of the trustees, from which the following is for the most part taken.

The Lyman School is now located upon a farm of one hundred and seventy acres, and is organized upon the family system; that is, the boys live in cottages sufficiently removed one from another to make each household wholly independent of the rest. The number of cottages has been increased from three to seven, to meet the demand. Each house is provided with its own school-room and workshop, so that classification according to character is made possible, but has in fact proved to be neither practicable nor desirable because the boys are now so nearly of an age when they enter the school,— i.e., over twelve years and under fifteen years,— and because they are committed mostly for the same class of offences, those against property.

Those who "on account of extreme youth or seeming penitence " have been committed to the custody of the State Board do not come to the Lyman School unless after a fair trial they prove unmanageable; and, whereas one hundred and forty-nine young offenders were last year committed to the Lyman School, sixty-eight others, convicted of the milder class of offences, but apparently innocent of vice, were committed to the custody of the State Board, and placed at the State Primary School at Monson. To these were added from

A CLASS IN THE LYMAN SCHOOL FOR BOYS, WESTBOROUGH.

time to time, by transfer from Westborough by the trustees, several more who were found not to be in need of the discipline of the Reform School.

As a matter of experience, the most advantageous classification proves to be by school standing. This secures graded schools, but breaks the strict separation of families, because, when boys rise in school grade, they must be either transferred from one house to another or live in one family and go to school in another. No evil effects are noted, however, from this slight amount of intercourse between the households; and the trustees are unanimously of the opinion that, if with their present experience they were planning the school anew for the class of boys now there, they would provide a general school-house and workshops. In this respect only would they modify the family system, and would on no account give up the separate sleeping and living rooms, each cottage having its own kitchen, dining-room, and play-room; for through these appliances the master is enabled to gain a close knowledge of the individual members of his household, while the influence of the matron, who often has young children of her own, introduces elements which do much to counteract the unnatural conditions of institution life, always so much to be deprecated.

In the arrangement of the houses and the discipline of the boys every aspect of a prison is discarded; for it is found that, when boys do not feel themselves imprisoned and are treated as responsible moral agents, they can be trusted with their freedom to a surprising degree. True, every year there are a number of runaways; but no effort is spared to find and bring these back, and the trouble of so doing is more than offset by the benefits of freedom to the great majority who do not abuse it. Of the 351 inmates who have been in the school within the year, 34 made successful escapes: 13 of these were captured the same day, 13 within a week, 6 after a somewhat longer period, and only 2 are still at large.

Runaways, when captured, may be punished by a simple loss of credits and a whipping, or confinement in the lock-up may be added. The lock-up is a room of not less than 240 cubic feet, and is well ventilated and lighted. The trustees realize that even such confinement is subject to grave objections, but in some cases it is hard to find a substitute for it. Sometimes a boy who is evidently restless is kept in the lock-up at night instead of sleeping with the other boys in the open dormitory, or is made to stay by the master during play hours.

Persistent runaways, who show themselves unwilling to profit by an open school, the trustees believe should be transferred to Concord. Happily, however, no cases of transfer for such cause have occurred within the year. The trustees are persuaded that the only satisfactory way to hold boys is to convince them that there is only one successful way out of the school,— that of honorable release,— and to fill them with a law-abiding spirit.

The school is in no sense a simple place of detention. Its purpose is to be, in a broad sense, educational; and during the incumbency of the present superintendent constant progress has been made in developing appropriate methods for arousing the interest and awakening the faculties of pupils recruited from the truant and vagrant classes. From two o'clock to five and from half-past six to eight all assemble in their respective school-rooms. In addition to the ordinary lessons appropriate to their years, observation lessons by the collection and study of plants and minerals, drawing, mechanical and free-hand, singing from note, composition, and gymnastics have been successively introduced. The teaching of the school-room is in systematic relation to that of the manual training-room. Here classes in wood-work after the Sloyd system are held in the morning, every boy receiving one lesson, and some two lessons, a week. New-comers now receive twelve lessons in mechanical drawing before they begin to work with tools, as the pupils make their own working drawings from measurements given out by the teacher.

The principles underlying the system of education are explained in detail in the report for 1891, from which the following is quoted : —

The " Educational Sloyd" differs from the instruction that can be obtained in an ordinary carpenter's shop in providing a systematic series of lessons which require of the pupil practical exercises in multiplication, division, and fractions. He must discover for himself how many inches make a foot and how many sixteenths there are in an inch. By a carefully planned progression which he is able to comprehend, he is taught a new process with each new tool. Any imperfection in measurement or in execution brings its own penalty in results, which he can see and which he cannot evade; and, according to his faithfulness or his heedlessness, the completed work, whether a simple wedge or a dove-tail joint, becomes a source of satisfaction or of regret. He is now prepared to apply his skill to common carpentering, cabinet-making, or other trades.

At each step the work of the school-room is related to that of the manual training. Preliminary work in clay modelling and drawing prepares the pupil to understand the principles familiarly recognized in the workshop. Besides learning what any country-bred boy would be ashamed not to know about the grain of the wood and other practical matters, his eye is trained to a nicer perception and his hand to a nicer skill. His observation lessons now become interesting as he studies the bean plant in embryo and at various stages of growth, sketching it as well as he can, and describing it in his written exercise. The habit of thus recording what he has himself observed prepares him to reproduce what he gathers from reading upon any subject in which he is interested. The importance to this class of boys of forming a taste for good reading can hardly be overstated. Biographical sketches compiled from various sources, and read at the close of the summer term, showed that many of the Lyman School boys had been reading and studying intelligently and with a purpose.

An integral element in the school system is the military drill (all in uniform and armed with real swords and muskets), and the physical culture drill after the Swedish, or Ling, system. The latter is practised daily, and is admirably adapted to developing obedience, promptness, and self-control. Such exercises, valuable to every one, are especially so to those who, as is the case with many criminals, have ill-developed nervous centres. Both the military and physical culture drill are paid for from the Lyman Fund.

These various educational efforts have undoubtedly effected a marked change in the mental habits of the boys. A more alert bearing, a better tone of conversation, a greater interest in lessons and in serious reading, is noted. Only those who knew the school a few years ago, or who are familiar with juvenile reformatories of the old-fashioned type, can appreciate the extent of the advance. It is significant that whereas in past time, when the school was conducted upon the prison plan, the number of whippings and confinements in the lock-up are recorded during the six months of 1878 as averaging thirty-one a month to a hundred boys; in 1886, when the school had been reorganized upon the family plan, but was without any of the special training which has since been introduced, the punishments fell to an average of ten a month per hundred boys; and this year they have fallen to eight per month per hundred boys,— a total decrease of 75 per cent.

Such hours in the morning as are not spent in the manual training classes or in drilling are devoted, during the winter months or in inclement weather, to various industries,— heel-cutting, simple forging, weaving mats for hot-beds, chair-seating, and tailoring. These industries are slightly remunerative, but not sufficiently so to make it worth while to carry them on except for the sake of keeping the boys busy. They have, however, little educational value; and it is desired that occupations tending directly to develop skill in the workers shall be gradually substituted for them. At present much less time is spent at such uneducational work than formerly. Half a dozen or more boys work in the morning throughout the year in the printing-room : as many others work in the barn, and learn milking and the care of cattle, hens, etc. In each family from six to eleven boys must always be detailed for housework ; but such a rotation of duties is arranged that the same ones are rarely so occupied for more than three months at a time.

At the proper seasons outdoor work upon the farm and grounds is substituted for the indoor industries. A kitchen garden is allotted to each family, that the boys may raise the produce they themselves consume, thus enjoying a larger or smaller supply of fruit and vege-tables, according to their own diligence. All the boys, in one way or another, put some labor into this garden plot. Much work has also been done in the way of making roads and drains, carting and sorting brick for the new building, etc.

All commitments to the Lyman School are for minority. This amounts to an indeterminate sentence, the boys being released on probation long before their terms expire. In the first few years after the reorganization upon the family plan it was usual to release after about one year in the school ; but the trustees, noting the fact that many who did well in the institution and went out full of good reso-lutions fell back into evil courses, considered that such time of deten-tion must be insufficient to effect a radical change of character. It is evident that children who have grown up in the street, perhaps in the gutter, ever since they were born, fall into crime, not necessarily from innate viciousness, but from a bad rearing, from idleness, from laziness, and a lack of all habits of self-control ; and to implant better habits, first by enforcing hard work and strict discipline, and second by awakening the dormant faculties of these street Arabs, demands time as well as education. Therefore, with the increased advantages introduced into the school, the trustees have increased the time of de-tention from an average of seventeen months to an average of twenty-two months. It is now required that boys shall earn a certain num-ber of credits before they can become candidates for release. The names of those who have attained the honor grade are then presented to the trustees for action. This removes the element of arbitrariness from the length of the term : every boy knows that he decides the matter for himself by his daily conduct. Marks are posted weekly that all may realize how they stand. Exceptionally good boys can earn their release in a year ; a majority stay in the school for eigh-

teen months or more; and over thirty per cent. of this last year's re-
leases had been in the institution for more than two years. This
method of release and the lengthened detention have produced excellent results.

In considering the question of release, the trustees require a detailed report upon the home and its surrounding conditions, the
nature of the offence for which the boy was committed, whether he
had previously been before the court or been in other institutions,
and the superintendent's estimate of his character. Last year 60
per cent. were released to their parents: the rest are placed out with
farmers.

Previous to 1889 the boys in places were visited by agents of the
State Board of Lunacy and Charity who had other and more pressing
duties; also, *i.e.*, attendence at trials of juvenile offenders. Since 1889
the Board has employed a visitor whose sole business is the supervision of Lyman School boys, whether in places or in their homes;
and all are held now to a strict probation. Those who are idle or
who run away from their places are recalled to the school, no pains
being spared to capture runaways; and those who prove incorrigible
are transferred to the Massachusetts Reformatory at Concord.

Their were: —

In the school Sept. 30, 1891,	200
Committed by court,	125
Recommitted by court,	2
Returned from places,	28
Total,	355

Of these 355 there were: —

Released on probation to parents,	75
Released on probation to places,	45
Transferred to Massachusetts Reformatory,	5
Transferred to Bridgewater,	5
Discharged as unfit subjects,	2
Runaways,	2
Returned to court,	1
Died,	1
Remaining in school Oct. 1, 1892,	219
Total,	355

SHOWING CONDUCT OF THE 506 BOYS ON PROBATION.

The following statistics are from the reports of visitors employed by the State Board of Lunacy and Charity, and not in the employ of the school : —

Condition of all boys who have been released on probation up to March 30, 1893 : —

Total, ... 506
Doing well, ... 67 %
Not doing well, ... 5%
Have been sent to other penal or reformatory institutions, .   19%
Whereabouts and condition unknown, ... 9%

Condition of all boys under twenty-one who have been out at place one year or more : —

Doing well, ... 67½ %
Not doing well, ... 3%
Have been in some other penal institution, ... 17%
Condition unknown, ... 12½%

Condition of all boys who have been out on probation two years and over : —

Doing well, ... 60%
Not doing well, ... 7%
Have been in some other penal institution, ... 22%
Condition unknown, ... 11%

Condition of boys on probation who complete their nineteenth year before Oct. 1, 1893 : —

90% have been out two years or more.
Doing well, ... 73%
Not doing well, ... 2½%
Have been in some other penal institution, ... 15½%
Condition unknown, ... 9%

Condition of boys on probation who complete their twentieth year before Oct. 1, 1893 : —

90% have been out three years or more.
Doing well, ... 56%
Not doing well, ... 7%
Have been in some other penal institution, ... 26%
Condition unknown, ... 11%

Condition of boys on probation who complete their twenty-first year before Oct. 1, 1893 : —

All have been out three years or more.
Doing well, ... 42%
Have been sent to some other penal institution, ... 35%
Condition unknown, ... 23%

"Doing well" means that, in spite of the scrutiny to which they are naturally subjected, the conduct of the boys so classed has been sufficiently satisfactory to the neighbors and employees to prevent any unfavorable report.

AVERAGE AGE OF COMMITMENT FOR TEN YEARS.

	Years.			Years.
1883,	15.33	1888,		12.92
1884,	14.08	1889,		13.07
1885,	13.5	1890,		13.15
1886,	13.25	1891,		13.89
1887,	13.56	1892,		13.73

Average for ten years, ... 13.54

AVERAGE AGE OF DISCHARGE FOR TEN YEARS.

	Years.			Years.
1883,	15.83	1888,		14.96
1884,	15.79	1889,		15.17
1885,	15.86	1890,		15.1
1886,	15.41	1891,		15.48
1887,	15.56	1892,		15.63

Average age for ten years, ... 15.48

SHOWING NATIVITY OF PARENTS OF BOYS.

	1883.	1884.	1885.	1886.	1887	1888.	1889.	1890.	1891.	1892.
Fathers born in the United States,	—	—	—	—	12	29	7	7	10	12
Mothers born in the United States,	—	—	—	—	7	32	13	4	10	7
Fathers foreign born,	—	—	—	—	8	63	11	5	18	5
Mothers foreign born,	—	—	—	—	13	58	9	4	5	12
Both parents born in United States,	—	—	—	—	15	20	20	22	20	22
Both parents foreign born,	—	—	—	—	43	45	71	52	53	54
Unknown,	—	—	—	—	25	13	13	11	7	23
One parent unknown,	—	—	—	—	—	—	—	—	8	16
Per cent. of American parentage,	—	—	—	—	24	29	20	26	26	25
Per cent. of foreign parentage	—	—	—	—	51	63	72	60	61	50
Per cent. of unknown,	—	—	—	—	25	8	8	11	13	25

NOTE.— There was no such division of the table previous to 1887.

SHOWING NATIVITY OF BOYS.

	1883.	1884.	1885.	1886.	1887.	1888.	1889.	1890.	1891.	1892.
Born in the United States, ...	94	128	61	50	80	89	105	77	86	105
Foreign born, ...	6	24	4	9	13	10	17	14	23	19
Unknown, ...	—	—	—	—	—	—	2	1	—	1

AVERAGE TIME SPENT IN THE INSTITUTION FOR TEN YEARS.

	Months.			Months.
1883, ...	12	1888, ...	17.58
1884, ...	13.54	1889, ...	17.3
1885, ...	15	1890, ...	18.38
1886, ...	15.93	1891, ...	22.6
1887, ...	17.82	1892, ...	22.1

BOYS RETURNED FROM PLACE FOR ANY CAUSE.

1883, ...	14	1888, ...	34
1884, ...	33	1889, ...	20
1885, ...	28	1890, ...	14
1886, ...	39	1891, ...	21
1887, ...	27	1892, ...	30

It is believed that the number of boys returned to the institution as unsatisfactory has been diminished by the increased length of time spent in the school, since during the first five of the ten years tabulated 536 boys were placed out on trial, and 141 returned; while during the second five years 505 were placed out, and 124 returned, which shows something over eight per cent. in favor of the lengthened stay.

COST OF MAINTENANCE: SALARIES AND ALL CURRENT EXPENSES.

Weekly per Capita Cost for Ten Years.

1883, ...	$6.14. Congregate.	1888, ...	$4.40. Cottages.
1884, ...	4.46. Congregate.	1889, ...	4.26. "
1885, ...	5.60. Cottages.	1890, ...	4.29. "
1886, ...	5.90. "	1891, ...	4.31. "
1887, ...	5.56. "	1892, ...	4.76.* "

Average per capita cost for ten years, ... $4.97.

* Includes extraordinary repairs in sanitary arrangements.

Weekly per Capita Cost for the Past Year.

Salaries, ...	$1.72
Provisions and groceries, ...	.98
Clothing, ...	.49
Furniture, beds, and bedding, ...	.20
Fuel and lights, ...	.41
Farm tools, live stock, and general farm expenses, ...	.25
General repairs, ...	.40
All other expenses, ...	.31

The appropriation last year was $27,500 for current expenses, and $19,085 for salaries,—a total of $46,585. The net per capita cost was $4.76. These figures do not include the expenditure of $1,510.92 from the Lyman Fund.

No account is here made of money earned from labor of boys or otherwise, for this should be accounted for in a separate table. The amount expended for salaries and current expenses each year is divided by the average number of boys for that year.

There will be no attempt made in this short pamphlet to deduce from the lists given any generalizations or theories. Suffice it to say that the history of each boy and girl is recorded at the State House, and duplicated at the schools at Westborough and Lancaster, and annually summed up on catalogue cards for convenience in making the analyses. The figures are obtained from reports made by impartial visitors, not from any mere guess-work by superintendents or trustees.

Statistics of great value might be compiled from a series of similar records of the conduct of probationers from the reform schools throughout this and other countries.

	1873.	1874.	1875.	1876.	1877.	1878.	1879.	1880.	1881.	1882.	1883.	1884.	1885.	1886.	1887.	1888.	1889.	1890.	1891.	1892.
New commitments, ...	140	110	124	132	120	134	102	95	71	108	100	138	64	59	93	99	124	92	109	125
Whole number in school during the year, . . .	480	499	494	524	509	462	457	353	341	290	247	274	247	198	214	255	296	295	315	374
RELEASED FROM THE SCHOOL:																				
On probation to parents and others, . . .	110	141	119	138	186	120	216	116	113	146	125	107	126	95	83	96	99	91	99	120
To other penal or reformatory institutions (incorrigible boys), .	9	3	4	13	13	1	1	3	3	4	6	13	21	4	4	11	3	8	7	10
To hospitals for special treatment, . . .			1					1	1			1					3	4	2	2
Died, ...	1	3	2	2	2	2	2					1		2					1	1
Returned to court over fifteen years when committed,	2				2	2	2	2	7		8									
*Expiration of sentence, ...					2			2												1

*These are the only boys held in the school till their sentences expired within the last twenty years.

THE STATE INDUSTRIAL SCHOOL FOR GIRLS AT LANCASTER, MASS.

The State Industrial School for Girls at Lancaster was established by the legislature in 1855, and opened in August, 1856, "for the instruction, employment, and reformation of exposed, helpless, evil-disposed, and vicious girls" over the age of seven and under the age of sixteen, who had committed any offence punishable by fine or imprisonment other than by imprisonment for life. Girls who were found in want, abandonment, or beggary, were also admitted. For the first ten years the average age for commitment was thirteen, the average age of all present in the school in 1866 being fourteen. It was then apparently expected to serve as a training school for girls needing care rather than correction. At present, however, only those needing correction and restraint are sent to this institution, there being other and better provision, both public and private, for young children. Few girls now enter the school younger than thirteen. The limit of all for commitment is seventeen; average age in the school, fifteen.

The Industrial School is excellently equipped for the work it has in hand. Located upon a farm on the outskirts of a quiet country town, its ample acres free the inmates from the confinement that would be necessary in a more thickly settled district. The buildings consist of four family houses, standing from two to three hundred feet apart, in which the inmates live, an old-fashioned cottage occupied by the superintendent's family, a farm home and other farm buildings, and a chapel. The whole aspect of houses and grounds is pleasant and homelike. Each family house, occupied by from fifteen to twenty-five inmates, is under the charge of a matron, a housekeeper, and a teacher. The superintendent and all the officers, except the steward, the farmer, and the farm hands, are women.

In the administration of the school the trustees believe the following points to be of especial value : —

1. The girls are classified in the several family houses according to the nature of their characters and experiences before coming to the school. Reports made by the State agents who attend the trials of

ELM COTTAGE.

COTTAGES OF THE STATE INDUSTRIAL SCHOOL FOR GIRLS, LANCASTER.

juvenile offenders afford the basis for such discrimination, the superintendent supplementing this by her own estimate of the case. There
is no promotion from house to house; that is, good conduct within
the institution never allows one who has been guilty of most serious
offences to be transferred to a family containing more innocent girls.
But for bad conduct in the school or when out on probation a girl
may be transferred to the household containing similar offenders.
This method of grading reduces to a minimum the danger of contaminating the comparatively innocent, for no intercourse is allowed
between girls of the various houses, each family being kept to itself
either when at work or school or play. This prevents graded school-
rooms, and of course seriously hampers the teachers; but the trustees
believe that for such girls classification according to character is of
the first importance. Except when the institution is crowded, each
girl has a separate sleeping-room.

2. The occupations of the girls are not such as to bring in a
revenue, the aim of the school being to fit them as quickly as possible for life in the world; and the career for which it seems best to
train them is that of service in country households or in their own
homes. Book-learning is not neglected, every afternoon being devoted to lessons; but the emphasis of the training is upon the
domestic arts, and every girl who leaves the school is skilled not only
in one, but in all the domestic departments,— sewing, cleaning,
laundry work, and cooking. To accomplish this, as soon as she
is proficient in one branch she is promoted to another department
in the same house. This would be impossible, were the institution
relying on her skill to earn an income.

3. The household appointments are rigidly simple. No heat is
allowed in the sleeping-rooms. Furnaces cared for by the girls are
used in preference to steam heat. They have no set wash-tubs or
other labor-saving machines, for they must learn to contend with such
lack of modern conveniences as they will surely encounter in the plain
households where their work will be in demand. The matrons are encouraged to practise, and to teach the girls to practise, the small
economies of an old-fashioned farm-house,— repairing and dyeing
old carpets, upholstering shabby furniture, papering, painting, setting
window-panes, and often performing the simpler kinds of carpentering. The girls delight in such novel occupations, which give variety
and zest to a round of tasks that might otherwise grow monotonous.
The practice is to reward good work by promotion to some more

STATE INDUSTRIAL SCHOOL FOR GIRLS, LANCASTER.

skilled employment; and the success of this method in inciting girls, previously wayward, idle, and ignorant, to self-respect and a workman-like ambition to excel, is remarkable. "I am doing the officers' wash," or "Next week I shall be in the kitchen," is the usual form in which they appeal for approbation; and to be degraded to some less responsible position is felt by all as a heavy disgrace. This honor for work is maintained by example as well as by precept, the superintendent and steward, no less than the subordinate officers, sharing with the girls in the most menial services. Work is valued, not for its kind, but for its quality. The officers who teach the house work receive the same pay, and are as intelligent and refined, as those who preside in the school-room. One of the officers versed in music and other accomplishments, who had filled several offices in the school, when asked how she managed to do everything so perfectly, answered, "That is the only way to raise drudgery into art."

Outdoor work on the farm also proves an invaluable feature of the school. Under the supervision of a young lady employed for the purpose, the girls pass many hours planting, weeding, and gathering vegetables, cutting and husking corn, filling the silo, etc. Those who question whether this is "woman's work" would have their minds at rest, could they see the joyous interest of the workers or note the blooming health of even those who came to the school frail and sickly. Hysterics and fits of screaming and of noisy disobedience, which used to be occasional episodes of institution life, have of late years become unknown; and the physician and superintendent attribute much of this improvement to the way the girls work off their bad spirits as well as their high spirits in a vigorous outdoor life.

4. A long probation under supervision is the correlative of a short period of detention in the institution. While they are all sentenced for minority, a year or fifteen months in the school is generally enough to teach them how to work and how to control themselves; but to lead them to choose right living in the face of temptation is necessarily a much longer task. Accordingly, they are released, not to absolute freedom, but to carefully selected homes, where during their whole minority they are subject to supervision and to recall for bad conduct. The system of volunteer local visitors, organized under the State Board of Lunacy and Charity, provides a kind of oversight and influence which would otherwise be impossible. During this long period of probation, lasting sometimes for six or seven years, many who were believed and who believed themselves to be

reformed fall back into evil ways; while others, of whom it seemed impossible to expect anything, do well. It is certain that the influence of the visitors succeeds in upholding many weak girls in virtue, while their careful oversight can detect many lapses from virtue which would otherwise escape the knowledge of the trustees. The efficiency of the State Board's salaried visitor and other assistants makes this unpaid service available.

It is found that girls who are allowed to go directly from the school to their parents so frequently fall back into evil ways that the trustees allow very few to go home on probation until they have first approved themselves in other places. All but six of the seventy-eight released on probation last year were sent to places. The demand for the girl's services in country households at wages of from $1.50 to $2.50 a week far exceeds the supply. A quarter of their earnings is, if possible, placed at interest till the depositor becomes of age or is married. Over $1,300 has been deposited this year. The superintendent opposes any attempt on the part of the girl or her employer to conceal the fact of her having been at the school. After having spent a year or more in the attempt to lead her girls to speak the truth and act the truth, she would not have them induced, through mistaken kindness on the part of their employers, to tell or act a lie. On the contrary, she tells them that it is the better girls who have not tried to conceal this, but have lived it down. Those who are out on probation usually keep up a close tie with the superintendent and the various officers, often returning to the school for holidays or visits.

Of the fifty commitments last year nearly half the number were for stubbornness on complaint of parents, who feared that disobedience was leading or had led to graver sins; and the rest were brought before the courts by the police, too often as notorious offenders. The trustees in their reports repeatedly urge that the former class should be increased at the expense of the latter; that is, that parents, friends, and officers of the law should more frequently interpose to check wayward girls in the first stages of a downward career. It often happens that, when first brought before the courts, girls are first put on probation in their own homes; but, being subject to no effective oversight or other influence likely to induce reform, too often their reprieve allows them to stain themselves deeper with sins that can never be wholly washed away. While the trustees are persuaded that the age limit of seventeen is none too high,—those of sixteen and over often proving as amenable to reforming influences as the younger ones,—they believe it to be a mistaken kindness which would leave a girl in bad company after the danger point has been reached, thus rendering the work of reform far more difficult.

The average number in the institution, according to the last report, was 89.2. The per capita cost was $4.46 per week. The total appropriation was $20,000, of which $8,000 was for salaries, and $12,000 for current expenses.

The following table gives an accurate presentation of the status on Sept. 30, 1892, of each girl who had been in the custody of the school Sept. 30, 1891, including those in the institution and those outside, with the reason for the recall of such as were returned to the school, whether for serious fault, for unsatisfactory conduct, or simply for change of place or on account of illness.

To sum up, the trustees believe the value of the Industrial School to consist in : first, its system of careful classification of the inmates ; second, its system of fitting them as quickly as possible to earn their way outside rather than using their work to secure a revenue for the institution ; third, its system of relying for discipline upon the general method of life and work rather than upon any artificial rewards and punishments ; and, fourth, its system of careful supervision during a long term of probation. The large proportion of its wards reclaimed to virtuous living attest the efficacy of these methods.

NOTE.—Three times every year the volunteer auxiliary visitors, women commissioned by the State Board of Lunacy and Charity, assemble at one of the schools or at the State House, where a welcome is extended to them, sometimes by his Excellency the Governor, and always by some members of the State Board. Then follows an executive session for discussion of such questions as social opportunities for the girls who have no mother nor sister to visit, the earning, spending, and saving of wages, the duties of the visitor to the employer, how to give her a clear understanding of the girl's weaknesses or dangerous tendencies without retailing her whole history with information which is intrusted to the visitor alone, to be used only with the greatest discretion. From these meetings the visitors go to the homes, often in remote districts, refreshed and stimulated to more intelligent work.

The visitors have made some mistakes, and in rare instances have neglected their duty A lack of business habits deprives some of them of much of the credit which their work deserves; for they too often fail to report quarterly the visits which they are known to have made, often much more than four times per year Meantime the cordiality with which many a girl has spoken of " my visitor," and has corresponded with her even when removed from her care, bears testimony to the real value of the relation that can be established between the two

A visitor should prepare herself for dealing with these girls by acquainting her-

	Sept. 30, 1891.	Sept. 30, 1892.
There remained in the custody of the State Industrial School for Girls, ...	272	283

I. SUPPORTED BY THE STATE:

	Sept. 30, 1891.		Sept. 30, 1892.
Remaining in the school, ...		91	
Of whom 45 had been committed in former years, 46 had been committed during the year ending Sept. 30, 1891.			
Remaining in the school, ...			82
34 had been committed in former years, 48 during year ending Sept. 30, 1892.			
Transferred in former years to the Reformatory:			
Prison for Women, ... 3		4	
Transferred this year, ... 4		1	
Transferred this year to institution not penal, . . . 1	8	4	9
Total still supported by the State, ...	99		91

II. NO LONGER SUPPORTED BY THE STATE, BUT STILL IN CUSTODY, ...

	Sept. 30, 1891.	Sept. 30, 1892.
II. NO LONGER SUPPORTED BY THE STATE, BUT STILL IN CUSTODY, ...	173	192
Subtracting those who were at large, having left places,	14	15
Those who were honestly self-supporting, still under twenty-one years of age, ...	159	177
These 159 girls were distributed as follows, namely: —		
With relatives or friends, still on probation, ...	26	
Conduct: good, ...		27
Not good, ...		3
At work in other families, ...	96	118
At work elsewhere, ...	1	
Had been married and were still subject to recall for misconduct, being under twenty-one years of age,	36	29
Total still in custody, but no longer maintained by the State, ...	159	177

self with the home and social life of those of a similar class in life whom she may see pouring out of factories or shops. She would soon become convinced of the need of the sympathetic care which she has it in her power to extend to those whom the school has trained for self-support, but whom no institution can fully prepare for resisting the evil influence of idlers or worse in the quiet village into which they are now to be transplanted. After a time the girl generally appreciates such disinterested effort in her behalf. One of the visitors, a graduate of Wellesley College, writes, " I have enjoyed my work very much on the whole, and have learned to believe in the system most thoroughly, so many of our girls here have done finely, and are coming out good strong women: it is an inspiration to think of them."

Total in custody, ...   272   283
    During the year ending Sept. 30, 1892, new com-
        mitments, ...   50
    Attained majority, ...   36
    Discharged by trustees, ...   1
    Died, ...   2
    Total who passed out of care of State, . .   39*
    Net increase, ...   11   283

PLACING OUT AND RECALLING TO THE SCHOOL.

A girl may be recalled by the trustees to the school, whether on account of misconduct or illness or for change of place. The figures on the following charts will show how often this policy has secured, even for a restless or troublesome girl, a satisfactory place at last.

During the year there were recalled to the school (10 of them more than once),   57
  Of whom for bad conduct (1 stealing, 1 intemperate), ...   8
  For no serious fault, ...   48
    For unsatisfactory conduct, but all again placed out, ...   6
    For illness or change of place, not implying misconduct, . . .   32
    Having left their places, but found with respectable relatives
      or at work, ...   10
  Total recalled (including 1 feeble-minded), ...   57

There has been an increase in numbers cared for by the school, an increase in placing out, an increase in per capita cost, a decrease in actual cost : —

	Average number in the school.	Number of commitments.	Number at work in families.†	Weekly per capita cost.	Total actual cost of the school.
1866, ...	144	59	53	$3.30	$24,753
1876, ...	121	53	40	4.05	25,683
1890, ...	94	56	90	4.08	20,000
1891, ...	89	46	98	4.38	21,000
1892, ...	89	50	118	4.46	21,320

*Of the 39 who during the year passed out of the care of the State, the conduct had been as follows : —

Married, conduct good at last accounts, ...   16
Unmarried, conduct good at last accounts, ...   9
Died, conduct good, ...   2

Total conduct good, ...   27 or 72%
Total conduct unknown, ...   4 or 10%
Total whose conduct had been bad (5 of them had been in prison), ...   7 or 18%
Discharged not a citizen, ...   1

      Total, ...   39

† Girls on probation to friends are not included in the above list. They are, however, visited, and subject to recall to the school.

In 1866, with an average of 144 in the school at a weekly cost of only $3.30, and only 53 self-supporting by work in families on probation, the total cost was higher by $3,433 than at present, when there are but 89 (average) in the school at a weekly cost of $4.46, and 118 at work in families on probation.

This does not include the comparatively small cost of visiting, being, perhaps, two-thirds of the time of 77 volunteer visitors and 1 salaried visitor; *i.e.*, $1,749.86,— *i.e.*, less than $6 per year for each girl visited.

SUMMARY.

Of the 272 girls who were in the care of the school Sept. 30, 1891 :

A. Honestly Self-supporting.

I. No Longer in the Care of the State:
Attained majority, conduct good, ... 25
Died, ... 2
———
27

II. In Care of the State, but no longer maintained at Public Expense:
Married, conduct good at last accounts, ... 26
On probation with friends, ... 27
At work in other families, including 6 returned for unsatisfactory conduct, but placed out again, ... 117
At an academy, paying her way. 1
———
171

Total who had become honestly self-supporting, ... 198

B. Conduct Bad or Doubtful.

I. Had attained Majority:
Having been transferred to Reformatory Prison, ... 5
Others, conduct bad, ... 2
———
7

II. Still in Care of the State, being under 21 Years:
In Reformatory Prison, ... 5
In almshouse, bad conduct, ... 2
At large or with friends or married, conduct doubtful, ... 7
Recalled, and remaining in the State Industrial School, ... 3
———
17

Total, conduct bad or doubtful, ... 24

C. Conduct not Known.

I. Had attained majority, married, conduct unknown, ... 4
II. Not yet 21, at large, having left places, ... 14
——
Total, conduct unknown, ... 18

D. Remainder.*

I.	In the State Industrial School through year, . .	. 23
II.	Recalled for illness or change of place, . .	. 8
III.	In the School for the Feeble-minded, .	. 1

32

Grand Total, ... 272

Ten girls who had at some time during the year been at large were found either at work or with respectable relatives. The same may be true of the fourteen still at large at the end of the year.

The above table is compiled from 272 catalogue cards. If similar tables could be collected through a series of years concerning the conduct of juvenile offenders valuable material might be obtained for the guidance of magistrates, practical philanthropists, and of students of social science.

The conduct of the graduates of an institution is the only fair test of its value to the community which is taxed for its support.

---

* Conduct while in the school is generally good; but, as there is little opportunity for misconduct, no account is made of it on these lists.

FROM THE SUPERINTENDENT'S REPORT OF 1891.

To the Trustees of the State Primary and Reform Schools:

Since so many inquiries have been made regarding the girls' dietary, it seems best that it be given in detail. While no fixed order of diet is followed, the statement submitted will give, as nearly as possible, a week's dietary as usually carried out. A rigid order of diet is not adhered to. In fact, the exact reverse is aimed at. Although the standard articles of food remain of necessity much the same, variety in serving does away with what there might be of monotony. To this end the housekeepers are instructed to so modify the dishes from day to day and week to week as to render them palatable in the greatest variety of forms. Each housekeeper, of course, has her different ways of doing this; but, virtually, the dietary for each house is the same.

To illustrate, griddle-cakes are served for the morning meal once a week, milk toast the same, each housekeeper suiting her judgment as to time, according to circumstances and convenience, usually utilizing these and similar dishes, when there is nothing left over from the dinner of the day before. It will be noticed in the statement that, as a rule, remnants of yesterday's dinner appear in the breakfast. This meal, therefore, is not only economical, but one easily prepared. Waste is not tolerated. All pieces of stale bread are reserved in toasts, bread puddings, "brown betties," etc.; remains of a meat or vegetable dinner, in meat or vegetable hash.

During the summer and harvesting months there are added all kinds of vegetables, garden sauce, and fruits in their season. These are served in abundance. The quantities consumed are surprising, being more relishable at this season than meats. Recognizing this fact, during the hot months a vegetable dish supplants the usual meat roast of Wednesday's dinner,— baked peas, pea soup, or onion stew, supplemented with sweet corn, cucumbers, and other vegetables, with a simple dessert of pumpkin pie or apple dumpling. During the early apple season sauce is served every night for supper, and throughout the year once or twice a week. Tomatoes are likewise abundantly used. In the months when eggs are plentiful they are frequently served, sometimes in place of Friday's fish. The latter, when used ("salt fish"), is served in various ways,— broiled, with milk gravy, fish chowder, fish hash, fishballs, etc. Corn bread or "Johnny cake" is supposed to form a part of nearly every dinner. Fresh, rich milk is provided the entire year, and as much of it as is wished.

SUNDAY.

Breakfast.

Warm brown bread or biscuit, butter, coffee.

Dinner.

Baked beans, brown bread, wheat bread, pickles, pie or pudding.

Supper.

Rice or crackers and milk.

MONDAY.

Breakfast.

Mush and molasses, bread, cocoa or milk.

Dinner.

Vegetable hash or cold corned beef from Saturday's dinner, potatoes, vegetables, corn cake.

Supper.

Bread, milk, gingerbread.

TUESDAY.

Breakfast.

Beans from Sunday's dinner, bread, cocoa or milk.

Dinner.

Fresh fish, baked with dressing or broiled with gravy, potatoes, corn cake, pickles, wheat bread.

Supper.

Bread, milk, bread pudding.

WEDNESDAY.

Breakfast.

Oatmeal, molasses, bread, cocoa or milk.

Dinner.

Roast meat, potatoes, tomatoes, gravy, Johnny cake, wheat bread.

Supper.

Bread, milk, sauce.

THURSDAY.

Breakfast.

Griddle cakes and molasses, bread, cocoa or milk.

Dinner.

Beef stew, vegetables, bread, "brown betty."

Supper.

Bread, milk, doughnuts or gingerbread.

FRIDAY.

Breakfast.

Soup from Thursday's dinner, mush, bread, cocoa or milk.

Dinner.

Potatoes, salt fish, milk gravy, or pork scraps and fishballs, tomatoes or pickles, corn cake.

Supper.

Milk toast, bread, milk, sauce.

SATURDAY.

Breakfast.

Fish hash, bread, cocoa or milk.

Dinner.

Corned beef, potatoes, vegetables of all kinds, brown bread.

Supper.

Bread, molasses, milk.*

Respectfully submitted,

L. L. BRACKETT,
Superintendent.

---

* The approximate cost of food divided by the number of persons in the institution — *i.e.*, an average of 89 girls and 19 officers and employees — is 16 cents per day.

The Catholic Protectory

OF NEW YORK:

ITS SPIRIT AND ITS WORKINGS

FROM ITS ORIGIN TO THE PRESENT.

PREFACE.

We herewith present a short sketch of the Catholic Protectory of New York from its origin to the present. The sketch must needs be incomplete. We cannot enter into details concerning the management, the persons who have been connected with the institution, or the results that have been reaped during the past thirty years. What crimes have been prevented, what homes have been made happy, what human misery has been alleviated, what brands have been snatched from the burning, what myriads of useful men and women have been made an honor to the state by this institution, it is beyond the power of human pen to record. Suffice it to say that no one who has not visited the Protectory, and looked into its workings can form any conception of the good that is done within its precincts.

New York, *May 4th,* 1893.

NEW YORK CATHOLIC PROTECTORY.

I.

Few institutions in the country deserve more attention than The New York Catholic Protectory. Its object appeals to every lover of his kind. Its results are a fitting subject of encouragement to every student of social economy. The extent, variety, and novelty of some of its workings will more than repay the student who takes an abiding interest in the progress of the human race.

The sad condition of juveniles throughout the United States, was a fact so generally admitted as to excite no discussion. But while this deplorable condition was acknowledged to exist in every part of the Union, the extent of the misery was specially noticeable in large centres like New York. This had repeatedly called aloud for a combined effort, in which authority, wealth, and good-will would form a trinity, giving one another the hand of fellowship.

One of the city papers wrote:

" It is not uncommon, even in the cold winter nights, to find hanging over the gratings of some printing office, a prostrate form, thinly clad and emaciated, seeking to nurse the vital spark of life by the genial heat that arises from the engine-room beneath the pavement. These are what are called in Paris the *gamins* of the street; here they are denominated ' outcasts,' or, to use the more charitable expression of benevolence, ' our destitute children.' "

Catholics felt that an immense portion of this work of regeneration must fall to their share. They were to be among the foremost in reclaiming the wayward youth of New York and vicinity. Here was a herculean task! Numerous methods were proposed and commissions by the St. Vincent de Paul Society formed, but as available funds were entirely inadequate, no decisive and definite form was given to the work until the latter part of the year 1862, when a number of prominent gentlemen met in

5

Manhattanville, at a "confirmation" in the Church of the Annunciation, then under the pastoral charge of the Rev. John Breen. The occasion was most auspicious for the commencement of such a work, and the gentlemen assembled under the hospitable roof of the parochial mansion were determined that nothing on their part should be left undone towards the practical fulfilment of this noble purpose. The subject was debated with considerable earnestness and zeal, and as a pledge of their determination and good-will, several of the gentlemen present subscribed five-thousand dollars, others $2,500, others $2,000, others smaller sums, until a sufficient amount was subscribed to assure confidence in the financial success of the undertaking.

It is but just to say of the great departed John Hughes, the illustrious Archbishop of New York, that he had long desired the opening of a Protectory for the destitute children of his charge. But he never could be induced to attempt the work until he was assured of having a religious body to conduct it. In January, 1859, he made application in writing to the Superior-General of the Brothers of the Christian Schools, through Rev. Brother John Chrysostom, then at Manhattan College, for Brothers to take charge of a Protectory. Brother John, in answering, said: "I feel that our Superiors will be happy to co-operate with the noble intentions of your Grace, as soon as possible."

During the discussion at Rev. Father Breen's, his Grace's only objection was that he had not yet got the Brothers. Rev. Brother Patrick, then present, assured his Grace that the Brothers would be given as soon as the premises were ready. His Grace said: "Then, gentlemen, in God's holy Name, let us begin the good work." Much enthusiasm, joy, and satisfaction were manifested at the happy turn the affair had taken, and the auspicious assurances of the future success of the project.

The work took practical shape when, on the 2d day of January, 1863, a portion of the twenty-five gentlemen selected by the Archbishop met and presented the "Articles of Organization of the Society for the Protection of Destitute Children." As there was not a sufficient number present, a call was agreed upon for a meeting of organization, to be held at the pastoral residence. No. 15 Barclay St., February 11, 1863.

It was thus under the influence and encouragement of Rt. Rev.

Monsignor Quinn, then Rector of St. Peter's, that some of the
first steps towards organization were taken; and for two years
afterwards, the late Dr. Ives daily sat at his hospitable table,
seeking encouragement and direction from the generous patron.

At this meeting were present:

Dr. Henry J. Anderson, Charles O'Conor, Chas. M. Connolly,
Eugene Plunkett, Dr. Donatien Binsse, Dr. L. S. Ives, Rev. Wm.
Quinn, Joseph Fisher, Daniel Develin, John Mullen, Lewis J.
White, John McMenomy, Florencio Escalante, Eugene Kelly,
Henry L. Hoguet, and Edward C. Donnelly.

These Catholic gentlemen observed with feelings of deepest
pain that, year after year, hundreds, yes, thousands of Catholic
children, were lost to the faith through a system which ignored
such a principle as religious rights in the helpless objects of its
charity. These children, under the system to which they were
subjected, were sent out West or placed in the hands of prosely-
tizing agents, who the better to conceal the origin and Catholic
parentage of these waifs, changed their name and distributed
them wherever their judgment or interest might select. After a
careful consideration of the whole subject, and calculating the
measure of the responsibilities which they would incur and the
means at their disposal, these gentlemen determined to act,
and to do so promptly.

A committee of seven was appointed to go to Albany and obtain a charter. They were also empowered to frame a set of By-
Laws, and to present the same to the Board.

On the 14th of April, 1863, through the untiring endeavors of
a friend of the Brothers and the cause, the Legislature granted the
charter, under the title of "The Society for the Protection of
Destitute Roman Catholic Children in the City of New York."

The incorporators were:

Felix Ingoldsby, Chas. A. Stetson, Eugene Kelly, Chas. M. Con-
nolly, Daniel Develin, Andrew Carrigan, L. Silliman Ives, Edward
C. Donnelly, Edward Frith, Henry J. Anderson, Joseph Fisher,
Eugene Plunkett, John McMenomy, Donatien Binsse, Lewis J.
White, John O'Brien, John Milhau, Bernard Amend, John E. Deve-
lin, Stephen J. Philbin, Florencio Escalante, John O'Conor, Henry
L. Hoguet, James Lynch, Frederick E. Gibert, and Daniel
O'Conor.

In an address delivered before the friends and patrons of the Catholic Protectory, Mr. John Mullaly, who was himself present at that memorable meeting, said:

"Among those who took deep interest in the work, I may mention a name that is respected, not alone as that of one of America's greatest jurists, but as belonging to a man of irreproachable integrity of character, Charles O'Conor. Mr. Charles M. Connolly, one of the most honored representatives of the mercantile community of this great metropolis, distinguished by his generous support of every deserving charity, and an ardent admirer and patron of art. Daniel Develin, so well and honorably known to New Yorkers, a gentleman of large benevolence, high character, and finely cultivated mind. Mr. Connolly and Mr. Develin are no longer among us, but the part they have taken in the great work has entitled them to the lasting gratitude of the thousands whom they have been instrumental in saving. Mr. Eugene Kelly, another name justly distinguished in the Empire City as one of its leading bankers and financiers. Mr. Henry L. Hoguet, well known among our prominent merchants, a gentleman of high integrity of character. Mr. John E. Develin, a most enthusiastic supporter of the project from the beginning, and a generous contributor to its maintenance, who has given it all the aid of his legal experience and knowledge, and been thus largely instrumental in its success. Mr. Joseph Fisher, another well-known and respected merchant of New York. And Mr. Andrew Carrigan, so long and favorably known through his connection with the Emigrants' Industrial Savings Bank:—such were the names of those Christian gentlemen who had met on this occasion, truly in God's service."

"But there was one gentleman among the laymen whose name deserves special mention. This was the late Dr. L. Silliman Ives, who was one of the first to suggest, and one of the most enthusiastic advocates of, the Protectory. He entered into the matter with all his energy, for it was a subject he had deeply at heart, and volunteered his services for the direction and supervision of the institution. I have been particular in giving the names of the gentlemen connected with the origin and early history of the Protectory; because, while we admire the work, we should not forget the men by whom it was commenced, and these men deserve to be honored as the founders of one of our noblest Catholic charities."

Among the salient features of the charter we may quote the following:—

" Such corporation may take and receive into its care:—

" 1. Children under the age of fourteen years, who, by consent in writing of their parents or guardians, may be intrusted to it for protection or reformation.

" 2. Children between seven and fourteen years of age, who may be committed to the care of such corporation as idle, truant, vicious, or homeless children, by order of any magistrate in the city of New York empowered by law to make committal of children for any such cause.

" 3. Children of the like age who may be transferred, at the option of the Commissioners of Public Charities and Correction of the City of New York, to such corporation.

" The said corporation shall have power to place the children in their care at suitable employments, and cause them to be instructed in suitable branches of useful knowledge, and shall have power at discretion to bind out the said children."

It may be observed that no provision, or appropriation of money from any source was included with the charter, therefore, " the next point was to obtain the means to meet the immediate wants of the institution, and for these an earnest appeal was made for collections and subscriptions, which appeal was generously and promptly responded to, a host of friends putting down their names for sums varying in amount from two thousand five hundred dollars and five hundred dollars to ten dollars. This was most encouraging, and calculated to inspire the highest confidence in the ultimate success of the work; but I doubt if those gentlemen, in the highest flight of their enthusiasm, ever dreamed that within the brief space of a few years the Catholic Protectory would have grown to its present extent and usefulness.

II.

The celerity with which the work was prosecuted showed how deeply in earnest were the men by whom it had been conceived and undertaken.

For the immediate accommodation of the youthful inmates two private dwellings in Thirty-sixth and Thirty-seventh Streets, near

Second Avenue, were procured, and here, under the pastoral care
of Father Clowry, who attended to their spiritual wants, the boys
found their first home and shelter, under the paternal care of
Brother Teliow, to whose untiring zeal and devotedness so large a
share of the success which has blessed the progress of the New
York Catholic Protectory is due.

Before entering upon other details, it may be well to say some
few words about the Brothers of the Christian Schools, to whom
the boys of the New York Catholic Protectory were given in charge
by Archbishop Hughes.

Rev. B. L. Pierce, chaplain of the House of Refuge, in his book
entitled *Half a Century with Juvenile Delinquents,* makes the following statement:—

" The officers of the Boys' Protectory belong to the order of the
Christian Brothers.* They give themselves to the Church when
they take the vows of the order, to be teachers wherever they
may be appointed to labor. They will never be priests; they are
expected to pursue no form of business hereafter, but for life will
remain in the office of instructors. Their salaries are simply the
requisite provision for their living, sick or well. These men are
constantly with the boys in school, work, recreation, and in the
domitory; and it can be easily seen what a moral power they are
able to bring to the aid of the superintendent in his work of reforming the young persons thus placed in his hands." It may be
here remarked that the superintendent is the Brother Director of
the community of Brothers.

Thus also speak the SELECT COMMITTEE of 1875:

" While conducted under the management of the Christian
Brothers, a benevolent society attached to the Roman Catholic
charge, and while especially designed to receive Roman Catholic
children, there seems to be no disposition to proselytize, when
those of other faiths are committed to its custody."

Notice of these partial arrangements had only time to reach the
poor, or the benefactors of the poor, when applications in behalf
of unprotected children became so numerous and pressing as to
compel the Executive Committee, in view of their necessarily limited means and accommodations, to restrict the number of inmates
to such boys as might be committed from the courts, or transferred

---

* The legal title is: " The Brothers of the Christian Schools."

to their care by the "Commissioners of Public Charities and Correction." Hence the records of their office show that, but for the want of sufficient room, at least double the number which they now report might be enjoying the blessing of the institution.

Owing to the difficulty of renting suitable buildings, the committee were unable to make provision for the reception of girls before the first of October. About that time, however, they succeeded in procuring a building at the corner of Eighty-sixth Street and Second Avenue, well suited to the purpose. This they were enabled to place under the direction of the Sisters of Charity, a religious order whose members, by their noble and generous self-devotion in the care of the sick, the forlorn, the destitute and helpless in every form, age, and condition in life, have been the theme of praise in story and song in every clime and tongue, and from persons of all shades of belief, race and religion; an order which needs only be named to insure the most unqualified respect and confidence.

The houses in Thirty-sixth and Thirty-seventh Streets were found to be inadequate for the accommodation of the daily increasing numbers, and the managers were, within eight months of the day of opening, forced to seek other and more commodious quarters. Two buildings were then rented in Eighty-sixth Street, near Fifth Avenue, and so soon as convenient the boys moved into them.

The difficulties experienced in securing accommodation—in obtaining the considerable sums necessary for the inauguration of so vast a work—were but a minor portion of the onerous task placed upon the management. The far more difficult problem of finding employment adapted to the capacity of the children, and which would be useful to them in after life, had to be solved.

" Like all other truly great religious and benevolent enterprises, it had to pass through a trying ordeal, and required the most unwearied presistence and indomitable resolution to carry it to a successful completion. But there was an imperative necessity for the work, and those who put their hand to the plough were not the men to look back. All honor to them for the noble impulse which led them to conceive and to triumphantly accomplish an undertaking of such magnitude and such true Christian philanthropy!"

Most of the children received, particularly during the first few years, were the victims of indolent or vicious habits, which time, patience, and God's grace could alone eradicate. Experience has taught that, to succeed in this work of reformation, constant occupation, pleasantly diversified, is essential. Industry is essential to a proper cultivation of the mind and heart. But industry in one unvarying line of duty will soon dull the mind of a child, and fill the heart with discouragement. Change and relaxation are demanded. Attention must be given to the play-ground; out-door labor must not be overlooked. The play-ground succeeds the school-room; the work-shop succeeds the play-ground. But there is another advantage in the introduction of trades. A feeling is thereby produced in the minds of the children so engaged that they are doing something for themselves—acquiring a skill which may lead to a prosperous and respectable position in life. Besides, we are enabled by this means to hold out an incentive to good conduct in the shape of promised remuneration for the work they do, that would otherwise require skilled help; the sums pupils thus secure may aid them in entering upon business for themselves. These sentiments have actuated the management of the Protectory from the beginning.

It will be remarked that thus far, the managers of the New York Catholic Protectory have relied chiefly upon private generosity to sustain the work. But, beginning with 1864, we find that the State and other authorities recognized the work as of public utility, and that they assisted it accordingly. Up to this time, the following sums have been received and disbursed:

From annual contributions, ... $6,125 50
"   donations, ... 4,586 00
"   the proceeds of trades, ... 411 35
"   the contributions of parents or guardians, . 728 15

$11,851 00

And that they have expended:

For rents, ... $1,250 00
"   furnishing houses, ... 3,927 85
"   clothing, ... 1,401 50
"   subsistence, ... 1,952 17

$8,531 52

For incidental expenses, ... 779 95
" office, ... 429 20
" salaries, ... 1,305 00

$11,045 67

In addition to the contributions to defray the current expenses of the establishment, the managers have secured, as a building fund, the sum of about $30,000, which, with a legacy of $25,000 left to the institution, will enable them, so soon as they can secure the proper site, to commence the erection of suitable buildings— buildings that may furnish protection for at least 1,500 ' destitute children,' thus relieving the city of the permanent charge of that number, besides making provision for the temporary discipline and protection of many more.

III.

While the New York Catholic Protectory thus pursued its mission, each day's experience more fully proved the necessity of moving out of the city. Apart from the fact that it was impossible to secure sufficient accommodation in the heart of a great metropolis, the managers became daily more convinced that the influence of surroundings in a vast city like New York was against their work. The problem which then propounded itself was to secure "proper location elsewhere." In the minutes of one of the regular meetings held at this time Dr. Ives said:

" In view of the circumstances, and in the firm conviction that the prosperity, IF NOT THE VERY EXISTENCE of our institution, depends upon the immediate erection of a building somewhere outside of New York City, every exertion possible has been made by the Executive Committee to discover a suitable place for this purpose. We have visited all the islands in the East River and found in them all some fatal objections. We then turned our attention to the mainland and could discover nothing within the limits of the city which seemed to promise any better accommodations. After consulting our legal adviser we felt justified in looking beyond these limits. An advertisement of the sale of a farm near the village of West Chester induced us to visit and examine it. Four members of the Executive Committee, Dr. Anderson, Mr.

Hoguet, Mr. White, and the President, with the Most Rev. Archbishop, the advisory Chaplain, and a number of the clergy, have
visited the farm, and after a thorough examination, have unanimously come to the conclusion, taking everything into consideration, that we are not likely to secure a more favorable site for our
institution. Your President, therefore, after making himself master of the facts relating to this property and to the terms of sale,
recommends its purchase by the managers."

It was, therefore, with no little satisfaction that they announced
the purchase, on the 9th day of June, 1865, of a valuable farm of
about 114 acres, with commodious barns, and out-houses, near the
village of West Chester, for $40,000.00, upon which they began
immediately to erect a spacious brick building, designed to accommodate from 600 to 800 destitute boys; while making arrangements to erect one, during the following summer, of equal dimensions, for the accommodation of girls.

We thus find the status of the development which the New York
Catholic Protectory had assumed when it left its straitened and
incommodious quarters in 86th Street, to take possession of its
large, and relatively comfortable home in West Chester.

When we consider how much had been effected at this stage of
our existence, we feel the full force of words written by the vener-
ated first President of the New York Catholic Protectory, Dr.
Ives, who in his lecture in Cooper Institute in 1864, said:

" This brings me to touch lightly upon another point, which is,
that education in a State, whether it relates to poor children or to
rich, will never be conducted with economy and success till it is intrusted to the different denominations of Christians. Otherwise it
is without earnest life, without decided character, without security
to morals, and without check to wasteful expenditure. It becomes, in short, or is liable to become, in the hands of designing
men, a system of fraud and peculation, which every wise man will
not hesitate to discourage. For this reason the late able and ven-
erated Archbishop of New York struggled for years against the
State system of education, and strove, by every just means, to get
by charter from the State the control of the training of destitute
Catholic children in this city. Just previous to his lamented death,
his efforts were successful, and the act of incorporation under which
our Society is at work is the happy result. Shall we succeed in

realizing his hopes? His first and last counsel was, 'Do not attempt too much at once!' The institution must have its tottering infancy, its gradual growth, before it stands up in the full strength of its manhood. It is still in its infancy. It has been able to provide shelter for only a small portion of those who have sought its protection." And it was still further to realize the mission of the New York Catholic Protectory that its field of action was transferred to its West Chester home.

The general principles which prevail in the management of the Protectory will be manifested by the following extract, wherein the love and interest shown, for and in the institution are illustrated:

" The great aim of an institution such as ours must be to render the inmates honorable in their dealings, and as far as possible, without infringing discipline, to give each pupil a chance to show his honesty of purpose and his appreciation of the trust placed in him. 'We admit that, now and then, a boy may be found who would take advantage of such opportunities to abscond, or to visit his friends, as he would call it; but it has happened more than once that the runaways, having gone but a short distance, began to reflect, and came back of their own accord. In pursuing such a course, what is lost for one is gained for hundreds: and if a child cannot be trusted while in the institution, little reliance or trust can be placed in him. Another happy result obtained by this training is, that the boys no longer regard the Protectory as a prison. In confirmation of which, I have only to state that, in case anyone should attempt an exit, hundreds would volunteer and could be safely trusted to pursue and arrest the delinquent. Indeed, it has occurred several times, that a couple of our boys, having been sent on an errand to the city, have there fallen in with one who had absconded, and have brought him back in triumph to the Protectory. We regard moral influence and reasonable vigilance as the best enclosure to the institution, and the best security against escape.

" Experience convinces us, more and more, that neither child nor man can be morally elevated and educated but in as far as he believes and loves."

" Trades have been carried on in the institution during the past year as heretofore, and attended with the same results. We hold

the system of trades to be the very best means for maintaining order and discipline in a house of this kind.   It fills up the time, and
diverts the young mind from the evil suggestions of the tempter.
Truth has said that idleness is the parent of every vice.   Hence
in the workshop we have found the most direct and effectual corrective for an idle, vicious boy.   There he can scarcely conceal
his evil passions and propensities, or find any way of evading the
watchful eye that guards him."

Another report informs us that:

" We learn from the many gratifying letters and accounts which
have reached us, that our labors are beginning to bear fruit, and that
many a young man, through the instrumentality of the Protectory
is now pursuing a course of virtue, usefulness, and honor, blessing
the day whereon he became an inmate of the institution which
taught him to walk in the path of duty."

IV.

Not only at home, but more especially abroad, has the excellence,
the taste, and the evident pride the Protectory children take in
their work been recognized and publicly extolled.   This was repeatedly shown by the comments of such journals as the London
Times, Standard, Globe, Chronicle, Post, the Dublin *Freeman*, the
Dublin Review, the *Pall Mall Gazette*, and other equally distinguished though divergent journals.   A few extracts from these must
suffice.   Says the London *Standard*, speaking of the exhibits made
by the Brothers of the Christian Schools at the International
Health Exhibition, London: "Most fascinating of all are the results in the New York Catholic Protectory.   The handiwork shown
is of a remarkably high order.   Take for example, the women's shoes.
They are of the very neatest, most finely finished, and of the best
make."

The London *Engineering* repeats in almost identical words:

"The boys at the Protectory show no mean skill in such handi-
crafts as chair-making, silk-weaving, printing, and electrotyping."

The "Official Guide to the International Health Exhibition,"
says:

" The work of the New York Catholic Protectory Society ap-

peals to all philanthropists, being the result of the efforts to reclaim the little waifs of New York City. These specimens of work are really startling, and go to show what may be done with those classes " of youth which in earlier years have had but few, if any, opportunities for development or self-help.

" The effect of such training must prove eventually of untold value to any country in which such work is faithfully done. But there is a double reason for such efforts being appreciated by the public, especially the tax-paying portion, when it is borne in mind that all this is done with such comparatively small cost to the public exchequer. This point can scarcely be too forcibly insisted upon. It places the work, the labor, the results of such institutions as the New York Catholic Protectory in a new and more advantageous light. Such statements as go to show how fair play to denominational institutions means economy in public administration, will be the most powerful form of argument which may be employed in bringing about a more kindly feeling among those who claim that the State and the State only should deal with juvenile delinquents, regardless of their religion. Dr. Ives, in the first annual report of the institution, struck the key-note of our standing in this respect. He wrote:

" When your honorable body considers that the institutions incorporated by the State for the relief of orphan and destitute children are generally full to their utmost capacity, and that from the effect of our unhappy war the number of these young sufferers is likely for years to come to be greatly increased : when you reflect upon what the managers, with much self-sacrifice, have already done, and upon what, from their limited resources, they have been compelled to leave undone ; with the facts that every dollar they have expended is a dollar saved to the tax-payers of the city ; and that every Catholic child they have been compelled to turn from them is a child to be provided for in some more expensive way ; the managers cannot doubt that your honors will regard the Society with favor, and extend to it a just and impartial liberality. . . .

" The managers regret that they cannot acknowledge the receipt of their quota of the State School Fund, to which, from the terms of their charter, they were induced to think themselves entitled, and hence had complied with the conditions on which it is usually granted; but being instructed that a special act of the Legislature is necessary to secure it, they trust that the deficiency may be supplied by the passage of such an Act during its present session. And also, that " The Society for the Protection of Destitute Roman Catholic Children," may in every particular, be placed on the same footing on which Protestant institutions of the like character have been placed by your honorable body.

" RELIGION, it cannot be doubted, is one of the most powerful instrumentalities in securing the economical and successful working of such institutions. But religion, to answer this end, must have its own distinct and explicit character—must operate through the hearts and minds of those who are governed by it. It can do nothing diluted with worldly policy or palsied by a professed neutrality. Attempted amalgamation has always either destroyed its life or changed it into hypocrisy. To be of service to any cause, it must be wielded by *each particular denomination of Christians, according to the faith by which each is actuated.* This is well understood by the statesmen of Europe. You can scarcely name a Government there, however despotic, which does not acknowledge this principle, in its legislation for all its educational and charitable institutions. Even in Austria and Bavaria, where Protestants are in the smallest minority, each denomination is allowed by law to train its destitute children in its own way, under its own direction, with its full quota of money from the general taxation or government funds. Surely in this free country we cannot be behind Catholic Austria and Bavaria in protecting the sacred rights of conscience, and in gaining to our institutions of charity that strength, efficiency, and economy which RELIGION, in its distinct life and supremacy, is so well calculated to give!" *

In the last annual report that he signed before his lamented death, Dr. Ives, in giving the history of objections against which he had to contend in obtaining a charter, so strongly states the truth and justice of the attitude of the Catholic Protectory towards the State that we can not do better than embody it in this sketch:

" In obtaining our charter we had to struggle against two objections urged with surprising zeal and pertinacity. The first, that ample provision for vicious and destitute children had already been made by the State, and that an increase would only tend to injure the existing institutions. The second, that these institutions were

* Report of Dec. 31, 1863.

organized on the fairest and most liberal basis by excluding all
distinctive religion; while the one, whose incorporation we sought,
was professedly sectarian in its character, being placed under the
exclusive control of Catholics.   Our answer to the *first* objection
was, that it had no support from facts, but was manifestly the
creature of unnecessary alarms, as a few years would give adequate proof.   And we now ask, if these few years—not quite four
since we entered upon our work—have not fully justified our answer?   The very men who opposed us in the beginning have recently confessed their error—confessed that the rapid multiplication of charitable institutions has not kept pace with the fearful
increase of destitution and delinquency among the children of our
city; while their reports show, that notwithstanding the large
number to which we have given protection, the institutions, for
whose welfare they seemed so much alarmed, are now crowded to
their utmost capacity and supported by most liberal grants from
the State.   Our answer to the *second* objection was, that if the
State had shown its fairness and liberality only by *excluding, in
fact, all distinctive religion* from its institutions, it was high time
that one institution, at least, should be organized on a different
basis; should professedly and really make *distinctive* religion its ac-
tuating and controlling power; as nothing short of this could so
sway the hearts of children as to make them in the end good
Christians and good men.   That the idea of making men *moral*
without instilling into their minds the principles of morality is pre-
posterous; and that, among a Christian people, the notion that
there are any other principles of morality than the distinctive
and unalterable " principles of the doctrine of Christ " is equally
so.   But the question was put:—*Has* the State succeeded in excluding from its institutions all distinctive religion, and all *sectarian teaching and influence?*   Inquire at " The Juvenile Asylum,"
" The House of Refuge," " The Children's Aid Society," " The
Five Points House of Industry."   Is not the *Protestant* religion inculcated in these institutions, and only the Catholic religion *ex-
cluded?*   Where among the managers of all these institutions is a
Catholic to be found?   Where among their superintendents, their
teachers, their preachers, do you find a Catholic?   Where among
their acts of worship is a Catholic act tolerated?   While, on the
other hand, who does not know that Protestant worship, in all its

various forms, is, without opposition, introduced? and Protestant doctrine, in all its shades and contradictions, is inculcated? Indeed, we did not find it necessary to debate this question. Protestant periodicals not only admitted but gloried in the fact. They boasted that the State is Protestant in all her institutions, and that it is an act of great indulgence on her part, that Catholicity is allowed to exist at all; that we as Catholics should be grateful that the power of the State has not been invoked to arrest our progress and put an end to our institutions. Can it, therefore, we enquired, be thought unreasonable, while such a spirit actuates the Protestant community, that Catholic parents should be averse to give up their children to Protestant institutions: to institutions, where Protestant dogmas and practices are enforced upon them: and where they are compelled to study books and listen to addresses in which the religion of their fathers is reviled? We pressed the inquiry further, and asked: Whether it was wise and statesman-like to introduce a system of compulsion where the rights of conscience are concerned? Where the faith of Catholic parents is outraged by forcing Catholic children into Protestant asylums? Whether peace and contentment in the community are likely to be the result of such a system? This was the line of argument addressed to the Legislature, which, against violent opposition, granted our charter. And we can assure that honorable body that they have reason to be proud of their firmness in sustaining our just and noble cause, which, in its four years' prosperity, has done so much to relieve the suffering and quiet the discontented. That the suffering must be relieved; that the multitude of little vagrants crowding our city must, on every principle of humanity, economy, and duty, have protection and training, cannot be questioned. Indeed, our government has here admitted its responsibility, and has inaugurated a policy to meet it. We ask, then (and we do it with all boldness), has not the State through our institution been enabled to reach an evil and accomplish a work which otherwise would not have been reached and accomplished? Has it not, through us, been enabled to bring within its embrace a class of destitute children that otherwise would have remained without succor? Has it not, through us, been instrumental in calling into exercise an amount of Catholic charity which otherwise would, at the most, have been but partially

secured? Has it not, through us, been the means of allaying that spirit of discontent and disorder so annoying to our police-magistrates, and so troublesome to the friends of the distressed; which arose from the want of a Catholic Protectory? Long will the scene be remembered in which, as our claim for an appropriation before a committee of the Legislature was bitterly assailed on sectarian grounds, an eminent Protestant lawyer arose and eloquently said, in reply: "Gentlemen, I think I am speaking for the whole bench of judges in the city of New York, while I affirm, that if the existence of the institution under the Society for the Protection of Destitute Roman Catholic Children in that city has no other claim upon us, it certainly deserves our regard and support, for *one blessing* it has achieved, and *that* is the removal from our courts of the cause of incessant litigation between parents and proselyters as to the legal disposition of poor children."

This generous defence of our Protestant friend, for which he has our thanks, was fully justified by facts at the time, and has been receiving the like confirmation ever since.

Dr. Henry J. Anderson was no less emphatic in reiterating the same truths, when, succeeding Dr. Ives, he wrote:

" This Protectory, therefore, has never asked for anything more than what is conceded to its sister institutions, viz: equality with any other protectory, to be counted a full sharer in the cost and compensations of the onerous responsibilities which such societies assume in concert with the city and the State.

" We may even say that, for reasons superfluous to repeat, it has hitherto asked for *less* than the recognized proportions hitherto established, when such enterprises have met the sanction required for their existence. At all events, so favorably has our society been impressed with the fair intentions and manly equity of the State, and her freedom from all narrow-minded jealousy of creeds, that not only have we refrained from asking her to relieve us from our full contingent of pecuniary obligation, but we have cheerfully raised from our own community (not overburdened with the means of doing it) twice as much, as near as may be, as has been contributed from every other source, including all that has been granted to these children by the city and the State. We believe that this will be found, on a strict examination, to be the largest contribution to the joint expenditure of any similar asylum recognized by the laws of New York, and liable to be visited as a co-operating agent in this special work. It is true that the Catholic orphan asylums and the Catholic day-schools have done immeas-urably more, as the so-called non-religious asylums and the non-religious day-schools (from which we are practically shut out) have done immeasurably less." *

V.

Here we record the death of Dr. Levi Silliman Ives. It has been stated that Dr. Ives died outside the bosom of the Catholic Church. The statement is absolutely false. Dr. Ives died in the odor of sanctity, fortified by all the rites of the Catholic Church, surrounded by Catholic friends, with a profession of the Catholic faith upon his lips.

Born in 1797 at Meriden, Connecticut; in 1816 a student for the Presbyterian ministry; in 1819 ordained an episcopal cler-gyman; in 1831 a zealous bishop of the Episcopalian Church in North Carolina, the Oxford movement, headed by the late Cardinal Newman, caused him to examine the claims of the Catholic Church, and in 1853 he received the grace of conversion. The history of his conversion he clearly and graphically narrated in his *Trials of a Mind in Search of Truth.* Coming to New York, he was for some time professor in Manhattan College. Soon his attention was attracted to the terrible evil of proselytism carried on in New York City. "His tender sympathies," says the poet John Savage, "and the necessities so sadly prominent in a great city, naturally led him to good works; and he desired to do some-thing in acknowledgment of the sublime light which had broken in upon his declining years. He desired to make amends in his full maturity for the want of the grace and benefits which had been denied to his earlier life." †

He saw thousands of the children of Irish Catholic immigrants brought up in institutions that had been turned into factories of sectarianism, their very names as well as their faith taken from them, and they, with false names and false principles, ticketed to the far West; and knowing the priceless value of the Catholic re-

* Fifth Annual Report, January 2d, 1868.
† Address delivered July 21, 1874.

ligion, the sight of this mistaken zeal grieved him as a crying injustice before God and righteous men. His soul became filled with
this idea, and he made it his life-work to do everything within his
power to remedy the evil. " Never," he said in a scholarly lecture
from which we have already quoted, " in the history of this city
has infant wretchedness stalked forth in such multiplied and such
humiliating forms. I speak not from hearsay, but of what my
own eyes have seen and my own heart felt. For the last ten years
I have been the close observer of what has passed among the ris-
ing generation in this great metropolis, and I cannot suppress the
humiliating conviction that even pagan Rome, in the corrupt age
of Augustus, never witnessed a more rapid and frightful declension
in morals, never witnessed among certain classes of the young, a
more utter disregard of honor, of truth and purity, and even the
commonest decencies of life. Extraordinary as this statement
may seem, it is a statement of fact." * The outcome of all this
solicitude is the institution that we are now sketching.

Dr. Levi Silliman Ives was one of those noble natures whose
every fibre quivers with generous impulse and elevated thought.
He lived only that he might do good. He bent all his energy—
all the powers of his beautiful soul and refined mind—to the raising
up out of the gutter of misery, the poor and destitute boy and girl
whom he found in the squalor of the New York festering districts.
His name should ever be held in benediction as the true friend of
the poor and the suffering. Dr. Ives was succeeded by Dr. Henry James Anderson.

VI.

The Protectory continued to grow in numbers and in efficiency.
An idea of the institution in 1867 may be best gathered from the
following financial statement:

The total outlay from the beginning (including what
   is now on hand, and in process of expenditure) for
   the purposes for which the Society was incorporated, is $469,034 02
Towards which the public grants in aid amount to   164,807 49
                                             ——————

Due to private and voluntary liberality,   .   . 304,226 53

* *The Protection of Destitute Catholic Children.* A lecture delivered at
Cooper Institute, November 23d, 1854, pp. 5, 6.

It is not surprising, then, that the Catholics of New York take an honest pride in the New York Catholic Protectory. Their practical proofs of this interest are beyond calculation, but, perhaps, the most striking in point of union of aim and purpose, and extent of success, was the General Fair, got up expressly to install the destitute Catholic girls of New York as comfortably as the boys had already been provided for. The following succinct statement will prove interesting:

" In referring to the part which we have endeavored to perform in this joint exercise of the Christian maintenance of the poor, we should do wrong if we did not specially bring to the notice of your honorable bodies the results of our appeal since the last legislative year to the generosity of the public, to make up an ample *building fund* to be sacredly appropriated to the benefit of poor friendless little *girls*, left either destitute or dangerously exposed. The fair for their relief was opened on the 20th of May, 1867, and closed on the 21st of June. With very few exceptions, and those too insignificant to record, our efforts were most generously seconded throughout the city, without distinction of sect or party, birthplace or creed.

" We shall never forget the promptness with which the municipal authorities, irrespective of all previous predilections or opinions, united in granting, not to us of course, but to *our* and to *your* homeless little ones, the use of public ground for the full space of time we required. The reverend clergy threw themselves into the work with an energy inspired by their frequent dealings with a destitution which they unanimously resolved should be relieved. The conferences of St. Vincent de Paul, twenty or more in number, devoted themselves unweariedly, day and night, to the hard work assigned to them. The city officials, and the metropolitan police, so far as they were detailed to our assistance, did more for us than we could ask. But, most of all, it is just and necessary to mention prominently in this report the enthusiastic and successful perseverance of the lady-directors and promoters of the fair. Without their aid, without their singular assiduity and zeal, what could the managers of this society have effected, with all their eager desire to merit the confidence of your honorable bodies, and to prove their sense of the proper value of your sympathy and kindness? We forbear to say more, for more we could not say

without betraying the unfitness of mere words to make known
what the Catholic ladies of New York can accomplish when their
hearts are in their work. To all, then, without exception, who so
generously contributed to the gratifying result, we promise, in behalf of the poor girls who yet await the application of this measure of relief, the certainty of their grateful and perpetual com-
memoration of an act of such substantial charity as the great
Catholic fair of '67. It is scarcely necessary for us to add that
the collection which, all expenses paid, has netted over $100,000,
will be jealously protected and religiously applied in strict conformity with the pledges so solemnly given at the time. The
work has been fairly commenced."

Thus assisted, the sum realized was "sacredly appropriated"
to the erection of a fitting home for the large number of destitute
girls who looked to the New York Catholic Protectory for relief.
But, while thus occupied, the managers were not unmindful of the
unceasing demands made upon them by the boys' department, and
in the same year that beheld the girls' building just begun, a long
two-story wooden building was erected at a cost of $14,696.94,
and of which, in the report of that year, we read: "The acquisition of a new frame building, sufficiently large to accommodate
250 small boys, has afforded us the long-desired advantage of separating the junior portion of the children from the senior." The
following year (1868), while the girls' building was in rapid progress of construction, the increasing demands for more and better
accommodations for the boys became so urgent that the erection
of a large building was imperative. Accordingly they wrote:

" The managers have the pleasure to announce that, owing to
the successful application of the industry of our boys, under the
skilful direction of the Christian Brothers, they have been enabled to
contract for the erection of the foundation of the main or central
portion of the Boys' Building; the part now finished and occupied
having been intended to constitute the northern wing of the edifice
as originally designed. The cost of this foundation, about eight
thousand dollars (all work and material included), will be assumed
by us without a call upon your honorable bodies for assistance in
this particular; and we are encouraged by the Brothers to believe
that, before we look elsewhere for help, we shall even make some
creditable progress in the superstructure, out of funds which the

labor of the industrial departments (as conducted by these devoted men) will be sure to supply.

" The necessity of a large additional building for the reception and training of the children sent to us by the established judges of the laws which govern such committals, is doubtless as obvious to your honorable bodies as to ourselves. That we shall continue to be able to extend to the city and State, for this inevitable re-sult of our present policy of mixed relief, a larger share of private contribution than other associations less happily organized in the material points of economical constitution and traditional experi-ence, we most firmly believe; and the thought that we shall there-by bring down the quota of the public burden to a *minimum* not hitherto attained, will be one of those rewarding consolations which we trust we shall be permitted to accept."

Of the Girls' New Building the President wrote the following year (1869): " We are happy in being able to state that the seventh year of our corporate existence has been carried on to completion one of the main features of the institution, namely, the large and commodious structure known as the Girls' New Building, into which about 200 girls were removed last November." He further says "The Girls' New Building is furnished throughout, and contains 520 beds, which enables the Sister to add over 300 inmates to her already numerous family. The entire cost of this large addition to the buildings and outfits of the society, amounting in the aggre-gate to nearly $200,000, has been defrayed from private charity, and loans obtained on mortgage, without our having had recourse to the contributions of either city or State for that purpose. A tract of about 20 acres of land has been purchased and added to the ground previously laid out for that division of the Protectory.

Of the Boys' Building above mentioned, he continued:

" We are now engaged in the erection of the main central build-ing of the Boys' Protectory, the dimensions of which are 228 feet long, and varying in width from 52 to 113 feet, basement, four stories, and mansard roof."

This new building well deserves the description found in the Eighth Annual Report, which we here reproduce:

" Having now occupied our new building for the space of about one month, it is but due to all who are concerned or interested in the welfare of the Protectory, that we avail ourselves of this opportunity to testify our unqualified satisfaction in reference thereto.

" In the first place, we revert with pleasure to the formal occupation or inauguration of the new building, which very appropriately took place on last Thanksgiving-Day (November 24th). That auspicious event will ever form a bright picture in the history of the Protectory, and will long be remembered by its inmates, friends, and benefactors. Honored on that happy occasion by the presence of His Grace, the Most Reverend Archbishop McCloskey, the Hon. Oakey Hall, Mayor of our city, and a large number of other distinguished gentlemen, the Protectory will ever look upon that affair as a glorious and triumphant celebration of its success. Among the various encomiums bestowed upon the institution by the distinguished speakers of the occasion, the speech of his Honor, the Mayor, was peculiarly striking and felicitous. In responding to an address of welcome delivered on the part of the institution by one of its youthful inmates, his honor, in his usual happy style, remarked that, among the many institutions of the kind which he had visited he acknowledged the Protectory to have borne away the palm of excellence.

" The building itself is allowed on all hands to be a model of masculine strength and beauty, combined with ample capacity and every desirable convenience. The admirable interior disposition and arrangement of the many apartments make them perfectly and fully adapted to their respective purposes, while the appliances for supplying water, heating the apartments, lighting, ventilation, etc.. are in all their details most complete. The same may be said of the culinary department, where every advantage has been taken of the latest improvements, to make it in every respect complete and satisfactory.

" The uses to which the various portions of the building are now applied, are as follows, viz:

" The basement comprises a store-room for provisions, a bakery, and a lavatory.

" The first story contains, besides the grand entrance and office, an immense refectory, and the kitchen, with its accessory apartments.

" The second story is divided into three parlors, a library, the Brothers' community-room, a series of private sleeping-apartments, bathrooms, etc. The third and fourth stories form two immense sleeping apartments, besides several private sleeping-rooms. The fifth story, or mansard, forms our spacious chapel, besides which it contains an infirmary and several private rooms. Above this rise the tower and steeple, to the height of 225 feet, surmounted by the cross. The cost of this building thus far is $244,095.62.

" As accessory to the new building, and constructed at the same time with it, must be mentioned the boiler and engine-house, a substantial brick building located within eighty feet from the north side of the main building. Within it are two large steam-boilers feeding two pumps and one engine, besides supplying steam for heating every apartment in the vast edifice, as well as for culinary purposes. The steam-pumps draw water from a reservoir at the distance of 500 feet, and force it up into three large tanks in the upper story of the new building, whence it is distributed into every apartment where needed. *

" We are, at present, engaged in constructing a new reservoir, sufficiently large, not only to supply the house with water at all times, but also to yield in season a good supply of ice for summer use. We intend, moreover, to construct it in such a way that in the winter time we may, with its waters, readily overflow our adjoining meadow, and thereby give our youngsters, at their own door, a fine chance for the healthful sport of skating."

This proposal has been more than realized, as any one who visits the New York Catholic Protectory during the winter months may attest. Indeed, we doubt if Canada offers any more exciting scene in any more agreeable display than that furnished by several hundred of the Protectory boys enjoying the exhilarating exercise of a first-class "skate."

And elsewhere, we are informed in the Brother Rector's report that:

" The system of encouraging youths who labor in the various departments, by a certain remuneration, we have practised during the past year with very satisfactory results. Not only does such a course infuse a spirit of emulation into the young worker, and give life and animation to his efforts, but it also tends most admirably to the successful working of the affair as a whole. We have had in the past year 75 youthful workmen, to whom we have awarded a suitable sum per month. The result is, that they take an interest

* The water supply has since been largely increased.

in the work set before them, and endeavor to give satisfaction
to those who are placed over them."

VII.

In 1869, a tract of twenty acres was purchased and added to the
Protectory grounds, and the following gifts were recorded:

From the late Thomas McKenzie, bequest of real estate

valued at	$25,000.00
Gift from Irish Emigrant Society, ...	5,000.00
Bequest of John F. O'Connor, ...	5,000.00
Bequest of Very Rev. M. M. Carron, ...	2,000.00
Bequest of James T. Fagan, ...	500.00
Bequest of P. McGuinniss, ...	250.00

The Ninth Annual Report sums up the condition of the Protectory as follows:—

"Since its origin in 1863, 5,911 children have been sent in as
wards to the Protectory, and enjoyed the advantages for a shorter
or longer time of its tutelary care. The whole amount expended
since the commencement of operations, and chargeable to the work
assigned to us, is $1,430,706.85, no part of which has been paid out
except in due regard to the joint interests equally concerned, viz.,
those of the city, and those of the beneficiaries of the trust.

" Towards this unavoidable expenditure, incurred only for such
purposes as the law directed or allowed, the authorities which in-
spected and approved the work, appropriated less than half the
cost, viz., $674,110.53. The remainder, $756,596.32, has been
raised and applied without troubling the public exchequer with the
presentation of a single bill. Private benevolence has contributed
$413,897.18, the children themselves, through their labor, $102,791.-
52, and the credit of the Protectory $244,019.71."

Sacrifices, such as these figures imply, must have some very
powerful motive to put them in motion, and, above all, to keep
them in active existence. It may be safely said that the desire to
see these poor children thoroughly educated is the prime cause
which enables and induces the Catholic of New York to undertake
such herculean tasks and to bring them to successful issues. What
this education is, which the New York Catholic Protectory seeks to
give its inmates, what the Protectory's objects are will be best un-

derstood from the words of the illustrious founder of the institution, who wrote:

" We regard the education of these poor, neglected, or destitute
children paramount to all other duties. Their future welfare is, in
a great measure, in our hands. Our special endeavor is to educate
them, in the true and broadest sense of the word. Hence, whilst
we impart instruction to them in the various branches of learning,
as reading, writing, arithmetic, etc., and even cultivate music in
those who evince a disposition favorable thereto, we are far from
considering these items as constituting the sum of their education.
Our great aim is to mould their hearts to the practice of virtue, and
while we make them worthy citizens of our glorious Republic, to
render them fit candidates for the heavenly mansions above. In
one word, whilst we labor to cultivate their minds, we emphatically
devote ourselves to the forming of their hearts. The proficiency
of the boys in their class-rooms speaks for the one, and their general good conduct for the other."

But while thus giving a strictly religious character to all their
teaching, while seeking to impregnate the atmosphere in which
they live and move with a thoroughly Christian aroma, there is
nothing morose, rigid, or constrained in the system of government.
We may justly repeat with one of the Annual Reports:

" We have reason to be consoled by the respectful, docile, and
orderly deportment of our boys, by the affection they manifest
towards us, and by the interest they take in the prosperity of the
institution."

The kindly spirit which has been so distinguished a characteris-
tic of the New York Catholic Protectory has frequently been noticed by visitors who have made a careful study of its workings.
Thus the following, from a well-known authority, is but the echo
of the almost universal verdict of the public:

HEALTH DEPARTMENT,
BUREAU OF VITAL STATISTICS.

DEAR BROTHER TELIOW:

You will please accept my hearty thanks for invitations to be
present at the festivities of your great family. But duties I cannot leave compel my absence on this occasion.

The assemblage of two thousand children upon Westchester

plains, where they feed on wholesome foods for mind and body alike, while some thoughts, hopes, and affections, may still cling to homes and parents, humble and needy though such parents may be, very deeply moves my desires for your success, and their welfare, present and future.

The fact that you and your Christian Brothers inculcate and secure obedience, order, cleanliness, and diligence in all these dear children, but, paramount to all, a reverence for their Creator and His divine behests, is enough for me, for these virtues will enable you to place them in suitable employments, or start every one of them onward to a life of prosperity and future happiness.

The good tidings of health and happiness which your kind physician has conveyed to me, enable me to join you and the children in their joyful emotions to-day.

With great regard,

ELISHA H. HARRIS.

Here is another unsolicited piece of evidence bearing upon the same point:

FIVE POINTS HOUSE OF INDUSTRY,

May 28, 1878.

DEAR SIR:

I desire again, in this formal manner, to tender my sincere thanks for your courtesy shown to Mr. Camp and myself on our visit to your institution yesterday. The visit, as we said, was one wholly for information which might be useful to us in our work. I was both surprised and delighted with what I saw, and you are certainly doing a most excellent work in an admirable manner. You have the right ideas in regard to fitting these children for usefulness, and are fortunate in being able to put them in such a practical shape. I think no candid person can take in such a knowledge of your general work as we did without commending it. I shall always be glad to say a word of commendation, whenever an opportunity offers, for the thoroughly good work you are doing for the poor Catholic children.

Sincerely yours,

WILLIAM F. BARNARD.

VIII.

The good work which we have found so many different writers
describing so pleasantly was pursuing the even tenor of its way,
with never a cloud, apparently on its horizon. The money so
"sacredly devoted" to the erection of a noble pile had attained
its object; the Brothers' New Central building was an accomplished
fact; new and extensive plans were maturing, which, in their own
good day and time, would add to the beauty of the surroundings,
while augmenting the measure of usefulness already attained by
the New York Catholic Protectory, when, on the night of the 15th
of July, 1872, the magnificent building occupied by the girls was
reduced to a mass of ruins.

Of this catastrophe, so crushing in its extent, and which, under
less admirable discipline might have added hundreds of living holo-
causts to the mere pecuniary loss, we shall not venture to speak
beyond thanking the Author of every good and perfect gift, who
was pleased to temper this trial by removing from it the most ter
rible portion of its possible results, and for having brought from
out the fiery furnace, without exception, every little one confided
to the tender care, and, as this occasion fully demonstrated, to the
more than motherly vigilance and devotedness of the daughters of
St. Vincent de Paul.

"Let no big girl pass this way without a baby in her arms"
were the only words spoken, but they acted like a charm. Hasten-
ing to the neighboring dormitories, with flames licking up the
building on all sides, each big girl became a heroine. Each one
brought the required "passage money" in the shape of a little
babe, many still sleeping in the arms of their rescuers. Thus, the
presence of mind, the genuine heroism of a daughter of St. Vincent, saved the situation, and sent a thrill of joy into every Christian heart when the word went abroad that though the walls of
the Female Protectory were no more, the children, without exception, lived, and called upon the generous public of New York for
protection.

None but those who had labored for years to secure the erection
of the ruined building can fully experience the meaning of such a
loss. We therefore prefer to allow one of those most deeply interested to describe the situation in a few lines:

Says the Superioress then in charge of the Girls' Department, and whose coolness and determination so largely contributed to the saving of every child in the building:

"But the real self-sacrifice of those who aided us in that terrible scene, and the generous devotedness of those who, since the fire, have shown themselves true friends of the institution, can never be sufficiently admired and appreciated. Adversity tries friends, it is said, and truly this reverse has shown us friends in such goodly numbers as we had never dreamed of. And firstly, the Christian Brothers, at all times and everywhere worthy of their name, on that memorable night thought no sacrifice too great if they could save a little one from death, or rescue from the flames some article of value. After the fire they kindly offered a portion of their house to the children, and we gladly availed ourselves of the offering, quartering five hundred girls with them, besides sending over all the smaller boys from the frame building.

"The larger boys belonging to the Christian Brothers deserve praise for their exertions amid the dangers of the fire. Through their noble conduct, though at the peril of their lives, several sewing machines were saved from destruction. The larger girls also behaved admirably, using their utmost dexterity to assist the Sisters in rescuing the younger children, carrying those who could not walk, etc.

"It was a scene well calculated to arouse the deepest sympathy. Five hundred poor children thrown at once out of shelter without food or clothing, their home a smouldering ruin! Providentially it was summer, or we must inevitably have lost by cold and exposure many of the little creatures whom it had cost us so much to save from the flames. Assistance of every kind poured in from all quarters; many parties in the neighborhood placed themselves and their homes at our disposal; indeed, nothing could be more generous than the conduct of the people of every class and condition."

IX.

Among the cardinal truths daily instilled into the hearts and minds of the little ones of the New York Catholic Protectory is that of unceasing devotedness to the Holy Father. But a short time before the burning of the new building, the little girls had sent about one hundred dollars, out of their own savings, as a gift to the successor of Peter. Needless to say that the widow's mite did not call for more praise from the lips of Our Divine Lord Himself than did the pennies of those little ones, poor among the poorest, from the lips of him who is the visible successor of the Saviour of men upon earth. We may therefore rely with almost implicit assurance upon the following details selected from the correspondence of the " New York Tablet: "

"What a tender beauty there is in the relations which subsist between our imprisoned and despoiled Holy Father and the members of his flock, even to the humblest of its poor little ones ! Cardinal Prefect Barnabo has presented to His Holiness, the Pope, on behalf of 500 orphans of the Catholic Protectory of New York, a handsome gift. The little ones have remitted 514 francs in gold from their savings for the personal benefit of the Holy Father. The remittance is accompanied by a touchingly simple note, wherein the children request the President of their institution to convey in his own writing their tribute of homage to the Holy Father. In reply, the Pope expressed himself deeply grateful for the gift of the little orphans, and frequently exclaimed while he read their address, ' Poor little things, that they, too, should think of the Pope ! ' From his own hand a receipt was sent, conveying the apostolic benediction to the orphans of the Catholic Protectory; to their directresses, the Sisters of Charity; to the president and officers of the Protectory, and to all in any way connected with the institution. A few days after receiving the above gift, His Holiness heard the news of the burning of the Catholic Protectory of New York, a translation of the account of which was read to His Holiness by the Cardinal Prefect of the Propaganda. The Pope wept while he listened, and was forcibly struck by the coincidence of the fire having occurred not long after the letter containing the orphans' offering was posted in New York. He expressed his joy at the safety of all the children, and praised the heroism of the Sisters of Charity, who so nobly risked their own lives to save the Blessed Sacrament and the sick under their charge. He also likened their action to the miracle of St. John of God: who risked his life for twelve hours to rescue the sick and dying from a burning hospital. He then, of his own accord, gave the order to send to the Protectory the present we have described."

The Sister Superioress thus speaks of the gift sent by the Holy Father:

"Just as we were comparatively settling down, we were surprised by the very agreeable intelligence that his Holiness had joined the number of our benefactors, and from his own poverty had sent us a most interesting gift, consisting of a case in which are contained six small pieces of table furniture in *vermeil*, each piece, as well as the case, marked 'Pio IX.' This is indeed a valuable present, as, by subscription, every Catholic in New York may have a chance to possess, not a mere trifle (and even a trifle would be something great, after having been in the possession of so great a Pope),—not a trifle, we say, but an heirloom to descend through generations in the family of the happy possessor, and fraught with memories such as the history of time has rarely recorded."

We must look beyond the mere surface, if we would seek an explanation of such wide-spread sympathy; and we are under the impression that we are not forcing conclusions when we claim that the sympathy so generally manifested by every shade of person and party is the natural outgrowth of the kindly disposition always shown by both branches of the New York Catholic Protectory, in dealing with the parents and friends of the inmates; while this feeling was still further intensified by the continued anxiety shown by both Sisters and Brothers, in the after welfare and careers of those who have enjoyed the protection of the New York Catholic Protectory. In this way, the Protectory becomes the means of strengthening family ties; it brings parent and child under chastening influences, which strengthen as they develop, and which only show the vigor of their development when having left the Protectory.

These results have become so ordinary in the history of the after career of the protégés of the New York Catholic Protectory that they cease to cause surprise, in comment, but we can safely assert that, as time progresses, the number of youths who will try to give father and mother a helping hand will so increase that the civilizing influences of the New York Catholic Protectory will continue to be an acknowledged public fact.

Of the happy relations thus established between parent and child the following will give an idea:

"The managers are much pleased in being able to state that they continue to receive from many sources flattering accounts of their former wards, now scattered over various sections of the country, following occupations of different kinds, and filling positions, the necessary proficiency for which they acquired during their stay under the sheltering roof of the New York Catholic Protectory. But it is, above all, in the many cases of reunited family ties—the work of this institution—that the managers take especial pride: cases wherein the truant child has been returned to its family a well-behaved, obedient lad or girl, able and willing to perform his or her share of daily toil, with such skilled knowledge acquired in the industrial departments of the Protectory, as enables them to contribute to the general well-being of their families.

"We feel satisfied that, in many cases, much good is accomplished by respecting the bonds of family relationship. We never adopt the course of binding out in distant States children who have parents or guardians in or near New York.

"Believing, as we do, that our first duty to the waifs of society put under our charge is to preserve to them all those humanizing influences engendered by parental care, even when the parents themselves are degraded by extreme poverty and its frequently attendant vices, we use every effort to *preserve and strengthen such family ties* as our inmates have. We invite the visits of parents and guardians; and where no other means of communication between the children of the Protectory and their friends is possible, we encourage the use of correspondence by letter, to that end.

" By adhering to this plan, much good is frequently accomplished, youthful truants in most cases benefiting by the advice and solicitude of their loving parents ; and in some cases reformed and industrious children, graduates from the Protectory, have been the means of reclaiming from the ways of vice their erring, but still beloved parents.

"It is the practice of the officers of the institution to impress on parents a proper sense of their rights and duties in regard to their children; and in the prosecution of this work they have oftentimes received substantial aid from the members of the St. Vincent de Paul Society, who, in their visits of mercy among the poor of the city, are frequently brought in contact with the parents of children, inmates of the Catholic Protectory.

" The result of these ministrations has not unfrequently awakened the solicitude of parents for their children, and, when their improved circumstances have permitted, they have voluntarily applied for the charge and custody of their children; thus enabling the managers to escape the necessity of placing children as apprentices or otherwise with strangers, and also relieving taxpayers from the cost of supporting such children as can be properly provided for in their own homes."

X.

In 1874, Dr. Henry J. Anderson resigned, and in 1875, while making a tour of scientific observation in India, died. Dr. Anderson was well known to the Catholics of the United States as President of St. Vincent de Paul's Society, and of the Catholic Union. He had been identified with the Catholic Protectory from the start. Whether acting in committee or as President, he brought to his work the most conscientious exactness. The mathematical accuracy of his mind entered into the precision with which he did all things. He was the soul of punctuality. The many duties of the Presidency he unremittingly attended to, even while laboring under severe attacks of illness, until the end of 1874, when, having made arrangements for extended foreign travel, he positively declined a reëlection.

Thus, during twelve consecutive years, was the Protectory the object of Dr. Anderson's every-day laborious attention and solicitude. This ripe scholar, this distinguished mathematician, this learned linguist, this ex-professor of the first seat of learning in the State, did not consider it beneath his capacity to perform the dull routine work incident to the business requirements of the Protectory.

He attended daily at the office, not only supervising the administration of its affairs, but, with a patience and self-abnegation never to be forgotten, he entered into the minutest details of its workings, discharging himself a large part of the clerical duties, writing most of its correspondence, attending personally to litigious cases in court, in which his legal acquirements and high moral reputation were of great value to the Protectory.

Oftentimes did this great, good man himself convey the

wretched-looking objects of his solicitude from the courts to the
institution, happy in having rescued these waifs from the misery.
sin, or crime to which they had till then been exposed. All of
these services were rendered with a quiet, patient, unobtrusive,
but persistent tenacity of purpose, the source of which must have
been a heart brimful of Christian benevolence. Upon the resignation of Dr. Anderson, Henry L. Hoguet was appointed president
of the board.

XI.

At the Boys' Protectory, a new hospital was erected in accordance
with the requirements of sanitary science, and furnished with
every requisite for the treatment of disease. It accommodates
one hundred patients; the hospital has several wards in which the
sick may be classified.

The claim for a division of the larger and smaller boys, already referred to as of prime necessity, has been to some extent provided
for, as the following citation from the Report of 1882 will show:

"A great want was long felt in the institution: one thousand
boys had a common open space for recreation, and in this place
the larger boys exercised over the smaller ones an influence which.
to a great extent, proved an offset to the work of the school-room.
The diversity of character in so numerous a body required different degrees of discipline: this could only be effected by separate
departments, so situated that one should have no communication with the other. We can say that the splendid structure which
will soon enable us to meet partially the long but imperative demands, is an invaluable acquisition to the Protectory. Your un-
flagging zeal and fatherly solicitude for the welfare, spiritual and
temporal, of your young protégés, give us the assurance that as
soon as circumstances permit, you will make such improvements
in the playground as the situation demands. A play hall and
reading-room are also very much needed; as now situated we have
no place to protect our boys from the inclemency of the weather
but the class-room."

It will thus be seen that the New York Catholic Protectory has
faithfully striven to realize the vast mission confided to it. That
it has been successful thus far may best be told in the work of the

committee appointed by the State to "investigate the causes of the increase of crime," and who, after their visit, declared that: "This institution meets with the unqualified approval and commendation of the committee."

XII.

But one point remains to be mentioned, we refer to the health of the pupils. The medical report for last year mentions, "that although 543 children have been treated for ills of various description during the year, we have been blessed with comparatively good health, there never being more than ten or twelve inmates at one time in the infirmaries, and the death rate calculated on the entire number of inmates (1,828) at the Protectory is 4.60 per thousand, and if calculated on the average attendance (1,976), it is less than 7 per thousand, whereas that of the City of New York is 26 per thousand."

The annual report of 1883 thus sums up the work done by the Protectory, so far as figures may show that work:

About twenty-one years have elapsed since the foundation of the Protectory, and it may now be said to have attained its majority.

To such of the managers who witnessed its inception and took part in the first meeting after the granting of its charter, the appearance of this report must afford particular satisfaction.

It was then, in a measure, only an experiment, an undertaking which might, or might not be successful; now, though far from complete in all its requirements as regards buildings, it is in a position which offers a fair prospect of future success and of the realization of the aspirations of its founders.

"Since its organization, the Society has received, sheltered, cared for and instructed in useful trades nearly seventeen thousand children of the City of New York, most of whom, without its care and training, would have become a burden on the public, and many of them pests to society.

"During these twenty-one years the institution has expanded from the humble rented quarters in 36th Street and 86th Street, to the spacious buildings of the Male and Female Departments at West Chester; and from caring for one or two hundred children as the result of its first year's work, it now provides for two thousand and sixty-five, and during the year ending September 30, gave a home to two thousand, eight hundred and sixty-one children, two thousand and two of whom were boys, and eight hundred and fifty-nine girls."

XIII.

The years roll by, each year telling of some improvement made now in the male department, now in the female department of the Protectory.

In 1885, Brother Leontine was made rector of the institution. The report of the following year shows an improvement in the finances; it amends the regulations in case of fire, takes all possible precautions to be prepared for any emergency, day or night, and records the honors received by the boys and girls at the World's Fair and Centennial Cotton Exposition, held at New Orleans the previous winter. Silk-weaving was suspended as not being profitable, but the new tailoring industry promised excellent results.

In 1886, His Eminence, Cardinal McCloskey, died. The managers in the report of that year announced the death of His Eminence, paying a tribute of respect and veneration to the distinguished prelate who had been a warm friend of the institution, not only from the day he succeeded the great Archbishop Hughes, but while still the bishop of Albany. The death of Edward Frith, Esq. is also recorded. The managers take pleasure in calling attention to the increase of fifty-one thousand dollars in the assets, and the diminution of debt, owing to the excellent management of the Protectory in both departments.

This year Mr. Henry L. Hoguet presented to the Male Department of the Catholic Protectory a fac-simile of the magnificent monument erected to Blessed de La Salle by the people of France in Rouen. The figures represent the Founder of the Christian Brothers instructing youth. The group was designed by Falguières. In presenting the statue Mr. Hoguet took occasion to speak of the work of the Brothers as follows: "To the unselfish efforts of these gentlemen and to that of their respective predecessors in office, the history of this institution, since its birth twenty-three years ago, has been one of almost unalloyed success." Brother

Justin, in accepting the statue in the name of the Brothers took occasion to allude to the men who had been identified with the Protectory from the beginning in the following words: " All honor, Mr. President, to the commonwealth that is so deeply interested in the welfare of the unfortunate, and that so amply provides by its statutes for their security and happiness. All honor to the men that projected and carried into successful action this splendid institution; to the great Archbishop Hughes; to the illustrious Ives; to that revelation of gentleness and heroism, the late Cardinal Archbishop; to his amiable and distinguished successor, our present Archbishop, who has already taken a profound interest in this institution; to the good Dr. Anderson, and to all the benefactors of the work; to you, sir, who were one of its founders as well as one of its devoted benefactors; to Monsignor Quinn; to Father Clowry; to Brothers Patrick and Teliow; to the noble Sisters of Charity, and to all the gentlemen who have been, or who are members of the Board of Managers."

XIV.

In 1887 the report of the Protectory recorded the death of the Rt. Rev. Monsignor Quinn, Vicar-General of the Archdiocese, who had been identified with the institution almost from its first inception. The same report deplores the death of Judge Denis Quinn, who had been an active and efficient member of the Board of Managers.

The new Infirmary in the Female Department was erected at a cost of $37,876.22. The building gave complete satisfaction and won encomiums from those who examined it with care.

This year Mr. Augustin Daly and Mr. A. M. Palmer gave a theatrical benefit to aid the Protectory in repairing the losses sustained by the fires that destroyed the boiler and engine-house of the Male Department in 1886, and the conservatory of the same department in 1887. Owing to exceptional management the institution was enabled to redeem its bonded debt by $50,000.00.

The report of 1888 shows that 3,291 children partook of the benefits of the Protectory during the year just closed, with an average residence of 2,339 children daily. The average cost is estimated at $125.37 per child. From state, county, and city sources, the average receipts are $99.65 for the maintenance of each ward, whereas the average yearly cost has been $125.37 per child.

The management of the Protectory sustained two very severe losses this year: the first by the death, on February 23d, of John F. Develin, a man eminent as a lawyer, prized for his genial and brilliant social qualities, a warm friend of the Brothers, and one of the original incorporators; the second loss was that sustained by the death of James Lynch, one of the original incorporators of the Protectory. Both of these gentlemen gave their constant material aid and unremitting personal attention to the work of the Catholic Protectory.

Improvements to the extent of $10,000 were made in the new engine-house and hot-houses for plants. The work of the construction of a new gas holder and new gas retorts, which had been under way during the summer and fall of 1888, was completed in November of that year, at a cost of $4,500.00.

In November of that year the old frame building in the woods belonging to the Protectory, known as the Graduates' Building, but at that time quite unoccupied, was destroyed by fire. The cause of this fire still remains unaccounted for, and it can only be suspected to have been the result of the evil doing of persons thereafter indicted for arson in other Protectory buildings.

XV.

The desirability of removing the workshops of the Male Department from the buildings occupied as dormitories, class-rooms, and refectories, was long entertained by the officers of the institution, but lack of means had kept that project in the background until December, 1888, when the subject was again brought to the consideration of the Board of Managers.

This resulted in the adoption of a plan, and its submission to His Grace, Archbishop Corrigan, by which all machinery would be relegated to a separate building to be used for workshops alone.

His Grace was well pleased with the project, and with his sanction preliminary steps were at once taken to inaugurate the work. Plans for a chapel and lecture hall for the Male Department were also procured, but it was determined that the erection of these must

be delayed for another year, as all the current funds and the use of the credit of the institution would be required to meet the cost of the industrial building, as well as that of some other buildings to be mentioned hereafter.

On the 29th of December, a fire occurred in the purifying room of the gas house; the damage was slight, but this fire gave rise to painful suspicions as regards its origin, the correctness of which suspicions future events fully justified.

On January 11th of this year Hon. Morgan J. O'Brien, recently elected to the bench as Judge of the Supreme Court, sent in his resignation as manager of the Protectory, thus raising the number of vacant seats in the Board of Managers to six.

The election held at the subsequent meeting of the Board resulted in the following gentlemen being returned: MR. JOHN HARLIN, MR. MARTIN B. BROWN, MR. WILLIAM J. FANNING, MR. GEORGE D. WAGNER, MR. AUGUSTIN DALY, MR. THOMAS C. SMITH.

XVI.

Early in this year (1889) means were adopted to carry into effect the determination of the Board of Managers, who had resolved that application should again be made to the Legislature of the State for a pro rata share of school moneys for the city's children in the Protectory equal to that which is now and has been for many years paid to the Juvenile Asylum for the children committed to its care by the courts.

A bill was drawn in very plain language, covering this purpose in behalf of our children and the children of the Sheltering Arms (a kindred institution under the guidance and care of gentlemen of the Protestant Episcopal Church). This connection of the two institutions was had with the consent and approval of Rev. T. M. Peters, D.D., the president of the Sheltering Arms. The bill was presented to the Assembly by Hon. Joseph Blumenthal, member from this city, and referred to the Assembly Committee on Affairs of Cities.

After a delay of two or three weeks the bill was called up for hearing in Committee. Mr. Elbridge T. Gerry and Mr. Charles Black were present. The former appeared as the representative of the Asylum of the "Sheltering Arms," by request of its president,

Rev. Dr. Peters, and the Protectory was represented by Mr. Black. On this occasion Mr. Gerry described the good work being done by the "Sheltering Arms," "an institution which cares for a class of children not specially provided for, such as the delinquent, deaf, dumb, blind, crippled, deformed, and weak-minded." He stated that its work of educating these children was greatly circumscribed by lack of funds, and "this asylum and the New York Catholic Protectory" (which he spoke of as one of the best managed institutions of its kind in the world) were "the only two corporate institutions of this class omitted from the list of institutions which, by the law of 1882, known as the Consolidation Act, were made participators in that part of the public school funds annually distributed by the Board of Education to corporate schools, for the education of those destitute children, wards of the city, who through the force of circumstances were prevented from attending the public schools." He contended that it "would be doing an act of but simple justice if the legislature remedied this omission by passing the bill then under consideration."

At this point Mr. Robert Ray Hamilton, a member of the Committee, objected to any further consideration of the bill at this meeting, on the ground that it was a bill of importance, and one likely to cause a great outcry from those who were opposed to the Protectory being permitted to share in the school moneys. He thought the bill should be printed, so as to admit of general distribution, and its opponents be thus given a chance to be heard in opposition.

The Committee postponed the hearing for one week. And at the second hearing of the bill Mr. Black presented the Protectory's arguments in favor of its passage, which, briefly stated, were as follows:—"That the Protectory was an institution for the care and training of destitute Catholic children of the City of New York; that it was under the jurisdiction of the "State Board of Charities;" that the majority of its inmates were committed by the magistrates of the city through the agency of the Society for the Prevention of Cruelty to Children, and that the city was represented in its Board of Management by its Mayor, Comptroller, and Recorder; that these children, as wards of the city, were entitled to the benefits of an education, and inasmuch as they were in an institution on commitment of the city's magistrates, and thus pre-

vented from attending the public schools, they should receive a
share of the school moneys to provide for their education; that the
Protectory's managers were not asking for the passage of this bill
as a special privilege, but simply to place the inmates of this institution on an equal footing with the children of the sixteen other
institutions now receiving their share of this fund.   Of these sixteen institutions thirteen are under the control of the various sects
of Protestant belief, one under control of persons of the Hebrew
faith, and only two Catholic institutions.   The Protectory, therefore, should not be discriminated against on account of creed."

At this meeting the Committee decided to report the bill favorably to the House.

On the following Sunday evening the Rev. Dr. King, pastor of
St. Andrew's Methodist Church, and chairman of the Legislative
Committee of the " Evangelical Alliance," addressed his congre-
gation from the pulpit to the effect that Mr. Hamilton had just
sent him word that the Protectory had again introduced and was
pushing to final passage a bill by which it sought to obtain a share
of the school funds, and that it was his intention to proceed to
Albany the next day in order to organize a strong opposition to
its passage.

Dr. King went to Albany, but found that the general sentiment
there was in opposition to his views.   He and his friends then
sought to have the bill recommitted to the Committee, ostensibly
to a further hearing, but in reality in the hope that it it would be
killed by delay. The friends of the Protectory, confident in the
justness of their claim, expressed a willingness to have the bill go
back to the Committee for discussion.

The bill was recommitted.

On the day appointed for a final hearing the active members of
the " Evangelical Alliance " appeared in the persons of Rev. Dr.
Strong, its secretary, and Mr. Cephas Brainerd, its councillor.

The first named gentleman stated, that of the sixteen institutions
now receiving money from the school fund, all were non-sectarian,
except the Roman Catholic Orphan Asylum.   When his attention
was called to the names of the " Ladies' Home Missionary Society
of the Methodist Episcopal Church," to that of the " Protestant
Half-Orphan Asylum," that of the " Five Points Mission," that of
the " New York Juvenile Asylum," and the " Hebrew Orphan Asy-

lum," as specimens of what the Doctor called *non-sectarian institutions*, he did not renew his assertion of their being *non-sectarian*.

Dr. Strong's explanation that some of these institutions were non-sectarian, because their Boards of Managers consisted of gentlemen holding various forms of religious belief, can scarcely hold good, as it is well known that the fact of members of a Board of Managers of an institution varying in their religious belief does not disprove the fact that a particular form of sectarian worship is taught its inmates. If the Doctor's rule were to hold good, the Protectory would be a non-sectarian institution, as its Board of Managers has not always been exclusively composed of Roman Catholics.

The Protectory's position on this question was impregnable; the representatives of the "Alliance" knew it; they did not rely so much on argument as upon arousing religious prejudices, to defeat the bill; as the sequel will show, they had prepared for this effect.

Dr. Peters, of the "Sheltering Arms," had committed himself to the principle of the bill because he believed it to be just. But certain members of the "Evangelical Alliance" influenced Bishop Potter to use his authority as bishop to instruct Dr. Peters to withdraw the name of his institution from the bill, and, through this same influence, the trustees of the "Sheltering Arms" were induced to repudiate the action of their own president.

Dr. Strong, in the name of the Evangelical Alliance, presented a letter from Bishop Potter addressed to Mr. John Jay, in which the Bishop characterized the action of the managers of the Protectory in presenting the bill then under consideration in the Legislature as "*not manly, nor honorable, but sinister, disingenuous,* and in its ultimate effects altogether evil." (Surely, Bishop Potter would not have used this language if he had calmly and dispassionately possessed himself of the circumstances which preceded the presentation of the bill.)

Dr. Strong and his confrères made strenuous efforts to crush the bill at this stage, which proved futile, as it was evident to any impartial person that they were prompted solely by religious bigotry.

The Committee again reported the bill favorably.

The next move of the "Alliance" was an appeal to the prejudice of individual members of the Legislature; these gentlemen were in constant receipt of pamphlets, circulars, and manufactured petitions, in which the bill was stigmatized as pernicious and an assault upon the public schools; the ministers of non-Catholic churches throughout the State were urged to organize their congregations to oppose its passage. In spite of all these efforts to defeat the bill, when it was finally voted on in the Assembly it came within 12 votes of passing. On motion it was then tabled, and when called up for reconsideration, on the day before the close of the session, it was found that the bill had gained 4 votes, leaving it but 8 short of the number required to pass it. Although defeated this time, the justness of the claim of the Protectory remains unaltered, and it is to be hoped that some future Legislature will so recognize it.

The thanks of the friends of the Protectory, and of all lovers of justice, are due to Hon. Joseph Blumenthal, for his manly and skilful advocacy of this bill, and also to General James R. O'Beirne and Mr. Charles Black, for their earnest efforts for the success of the same measure.

XVII.

The Protectory fire company during the past year assisted at the extinguishing of several fires which occurred at West Chester. Wednesday, Nov. 20th, a fire broke out in St. Peter's Protestant Episcopal church in that town. The band of the Protectory was awaiting the arrival of the Delegates of the Superior Council of the Society of St. Vincent de Paul, on the 2 o'clock train of that day, when the church bells rung out the fire alarm.

The boys at once doffed their band uniforms, donned their fire clothes, hastened to the church, taking with them the fire engine belonging to the Protectory, and worked with a will at the fire, thus assisting in its extinguishment. A vote of thanks was promptly tendered to them by the vestrymen of St. Peter's Protestant Episcopal church.

The month of March, 1889, is rendered distressingly prominent in the history of the New York Catholic Protectory by the fact that on the 19th of that month an attempt was made to burn down the row of buildings on the Protectory grounds inhabited by many of the families of its employees, and while the possible loss of life by this dastardly crime was mercifully prevented, still great pecuniary loss resulted by the destruction of other buildings contiguous to those that were inhabited.

These buildings were burned on the 27th of the same month, and most undoubtedly their destruction was the result of arson by the same guilty parties. That fire consumed the large cow-stable and the horse-stable and wagon-house, thus entailing a loss of e[?] thousand dollars to the Protectory.

These frequent fires, and other attempted fires, pointed most[?] nificantly to arson as their cause, and aided by the very able, [?] seeing chief inspector of the New York police, Thomas Byrnes, [?] whose direction the case was submitted by the managers, the p[?] sumably guilty parties were discovered, one was brought to justice, and the other was acquitted.

In consequence of the frequent fires and attempts at firing buildings of the Protectory above mentioned, the matter of procuring fire insurance had become difficult; the rate of premium demanded by the underwriters was very high, and many companies refused to underwrite even at these high rates. To induce a sufficient number of first-class companies to underwrite it was determined by the managers that the institution should insure itself for one quarter of the whole sum requiring underwriting. Thus the sum now requiring insurance on all the buildings of the Protectory, and on all the contents thereof, is six hundred thousand dollars, of which three-fourths, or $450,000, is underwritten by responsible companies, and the other one hundred and fifty thousand dollars is at the risk of the institution.

At the request of the underwriting companies there has been established at the Protectory an enlarged and much improved system of external lights. A cordon of large Gordon gasburners has been erected on extra tall lamp-posts around the exterior of both the Male and Female Departments' buildings. Extra night-watchmen have been engaged, who have to record their passage around the lines of buildings by Watchman's Time Detector watches.

Washington's birthday was this year celebrated at the Protectory in a most patriotic manner. The presentation of a magnificent United States flag, the gift of Joseph J. O'Donohue, Esq., was made the occasion of an interesting discourse by the Hon. Morgan J. O'Brien.

On the 18th of May the Sacrament of Confirmation was conferred by Most Rev. Archbishop Corrigan upon 400 boys and girls of the institution, on which day the Protectory was honored by the pres[?]

ence of a large number of its friends. This gathering of the guests of the Protectory was made the occasion of several very flattering remarks, by prominent non-Catholic gentlemen, on the usefulness of the institution's work.

In June last the children were permitted to contribute their share of alleviation to the sufferers by the terrible disaster of the Johnstown flood by sending to the destitute children of that district 200 pairs of shoes of their own manufacture.

Having referred to the more salient points of the Protectory's history for the year 1889, it remains to briefly state the results of the institution's work as regards its inmates.

They numbered on October 1st, 1888, ...		2,369
There were received during the year, ...		851
Total number in care of institution, . . .		3,220
The regular discharges numbered . .	941	
Absconders, ...	8	
Deaths, ...	16	965
There remained in the institution, Oct. 1st, 1889,		2,255

The percentage of deaths, 16 out of 3,220 inmates, being 4 69-100 per thousand, compares favorably with 6 67-100 per thousand, this being the death rate presented by official returns of the Bureau of Vital Statistics of children of same ages in the city at large.

This economy of vitality, equal to two per thousand on the inmates of the Protectory, is the more remarkable as its wards are drawn from the very poorest, and at times from the most neglected classes of New York's juvenile population.

XVIII.

On May 9th, 1890, occurred the death of Henry L. Hoguet, the revered and esteemed President of the Board of Managers of the Protectory. For sixteen years he had guided its councils and had administered its affairs with signal ability, untiring labor, and generous zeal. Born in Dublin, Ireland, in 1816, in 1829 Henry Hoguet went to Paris, where he spent five years at the College of Charlemagne; in 1834 he came to this country, and entering upon a business career, by his energy, perseverance and integrity, he built up for himself a fortune, a name and a position that placed him among New York's foremost citizens. "His word," says Dr. Brann in a deserving eulogy, "was his bond, and he always had the confidence of his fellow-men." For twenty-five years he was president of the Emigrants' Industrial Savings Bank. In 1884, Pope Leo XIII. made him Chevalier of the Order of St. Gregory the Great.

The Catholic Protectory was to Henry L. Hoguet as the very apple of his eye. He took the deepest interest in it through all the phases of its growth and development. He spared neither time nor pains in looking into and directing its internal management to the best of his ability. The spirit that actuated Silliman Ives and Henry James Anderson, was also his, and he transmitted that spirit to his successors. Let those who came in daily contact with him, speak his merited eulogy. Sister Celestia writes:

" In him the children of the Protectory have indeed lost a father. He knew every one of the children; and for each and all he had a father's interest, a father's loving and careful foresight. They in turn responded as fully as children can to his devotedness. As soon as he appeared, every face would light up, every little heart grow glad, so true it is that childhood instinctively knows its friends. How beautiful is true charity! In Mr. Hoguet was certainly seen a more noble example than we often meet in this busy every-day world. In that better life, upon which we trust he has entered, may he receive his reward exceedingly great. His memory will ever be held in benediction within the walls of the Protectory."

The Rector, Brother Leontine, who loved Mr. Hoguet dearly, and was loved and esteemed by him, alluded to the deceased in the following terms:

" From the inception of the institution he has been one of its warmest friends, greatest benefactors, and ablest guides. By his death the poor, homeless child lost a dear and valued friend, society one of its supports, our country one of its truest and best citizens, the Church one of her most devoted and valiant sons. We deeply deplore his loss. He will ever be remembered by Brothers and boys as a sincere and valued friend. The beautiful statue of the Blessed De La Salle which he erected a few years since on the Protectory grounds has entwined his memory round the heart of every Brother of the Christian Schools." Henry L.

Hoguet was succeeded by Mr. Richard H. Clarke as President of the Board of Managers.

XIX.

Some important new features of an educational and industrial kind were successfully introduced in 1890 among the girls. September 9th, a Kindergarten class was put in operation with a goodly number of little boys and girls trained to habits of useful occupation, beautiful handicraft, innocent and intelligent amusement, with a competent teacher and a zealous Sister presiding over the school and its exercises. Thus young minds and young hearts were practised in graceful thoughts and words, their bodies in healthy exercise and development, their hands were trained to useful and pleasing works, their eyes to the beauties and combinations of colors, their ears to the harmony of music. The effect of this education upon the little children has proved most beneficial and agreeable. Boys and girls thus educated become better fitted for the subsequent, more productive and laborious trades to which they will be applied as they grow older.

Another new industry and training introduced among the larger girls was the establishment of a School for Cooking. A suitable part of the New Laundry Building has been set aside and fitted up and equipped with everything necessary for the purpose, cooking-ranges, gas-stoves, tables, dressers and sinks, and with the most modern and approved culinary utensils. Miss Juliet Corson, who is one of the most eminent and able of American women in movements for improving American cooking, promoting domestic economy, and founding cooking-schools, gave lessons to a class of twenty-five girls who were set apart to be educated as thorough cooks. One of the Sisters now continues the good work that Miss Corson had begun.

This year the management was pleased to report the completion, occupation, and application to their respective industrial uses of several new buildings. These buildings, and their dedication to the useful purposes for which they were designed, constitute one of the most prominent and important developments of the Protectory in recent times. The principal of these new buildings is the large industrial building or Trades School of the Male Department, which is built of brick and is substantially fire-proof, two-hundred and forty feet long, fifty feet wide, and four stories high. The trades that had heretofore been carried on in the main building were transferred to this new Industrial Building. Its ground floor is used and occupied as an engine-room, laundry for the Male Department, and as a store-room and shipping depot for the Shoe Department. Its first floor is used and occupied by the Shoe Department, and into it was removed and set in motion all the various machinery of our shoe factory, which is now in full operation. There were then two hundred and seventy-five boys engaged at shoe-making in this department, and their skill and proficiency, as well as their cheerful and healthy appearance, and their rapid and willing labor, awaken much interest and admiration. This department is greatly aided by the City Shoe Department, in which the commercial part of the work is transacted. The second floor is used and occupied by Printing and Electrotyping offices, and here was placed all the machinery from the old Printing Office, together with two of Potter Brothers' fine new printing presses. Ninety boys are trained to this excellent trade, of whom seventy-five are in the Composing Room, three at Electrotyping, eleven in the Press Room, and one at Proof-reading. The remaining floor of the new Industrial Building is devoted to stocking making machinery.

The efficiency of the work done in this new printing department may be best expressed in the words of the Reverend John Talbot Smith in the *Catholic Review*. He writes:—

"One of the features which attracts attention at the Male Department of the Catholic Protectory at West Chester is the spacious, airy, lightsome, and cleanly Printing Office. In two weeks time the boys had set up, electrotyped, and printed two hundred and twenty-five thousand copies of a quarto double-page circular issued to the Catholic people of New York, inviting them to the ceremony of the laying of the corner-stone of the new seminary. Twenty thousand additional copies of these circulars were printed in German, ten thousand in Italian, and five thousand in French. The circular was also printed in Bohemian, Hebrew, modern Greek and Syriac. This immense number of circulars was distributed in the various parts of the dioceses from the mailing-room of the Protectory. In addition to this work a number of railroad

posters, twenty thousand two-page programmes, and one hundred copies of the Latin Psalms, used in the blessing of the corner-stone, were printed. Moreover at the same time there was carried on in the same office the work of setting up, electrotyping and printing a sixty-two page Souvenir of the laying of the corner-stone, for which twelve illustrations were made, and of which five thousand copies were printed. When it is considered that this work was done by boys who had been trained and taught in this institution, and that the work itself was done in a manner to elicit the praise of everyone that examined it, it will be seen what a noble work the Protectory is doing."

Two other buildings have been erected and completed on the side of the Male Department; a cow-stable, which is one hundred and twenty-nine and a half feet long, thirty-five feet wide, and two stories high; and a horse-stable and carriage-house, which is sixty feet long, twenty-nine feet three inches wide, and three stories high.

On the side of the Female Protectory the Laundry and Cooking-school Building, which the Sisters appropriately called St. Vincent's Hall, was erected and completed. It is used and occupied as a Laundry for the Female Protectory and the new Cooking-school. It is eighty-seven feet long, forty-eight feet wide, and three stories in height. The Industrial Building and St. Vincent's Hall are connected with the Engine-rooms of the Male and Female Depart-ments respectively, by tunnels, so constructed as to contain all the pipes for water, steam, gas, and power, so that the same can be easily reached for examination and repair.

The cost of the several new buildings thus mentioned, and of their equipment for their respective industrial uses, stands as follows:—

The Industrial Building, cost $119,784.15
The Cow-stable, Male Dept., cost 12,241.89
The Horse-stable, Male Dept., cost . . . 10,183.48
The Laundry and Cooking-school, F. Dept. cost . 38,545.43
The Tunnel, Wall, etc., Female Dept., cost . . 14,424.48
The fitting up and equipment of the Industrial Building,
   including Laundry and Machinery, cost . . 4,883.13
The fitting up of the Laundry, Female Dept., cost . 4,772.34

Total, $204,834.90

These important structures and improvements added greatly to the efficiency of the institution as the agent of the city in caring for, educating, and restoring to usefulness and good citizenship the wards committed to its care, the waifs and poor children cast upon the public from the vast and increasing population of the metropolis. But these works in the meantime severely taxed the financial resources of the institution, and necessitated the addition of $100,000 to its mortgage debt, which now amounts to $180,000, including a mortgage of $13,000 on city offices and House of Reception, No. 415 Broome Street. But it is a source of satisfaction to know that even this amount is much less than the mortgage debt had been in the past; for on September 30, 1875, the mortgage debt was $262,000. So that with new buildings and improvements added to the equipment of the institution, which increase immensely its usefulness and capacity, and which are now completed and paid for, the mortgage debt is $82,000 less than it was at a period long anterior to these improvements. The net capital was also increased, and exceeded that reported Sept. 30 1889, by the sum of about $27,000.

On April 25th of the present year there passed away from us one who was associated with the birth of the institution and who was its best and truest friend. In the death of Brother Patrick, the Protectory lost one who was ever watchful of its interests, as his position as Brother Assistant brought him into the closest relations with the Brothers connected with the Protectory.

Brother Patrick always rejoiced in the part he had taken in the founding of the good work. Many of the prominent features of the institution were submitted to him and received the benefit of his suggestions. His fertile mind was ever planning greater completeness, and his great, kind, fatherly heart went out in loving sympathy for the friendless outcast and the vagrant boy.

The Protectory also experienced a great loss in the death of Sister Celestia, the Superior of the Female Department. She was a noble Sister of Charity, earnestly devoted to the interests of the institution, exceedingly kind and attentive to the children, and loved and respected by all who knew her. The grief shown by the children at her death spoke eloquently of the love they bore her, and was a grateful tribute to the memory of her, who in early life had left all that the world might give, to devote herself to the service of God and her neighbor.

XX.

While the whole number of children receiving the benefit of the Protectory from Sept. 30, 1891, to Sept. 30, 1892, was 3,204, the total number of days of their actual attendance and residence in the institution for that year was,

For Boys..	572,703
For Girls...	247,503
For Little Boys...................................	49,376
Total number of days of attendance and residence.	869,582
The average daily attendance of the boys was.........	1,565
The average daily attendance of girls and little boys was............................	811

And the total average daily attendance of inmates was 2,376

It should be borne in mind that the children designated as little boys are under the care and instruction of the Sisters, thus making their entire family of girls and little boys on the 30th of September, 1892, to be 806.

The financial management of the institution during the fiscal year has been successful and gratifying.

The gross annual expenses of the Male Department during the fiscal year, exclusive of new buildings and improvements, have been................	$184,290.63
The gross annual expenses of the Female Department during the same year, exclusive of new buildings, and improvements, have been.......	99,090.57
And for both institutions at West Chester.......	$283,381.20

Thus the average cost of maintaining each inmate for the year has been........................ $119.27

While we are allowed for this service a per capita of $110.00.

After the purchase of the house and premises No. 417 Broome Street, during the fiscal year ending September 30, 1891, in order to comply with the rules and requirements of the Board of Health especially relating to the provision of suitable and necessary isolation of children in case of contagious diseases or epidemics, it was found necessary to remove the old building 417 Broome Street, and replace it with a new one. This was done under the plans and superintendence of Mr. L. J. O'Connor, Architect. The new house was completed by February 1, 1892: three sisters were appointed to take care of the children during their quarantine therein prior to their transfer to the institutions at West Chester; a night-watchman was employed, and a suitable man was engaged to attend to the health, comfort, and security of the larger boys. The old building, No. 415 Broome Street, was repaired and re-arranged so as to conform to the plans and uses of the new building, and the re-constructed House of Reception was opened for the reception of children on May 27, 1892. On May 15, 1892, the House of Reception was blessed and dedicated according to the ritual of the Church, by the most Rev. Michael Augustin Corrigan, Archbishop of New York.

In addition to the foregoing amounts expended for
maintenance of children amounting to.......... $283,381.00

We have expended for the construction of the New
House, No. 417 Broome St., forming a part of
the House of Reception...................... 22,535.97

For permanent improvements in the Buildings of the
Male Dept. at West Chester................. 4,524.18

For the construction of a tunnel from the new Industrial Building to the Infirmary of the Male Department, for heating and other purposes....... 3,573.47

For permanent improvements in the Buildings of the
Female Department....................... 2,829.94

Making the total amount expended........ $316,844.56

In addition to these expenditures we paid out of the
income that year, a note for $15,000 which had
been given in the previous year ending Sept.
30th, 1891, for account of the purchase of the
land, 417 Broome Street.............. .... 15,000.00

Notwithstanding these important disbursements, we
paid off the entire mortgage debt on the House
of Reception in Broome Street, previously con-
tracted..................................... 13,000.00

GLOVE MACHINE SEWING ROOM.

And we reduced the mortgage on the properties at
West Chester by the payment thereon of....... 11,000.00

Making the total outlays for above purposes......... $39,000.00

Making the total expenditure for the year $355,844.76

The alterations and improvements needed and made
in the Old House, 415 Broome Street, cost..... $1,621.36
The furnishing of the House of Reception cost..... 1,244.51
The equipments of the Chapel in the House of Re-
ception 863.05
The furniture in the School-rooms in the House of
Reception......... .... 170.50

Total cost of equipment of House of Reception,
addition of erection of No. 415 Broome St., $3,899.42
The Board of Managers found itself near the beginning of the
fiscal year with the following obligations, present and approach-
ing, to meet:—
A floating debt of.................. .... $45,099.22
The note given in purchasing No. 417 Broome St... 15,000.00
The contract for the erecting of New House, No. 417
Broome St 22,535.97
Cost of the new tunnel........................... 3,573.47
Prospective permanent improvements at the Male
and Female Departments 7,354.12
Equipment of the House of Reception........... 3,899.42

In all............................,.. ...... $97,462.20
In order to meet these approaching obligations, they
negotiated a loan on bond and mortgage from
the Emigrant Industrial Savings Bank of $75,000,
which was secured on the real estate of the institution at West Chester, which loan was made in
August, 1891. Since that time, however, by
husbanding resources and by an economical administration they have paid the above sums
amounting to $24,000 on the mortgage debt. It
should also be mentioned that the floating debt

on the 30th of Sept., 1891, including the note of

$15,000, was.............. .... $60,099.

And on Sept. 30, 1892, the floating debt was reduced

to.................................... . 28,39

     Amount of reduction in the floating debt.... $31,700

Taking into view the general financial condition of the Protectory in the two years last past, the following figures will show result:

The debt on Sept. 30, 1891 was as follows:—

Mortgages payable............................ $215,000

Floating debt, including the $15,000 note......... 60,099.

     Total indebtedness on Sept. 30th, 1891 ... $275,099

. While, notwithstanding the increase in the mortgage debt of $75,000, the general or total indebtedness stood on Sept. 30th, 1892, as follows:—

Mortgages payable........ .... $231,000.00

Floating debt............... . ...28,398.83

     Total debt on Sept. 30th, 1892, was...... $259,398.83

Showing, in addition to permanent improvements, a

    reduction of the total debt during the year, of $15,700.39

The practice of making monthly payments on the principle of the mortgage debt was discontinued in 1889. It has been renewed in 1892 with a result of $24,000 paid thereon, and in reduction thereof, which was accomplished without any interruption in the provision and payment for maintenance of the other works above mentioned. At the same time the annual inventories show a substantial increase in the net capital of the institution.

It must be mentioned, however, that the foregoing works of purchase, building, etc., were so pressing, that the managers have been compelled to defer another important permanent improvement, the erecting of a chapel for divine service, for the boys of the Male Department. The Brothers and boys now and for many years have been using a loft, or upper room in the main building, for a chapel. It is wholly unsuited for the purpose, and it is also itself needed for dormitory service. The measure would also increase accommodations for reception of boys.

This year Mr. Richard H. Clarke resigned as President of the

Board of Managers. During the time that he held office he took the deepest interest in the institution, and gave to it in unstinted measure his time, his energy, and the best thought of his ripe, scholarly mind. Mr. Bryan Lawrence, one of the directors of the Emigrants' Savings Bank, is now President of the Board.

XXI.

We have here endeavored with the aid of the annual reports to trace in rude outline the story of the Catholic Protectory, through the varying phases of its growth and development from its first humble beginning to its present magnificent proportions. Much has been achieved. Much remains still to be done. He who visiting the Protectory on one of its holidays, notes the many gymnastic exercises or the splendid military drill through which the boys are put; their graceful delivery in the recitation of pieces; the sweet songs they sing, and the superb band of seventy-five pieces that discourses music more like professionals than amateurs; observes the boys in the base-ball field; looks into the work done by boys and girls in the class-room; or he who visiting the workshops of the boys, and the sewing-rooms of the girls, when in full operation, notes the industry and taste with which they perform their various duties—such an one can form some conception of the good that is accomplished by both departments of this institution. He can recount the useful men and women that are trained up to become worthy citizens of this republic, while retaining the faith to which they were born and which is their inalienable birthright.

CPSIA information can be obtained
at www.ICGtesting.com
Printed in the USA
BVHW051234210721
612411BV00006B/1161